BITZY'S STORY

# Healing the
# Pain of Silence

BITZY'S STORY

# Healing the Pain of Silence

*A Memoir*

## JessieMay Kessler

gatekeeper press™
Columbus, Ohio

Bitzy's Story: Healing the Pain of Silence

Published by Gatekeeper Press
2167 Stringtown Rd, Suite 109
Columbus, OH 43123-2989
www.GatekeeperPress.com

Photo Credits: Kevin M. Curtis, of Mystic, Connecticut

iStockphoto.com/deteetarkan (black wooden frame on the gray wall)

Library of Congress Control Number: 2021949759

ISBN (paperback): 9781662921292
eISBN: 9781662921308

*This book is dedicated*
*To all the parents and families,*
*Who give of their time, their money, and their love,*
*Who stand beside their sick children,*
*Giving comfort, consolation, and hope,*
*As the child and family*
*Move through the*
*Child's long term illness*
*And*
*To all the nurses,*
*Doctors, specialists, administrators, counseling staff,*
*office workers,*
*Food preparation people, and*
*Janitors,*
*Who stand behind the parents,*
*Cheering the families on to good health.*

My older brother, Owen, who is now ninety-one years old, wrote back this message when I suddenly remembered I needed to ask his permission to use the picture of him, the rabbit, and myself on my book cover of Bitzy's Story.

"About the book cover—fine, use the photo as you see fit. But, there is background information. The rabbit's name was Butch. And was one of the first litter of rabbits. (This was his 4-H club project for one year when he was about fifteen and I was five years old.) I had purchased three "purebred New Zeeland white rabbits"—two females and one male. I built three cages, and one morning when I looked out the window, there was rabbit fur in one cage. And squirming around in the fur were 12 little rabbits. A miracle had occurred because it was a male that had given birth. And to top it off, half of them were black! Ultimately, I had 64 rabbits! And Butch was the last to go."

From left to right are Owen, the rabbit Butch, and myself, Bitzy, about a month before I was diagnosed with rheumatic fever. The lurking illness explains the sadness in my face. I wasn't feeling very well, but nobody seemed to notice, including me.

Several of the photographs in this story were taken about fifty years after the story and are marked with a P. Life doesn't move too quickly in Shakerton, Massachusetts!!

# Contents

Bitzy's Story: Author's Explanation ................................................. 1

Chapter One:           That Horrible Awful Carol Simpson ........... 7

Chapter One T:          Horrible ................................................. 13

Chapter Two:           No Food in the Hospital ........................... 17

Chapter Two T:          Food Hospital ........................................ 25

Chapter Three:          To the Doctor's Office ............................. 29

Chapter Three T:        Doctor Office ......................................... 35

Chapter Four:           Only a Monkey to Talk to ......................... 37

Chapter Four T:         Monkey ................................................ 45

Chapter Five:           Staying Inside the Lines ............................ 47

Chapter Five T:         Inside Lines ........................................... 53

Chapter Six:            Horses on the Ceiling ............................... 55

Chapter Six T:          Ceiling Horses ....................................... 59

Chapter Seven:         Thanksgiving from a Bed .......................... 63

Chapter Seven T:       Bed Thanksgiving .................................... 71

Chapter Eight:          Yes, There is a Santa Claus ....................... 73

Chapter Eight T:        Santa Claus ........................................... 81

Chapter Nine:           Sunshine in a Basket ............................... 85

Chapter Nine T:        Basket Sunshine ..................................... 91

Chapter Ten:            Stepping Outside the Bed............................93

Chapter Ten T:          Red Ball ..............................................99

Chapter Eleven:        First Steps Then Blood Taken....................101

Chapter Eleven T:      Blood Taken ......................................109

Chapter Twelve:        School After School .................................111

Chapter Twelve T:      After School ........................................117

Chapter Thirteen:      Hailstorm Heat ..........................................119

Chapter Thirteen T:    Heat Hailstorm ...................................131

Chapter Fourteen:     Ugly Things ...............................................133

Chapter Fourteen T:   Thing Ugly...........................................137

Chapter Fifteen:        Back to Regular School..............................139

Chapter Fifteen T:      Regular School.....................................149

Chapter Sixteen T:      Second Dialogue With the Inner Bitzy ...153

Chapter Seventeen:    To Ride a New Bicycle .............................157

Chapter Seventeen T:   Ride Bicycle........................................165

Chapter Eighteen:     The Men's Maternity Ward.......................167

Chapter Eighteen T:    Men's Maternity..................................181

Chapter Nineteen:     Playing House.............................................183

Chapter Nineteen T:    House Play...........................................189

Chapter Twenty:       The Military Choir Mistress .....................191

Chapter Twenty T:     Choir Mistress ...................................195

Chapter Twenty One:   How to Get a Piano..................................197

Chapter Twenty One T:   Piano .................................................203

Chapter Twenty Two:   Increase in Family....................................205

Chapter Twenty Two T:   Family Increase..................................213

Chapter Twenty Three:   Setting the Dream ...............................215

Chapter Twenty Three T:   Dream.............................................223

Chapter Twenty Four:         My Soul Dog: Patches ............................... 227

Chapter Twenty Four T:      Patches ...................................................... 233

Chapter Twenty Five:         "Drops" Can Make Money ........................ 235

Chapter Twenty Five T:      Make Money .............................................. 239

Chapter Twenty Six:          Books, Letters, and Boys .......................... 243

Chapter Twenty Six T:       Pony .......................................................... 249

Chapter Twenty Seven T:    Final Dialogue with the Inner Bitzy ........ 251

Chapter Twenty Eight:        The Red Car .............................................. 257

Chapter Twenty Eight T:     Red Car ..................................................... 263

Chapter Twenty Nine:         Here's to the Older Man ........................... 265

Chapter Twenty Nine T:      Older Man ................................................. 275

Chapter Thirty:                Sharp Endings ........................................... 279

Chapter Thirty T:             Boy and Girl .............................................. 283

Chapter Thirty One T:        Wrapping It Up .......................................... 285

# Author's Explanation

LIKE THE STORY of the cobbler's children who never have shoes, it did not occurred to me that the depression, which slips in and out of my life, coming unbidden like a ghostly night invader, could be confronted with the same methods I use with my clients. I have been a therapist for over thirty years, encouraging my clients to record their dreams and bring them to sessions so that together we can ferret out the healing that comes by understanding the unconscious messages buried in the material.

The first step has been to admit to myself that there was a ghost of depression and that this entity would not rest until I faced the issues it represented. That first recognition came with a wake-up call of a dream I had about a Falling Down Woman. Why did she keep falling down even when I offered help? The events in *Bitzy's Story* that follow evolved as if some giant being was orchestrating the revelation in my life, the course of action, and the healing result.

Working with this material, I've concluded that children hide their fear, pain, and confusion during illness to protect their parents. By the end of the ailment, parents are thrilled with the child's return to good health. Not wishing to re-experience their fears of losing their child, the family speeds forward without processing the feelings created during the illness—the child lives with a silent legacy of unspoken emotions ranging from rage to fear.

*Bitzy's Story* deals with the events and unexpressed emotions revolving around my becoming ill at five years old with rheumatic fever and suddenly being separated from my mother—the first trigger for a chronic stress response. I've come to believe that any invading trauma sets off reaction in the ancient animal brain. If a life event renders us helpless, even for a short time—a beating, mental abuse, a rape, an illness, an accident by car or otherwise—we see ourselves as unfit and fear being forced out of the pack. Being outside the group means isolation and the loss of food—the ending of life. As if to protect from this impending doom, most individuals reacting to a traumatic event withdraw, hide, and await the dreaded outcome.

Children, who suffer through childhood illness of some duration, come away with emotional wounds that seldom show to the outside world. As adults, we appear to function well, even to the point of perfectionism but inside resides the constant fear that something is wrong with us, that we are not good enough, much like the abused child. It is as if a part of the personality is left back in the sickbed. Sometimes these feelings are conscious, but for most people they lay hidden, the only hint of trouble appearing when our personal lives seem to stagnate or be in constant turmoil, and we decline to talk about these illnesses; "It was a long time ago."

This book's language is that of the child reliving the events of illness and the gradual recovery. Each chapter ends with my processing comments derived from my now adult mind and my training as a therapist. It is an effort to explain how the child's reaction to sickness comes from their family history. *Bitzy's Story* illustrates that the child's illness also shapes other family members' emotions.

Some of the names and place-names in this book are fictitious to protect the individual's privacy, while others remain the same. By sharing my process of discovering this raw emotional material stemming from a childhood long term illness, I hope to encourage you to use these techniques to gain more meaning for your life. This may constitute a better understanding of a family member caught in this situation, help you to heal, or for you to give support to a child going through long term illness.

I use the technique of mirror dialogue in this book to show how one can draw out material from the unconscious brain to help heal the conscious individual's mind and heart. These dialogues and the therapist's notes will be in a different font to help you recognize the changes in perspective as you read through this book. You can read *Bitzy's Story* as she tells it. If you wish to gain a richer meaning from this book, I encourage you to read the 'Looking Through My Therapist Eyes' that accompanies each chapter.

Remember when you were a child and would walk up to a mirror putting your hands on it, mashing your face against the surface to look at the distorted character on the other side? Who was that creature looking back?

To revive this material while sitting at my desk, I close my eyes. Through imagination, I move to a mirror in my mind. Putting my hands against the cold glass surface I spread my fingers as if for support. Suddenly, I can see a tiny space between my hands and the image of my hands. I wonder who lives in that space. Leaning into the mirror I ask, "Is anyone in there who wants to speak to me?"

A little girl seated on the floor unwinds and stands up slowly but then pulls back. Her small face, which is framed by blonde braids, wears a frown. One shoulder seems cocked slightly higher than the other. "Who are you?" I ask.

In a soft voice lower in timber than the speaking voice of most children, she responds, "BitzyBird."

"Bitzy who?" I ask.

"My name, if you want to know, is Bitzy Sandler," she responds with some energy. (Even as this child comes out of the shadows, she refuses to use my given name, JessieMay Sanderson.) "I don't know why you'd want to know my name, now. You've never paid any attention before."

I'm taken aback by this puckish push of words and can't seem to think of what I want to know, so I blurt out, "What sort of name is that?"

"See, there you go again, making fun of my name. My big brother Owen gave it to me the day he brought that rat into the kitchen by the tail. Don't you remember he held that horrible big thing by its skinny tail, letting it swing in front of my nose? And when I screamed and pushed it away he chanted, "Na, Na, Na! Bitzy is a scaredy-cat. She's afraid of big old rat!" (When you read all the books in this memoir trilogy, you will read where my mother refused to let go of the name my grandmother gave to me when I was a toddler: My Little Bird. The family picked the name up, so I became Birdie. I hated the name because for me it represented that sick child who was damaged and unfit.)

"I remember the rat," I confess. "But I thought Owen put the rat into the old black woodstove. Or was it Mother that put it in?"

"See," Bitzy replies. "You only remember the parts that didn't frighten you. You forgot how I got my name. You forgot about me!"

Trying to keep my distance from this impish little girl, I ask, "Was the rat still alive when Mother put it into the stove?"

"Of course it was dead! But see, you've forgotten the things that confused you or hurt your heart."

"Touché, Little One! I've always wanted to forget that scene. Are there others I'm glossing over?"

"You bet!" Bitzy replies.

"Okay," I respond. "Let's get on with it"

I've had enough therapy to know that keeping Bitzy hidden has kept me arrested at some deep level. I wonder if Bitzy's illness causes me to believe I am somehow flawed and, therefore, not able to reach for my goals. Emotional fear and physical pain are hallmarks of depression: I experience both.

Many children, who face long term illness, cope with the fears of medical explanations which, are *not understood*, experience feelings of being abandoned in hospitals that mean *to help*, and manage the situation *by forgetting* to make it all go away. They put on a brave face by becoming super good children: each trying to do whatever the adults appear to want. Inside the child, the day's events lay down scars upon a fragile, developing sense of self.

Bitzy will tell the story from here on, well, at least most of it. She is the main character: a five-year-old girl who lives with her parents and three siblings, big sister, PollyAnne, ten years older, big brother, Owen, nine years older, and then little brother, Coppy, nine years younger than Bitzy. This family configuration makes Bitzy almost an only child. She doesn't mention that she grows up to become a therapist because Bitzy can't possibly know how this life experience will shape her future. Bitzy tells her experiences, in her child's voice, the way she remembers growing up in the 1940's and 1950's from age five to age fourteen.

Back row: Jordan, Baby Bitzy, Franklin
On the bench: Owen and PollyAnne

CHAPTER ONE

# That Horrible Awful
# Carol Simpson

M Y REGULAR SCHOOL bus had come and gone. I stood by the window, turning the handle of the silver pencil sharpener, grinding away on my yellow wooden pencil, that curse to all first graders. On tiptoe, I could see out the window. The sun, partly blocked by the brick school house, was causing shadows behind the playground's swings. The big silver swing-set with its straddled silver legs looked like a silly giraffe I'd seen in a book. The departing bus and the stringy shadows told me it was late afternoon: time to be going home! The year was 1945. I knew because Mother had explained that being born in 1940, I was always the same number as the year. I was five!

First grade wasn't what I'd expected. The other kids frightened me when they pushed and shoved me to get to wherever they were going. And the noise! Everybody talked at once, trying to get the teacher's attention. Teacher would say, "Now, quiet down, boys and girls. We must give everyone a chance to talk." I wondered if Teacher even knew I was there. I wanted to just go home. I couldn't think. In class, the other kids looked like they knew what Teacher wanted them to do.

In the morning Teacher had said, "Now, children, I want you to take out your yellow pencils. It is time for your penmanship lesson. Billy, you can pass out the lined paper." The other children bustled to her order. I fumbled in my desk. Where had that pesky yellow pencil run to this time? I hunted behind the new reading book and under the rumpled yellow papers. By now, everyone else was writing. The whole day went this way. Teacher finally told me to stay after school to finish my penmanship paper. This event was the first time in my life I'd ever had to stay after school! I was scared I was going to miss the second bus! What if Mommy didn't know where I was?

Teacher said, "Bitzy, the second bus, the one you will take, is fifteen minutes later than your regular bus. You will only be a few minutes late getting home." I must have looked scared because she went on, "Do you want to go to the office and call your mother?"

I shook my head, 'No.' *How could I tell her I didn't know how to use the telephone?* Once, when I was four, I was playing with the phone at home and got to talk to somebody. I was speaking French to the woman on the other end, the same French my sister was talking out loud as she did her homework for high school French class. Mother didn't yell at me, but she sure looked mad. She told me I shouldn't ever use the telephone again in that manner!

I did stay after school to finish my penmanship paper. Now, waiting on the gigantic swing-set and watching the fading sun move across my arms, I feel really sad, discouraged. Being only five years old, when I sit on the black rubber seat, I can hardly reach the ground with the toes of my new oxford shoes. The chains that hold up the seats are so thick it's hard for me to get a good grip. Sometimes my thumbs get stuck inside the links. It's kind of scary, but I can make the swings go. I'm worried that Mom will be mad at me for being late. One blonde braid tickles the side of my cheek as I start the swing to moving.

I'm thinking about Mother's being upset and look up to see Carol Simpson charging toward me from across the playground. I freeze to the swing. *Now, what is she going to do to me?* Carol lives across the street from my house. Both our families are part of the big green lawns and farm fields that make up the grounds of the Industrial School for Juvenile Delinquent Boys at Shakerton, Massachusetts.

Carol is a sneaky kid that treats you nice one minute and punches you the next. She's two years older and bigger than me, and she's still coming!

"Want a push?" Carol askes, nearly out of breath.

I shake my head, no, and brace my feet against the dirt under the swing. *You never know what Carol is going to do next.*

"Aw, come on, I'll just give you a little push. I won't put you up high."

*If she says she's not going to put me up high, that's just where I'm going. Carol will blow me into the sky, up, up over the silver crosspieces at the top of the swing-set. I'll fly right off into space and maybe never come back.*

"No! Don't . . . don't push me!" I say, struggling to get the words out. I back up, pulling myself and the swing cradling me, farther away from Carol.

"What! Are you afraid of me?" Carol steps closer.

I shake my head, no. But my heart is pounding a resounding yes. Once more, trying to avoid her, I step back, swing and all.

Carol moves forward again.

In a very clever move—at least at the time I thought it was smart—I step aside, wrapping myself and the swing chains around one of the sliver support poles of the swing-set, putting the heavy chains between Carol and me.

My move is too much for Carol, who makes a swipe at my face. I duck but now find my clever move has simply made me a prisoner locked in place by the heavy chains wound around myself and the support pole. I try frantically to unwind the chains.

The ducking move angers Carol, and she punches me with her fists. *Oh God, I hope that bus comes quickly. Carol's too big for me. She's going to beat me to death!*

Just then, the old station wagon—the school bus for the State School children—pulls up alongside the playground. Hearing the station wagon coming, Carol stops for an instant in her attack, giving me valuable time to get untangled. As the last chains let go, I grab my school papers off the ground and dash for the safety of the wagon and the driver, kind old Mr. McLaughlin. Carol being older and heavier, is slower to move: still, she is running fast behind me. Mr. McLaughlin must have seen the trouble, for he says to Carol, "How about you sit up here right behind me. That way you can get off the bus first and won't have to wait for Bitzy to get out." I often can't understand old Mr. McLaughlin and his Scottish accent, but today, I understand every word and will always be grateful.

Sitting in the very backmost corner of the wagon, I start to cry. School is just too much for me. Every day when I get onto the bus, I have to watch what I say, or Carol and her younger sister, Sally, will get me. The kids in school don't talk much to me. I think it's because I'm quiet, and they think I'm stuck-up. I'm not stuck-up: I'm just scared of them. Besides the trouble with the kids, I never seem to know what Teacher wants, or I'm looking out the window daydreaming and don't hear her directions.

Last year I wanted so badly to go to school. I even stopped sucking my thumb. Mother told me that though I was soon going to be the legal age of five and could go to school, if I didn't stop sucking my thumb, the other kids would tease me. I stopped. *Little good it seems to be doing me, now!* Feeling hopeless, I sit in the back of the wagon, mulling over my troubles, the silent tears running down my face.

The station wagon stops in front of my house. I wait, hunkered down in the back seat, for Carol to clear the bus first. I'm so tired of always having to be prepared for what she's going to do. I just don't want to face her. Besides, I don't want Carol to see that I'm crying. She'll tease and tell her sisters I'm a baby. *Well, I feel like one.* Now all is clear. I gather up my battered papers from the day and trudge up the walk to my house.

Once inside, I go to the living room. Mother looks up from her brown chair where she sits reading. "What on earth happened to you, Honey?"

I say nothing. I want to push my way into my mother's arms. Mother gathers me onto her lap and sits rocking me and soothing my back. "Come on," she says, "Tell me what happened. Did somebody hurt you?"

I shake my head in confusion. *I don't know if I want to tell her about Carol or not. It won't stop happening even if I tell her. Mother won't understand. She'll say, "Carol Simpson always hurts you, so why do you go back and play with her? Just stay away."* But I can't stay out of her *way when we both ride the same bus.* I decide not to say anything.

I shake my head in a nondescript way that could have been yes, or no, depending on how you saw it.

"Honey, you can tell me."

I'm still silent. The tears continue to run down my face. Mother wipes them gently with the corner of her soft apron. *There is nothing to tell Mom. The whole picture is so terrible there's no place to start!* More tears run down my face

Mother feels my forehead. "You seem feverish, Bitzy. This behavior isn't like you; crying over nothing. You never cry! Why won't you tell me what is wrong?"

I just burrow deeper into my mother and the tears flow.

Finally, Mother says, "Bitzy, I'm really worried about you. You never cry like this and won't talk to me. I wonder if you've caught something. I'm going to take your temperature. Lie down here on the couch, and I'll get the thermometer." With that she disappears upstairs.

I crawl up onto the couch, leaving my crumpled papers on the floor, symbols of my defeated spirit. Mother reappears with the thermometer, shaking it as she walks toward me. "Here, put this under your tongue . . . no talking for five minutes. I guess we don't have to worry about that this afternoon!" Mother smiles, pleased with her bit of humor.

Sitting on the side of the couch, she holds my wrist and counts. I wonder what she's doing, but it's so nice, not having to be aware of anything, that I let the thought go.

In a few minutes, my mother pulls out the thermometer, balancing it on the back of her wrist. "Well, this is strange. You feel warm and have a bit of temperature, but not enough to call you sick. All in all, I think you should go up to your room, wash your face clean, and rest on your bed for a while before supper. Sure you don't want to tell me what happened in school?"

I shake my head and start toward the stairs, the tears still trickling down my cheeks taste sharp and salty, bitter reminders of today's terrible events and what I can expect for tomorrow.

## Looking Through My Therapist Eyes

# Horrible

I recognize that all children come into life with characteristics that are inherently their own. Still, they also acquire behaviors and thinking patterns: beliefs, which are absorbed unconsciously from their parents. To better understand Bitzy, I need to share her parent's history along with the family stories.

In this chapter, it is Mother's background that sets up Bitzy's responses. The Grandmother, Mary Emma Moody or Grammy, as Bitzy calls her mother's mother, was a very strong woman, who gave birth to her sixth child, Jordan Elizabeth, Bitzy's mother, six months after her husband, Charles Moody, died suddenly of pneumonia. An event that left this woman of thirty-eight to raise the five other children and new infant in a small Colorado town, all alone, far from her extended family's support.

Can you imagine the devastation and the fear that must have permeated this woman as she finished carrying, birthing, and suckling this new child? As an infant, Bitzy's mother, Jordan, unconsciously absorbed this climate of being overwhelmed and fearful.

Mary Emma brought her six children back to New England and found interim lodging with her brother's family while she trained herself to do laundry in the Chinese's fancy manner. Once skilled, Grandmother established a laundry in the basement of the house she rented, in Medford, Massachusetts, while the older children pitched in to help with the business or raise Jordan. When did this mother have time to nurture Jordan, listen to her, affirm her existence, and teach her to express her feelings? A child caught in this environment soon understands that no one has the energy to pay attention to him/her and learns that they must not make demands.

A paragraph taken from Mary Emma's unpublished book, *Mary Emma of the Square House,* tells you in her own words how little instruction and nurture Jordan received from her mother.

> *"Jordan had not had her share of attention as I have written of the development of the family. Indeed as I look back upon the years of her childhood, it seems to me that I was always too busy with the necessary financial problems to give my last little daughter the attention a child should receive.*
>
> *She slept with me, and when at the end of the heavy day I crawled in beside her, I used to gather my sleeping baby into my arms and tell her how much I loved her, and the unspeakable blessing she had been to me in the dark years that covered all her babyhood. She called herself "Bay" from the time she could lisp. I have often wished I could have told my "Little Bay" some of the sweet things when she was awake that I told her when she was fast asleep, but the ability to express my affection only came with relaxation.*

By the time our story starts, Bitzy has already accepted that life experiences are frightening, absorbing fragments of emotional lessons handed down from the two previous generations. Having experienced earlier in life that Mother is not going to affirm her feelings, Bitzy chooses not to reveal her problems of being overwhelmed by what is happening to her; Carol Simpson, the Teacher, and the other children. Mother, functioning from her background, doesn't simply croon and cuddle her daughter, reflecting how awful things must be, which would, in turn, have brought about Bitzy's willingness to share her feelings. Instead, Mother starts to problem solve—there must be an underlying cause to Bitzy's discomfort—a bad event at school, a possible cold, maybe rest. The woman focuses on her own need to verify her conjectures by procuring the thermometer and taking the child's temperature.

In all respect to Mother, I must affirm that her ultimate actions of recognizing there was possibly an underlying cause to my behavior probably saved Bitzy and my life. But the process left both Bitzy and I mired in our fears and reinforced our previous wounds of not being heard emotionally.

# CHAPTER TWO

# No Food in the Hospital

I WAS WATCHING THE telephone poles going by. Lying down flat on the back seat of the car, dressed in my snowsuit and wrapped in a blanket, I could see the poles by looking up through the top edge of the car window: a telephone pole and then a tree, a patch of late-afternoon fall sky, then another pole. I was counting. The car was getting closer to my house. My face felt stiff and tight, still streaked with tears as if I had been crying straight for all of the past week—but it had only been three days. I could hardly wait to be home again finally.

Dr. Blackmore, the family doctor, had come to the house. Mother was worried and had called him in. He put that awful, flat stick in my mouth and, then, while I gagged and choked, he peered in saying, "Um . . . I'm not sure what to make of it." Turning to my mother, he continued, "Doesn't look really red, and yet you say there's daily fever? I don't know what to tell you. I think we should put her in the hospital for a few days, just to observe." I wasn't sure I liked Dr. Blackmore anymore after the gagging routine, but he had always made me feel better before. And what was a hospital, anyway?

I soon found out. Mother packed up a few things in a suitcase, a toothbrush, soft flannel pajamas, a hairbrush, and slippers. Then she bundled me up, even though it was only late September. Mother directed me toward the car, and we headed in the direction of the little local hospital in the next town of Airsville, Massachusetts. When we got there, everyone seemed so nice. Everybody smiled at me. The nurses were in crisp starched white. I noticed how the tops of their uniforms seemed to billow out from their waists, stiffly, like pieces of white cardboard, completely concealing the fact that they were women. I thought *it must be a bother wearing cardboard all day long. It's got to stick into you and get in your way.*

One nurse speaks to me. "Oh, it's so nice to have you here with us, Bitzy. We are really going to have a good time, you wait and see. How old did your mother say you were?"

"I'm five," I say. "I just started school."

"How do you like it?"

"It's okay," I respond. *Should I tell the nurse how scared I am going off to school in the old station wagon every day with those awful Simpson kids from across the street? No!* Somehow, I sense that the nurse doesn't care if Carol Simpson beats me up or not, so I tell her nothing. Mother helps the nurse undress me and put on the old, soft pajamas. They lift me onto the bed, swinging my skinny legs in under the stiff white sheets and light, white, cotton blanket. The nurse pats the cover down, saying to my mother, "There, she's all set. When you are ready to leave, Mrs. Sandler, ring the buzzer, and I'll come back to be with her."

Go! I didn't realize that Mommy wasn't staying with me. *Is she going to leave me?* Suddenly, I'm terrified. "Mummy, you can't leave! You aren't going to leave me here alone, are you?" I wrap myself around my mother's nearest arm, which supports her as she stands, arms straddling my body on the bed, balancing herself and leaning in toward my face. "Can't you stay here, too?" I plead. Any sense of an adventure has vanished. It is now sheer terror.

"No, Honey, I can't stay. It's against the hospital rules. But I'll come to visit you every day, right after lunch. We can play, and I'll read you a story."

"Mummy, don't leave me here!" I say as loudly as I dare.

My mother looks toward the window for an instant, and then, turning back to face me, she asks, "Which book would you like me to bring tomorrow?"

The change of subject doesn't fool me. "Why can't you stay with me? I don't want to stay here!" The tears flood my burning cheeks.

Mother puts an arm around my shoulders. "Well, you have to stay here, Honey, because we don't know for sure what is wrong with you. Do you remember how I have been taking your temperature every day? It's not a normal temperature, and the doctor thinks it would be better if you were here, where they can keep an eye on you. That way, they can find out for sure what's wrong." Mother sounds so calm and reassuring, but I still hurt inside.

My heart feels like someone has taken ahold of both sides of it, sort of like it's a cooked pancake, and is pulling it apart with their bare hands until it breaks into smaller, useless pieces.

I remember how last summer Mother went away for a week, leaving me at home with Daddy, PollyAnne, and Owen. My heart felt the same way while she was gone. Later they found out that I'd caught Scarlet Fever and had been sick the whole week, but nobody paid attention, and nobody felt my heart but me.

My mother's mother, Mary Emma Moody, my Grammy, had come to take care of us, and she did everything the wrong way—not like my mother did things. She cooked meatloaf in the wrong pan and put dishes in the wrong closets. She made a terrible mess. I tried to point out to her that she was making a lot of mistakes. She said that I was very rude and a badly behaved child—couldn't understand what had gotten into me.

"Please don't go, Mummy." I plead softly, "Please, please don't go." The tears are now streaming down my face, making huge dots on my faded flannel pajamas.

"Oh, Honey, believe me, I don't want to leave you, but I have to for your own good!" Mother pulls me into her chest as if I'm a rag doll, overlapping her arms around my back. She holds me with my face mashed into her shoulder for a moment: then, plumping the pillows with one hand, she pushes me back into their crispness. "You're going to be fine, just fine, and I'm going to call the nurse. You can rest right here, and soon it will be suppertime. They'll bring you a tray with all sorts of nice things to eat. You'll see. There, I'm pressing the buzzer.

The nurse will be here in a moment. I've got to go." And with that, Mother pulls herself from my efforts to cling to her, grabs her coat and pocketbook, and walks out the door.

As if by magic, the nurse comes through the big doors. "Now, don't you look pretty in your pajamas! Did Mommy get those new for you?"

"I'm heartbroken and could care less about stupid pajamas. I tearfully shake my head.

"They're not new?" the nurse persists. "Well, they certainly make you look pretty, except for those little tears." She kindly wipes the moisture from my face with the edge of the sheet. The white surface feels scratchy against my skin and smells of bleach. It doesn't do any good, for as soon as my face is dry, there are more tears.

"You'll feel better in a bit. We're going to get you all fixed up here so you can go back home and play."

The words, 'back home' hit my torn heart. Tears flood my pajamas, and I pull the sheet up under my chin in an attempt to hide from this kindly but terrible nurse.

Shortly, the nurse, seeing that she is not getting anywhere, says, "I think I'll leave you here for now. Tomorrow there's going to be a little boy over in the next bed. Maybe you'll be able to play with him a little. In a while, I'm going to bring you the nicest supper you have ever seen."

I stare at her hating her for being in my pain and wishing she would shut up and go away.

"And one last detail," the nurse says. "See this thing, here?" The woman is holding a brown rubber cord, with a funny sort of metal piece at the end. "When you press this little spot, it tells me that you want something. That's how you can call me if you need to." With that bit of information, the nurse disappears.

I'm alone, all alone! I ache from somewhere deep inside me. The pain is everywhere, and the tears just keep coming. Sliding down into the stiff pillows, I curl up as small as I can and pull the covers over my head. *Maybe, if I make myself small enough, I'll vanish and reappear at home. I hate it here. I don't want to be in this horrible place!*

The next day comes early, but having no sense of time, I know my mother had said she would come to visit me today, and it is now today. That's the first question out of my mouth: "When's Mummy coming?"

The nurse explains that first, I will have breakfast, and then they will bathe me in bed. "Won't that be fun?" she says.

*I think that's a pretty dumb idea. With a bath in the bed you'll get the bed all wet, and the water will fall off onto the floor.*

The nurse babbles on, "Then we will get you lunch, and after that, your Mommy will be here."

Mother's visit sounds like forever away.

Breakfast doesn't look any better than supper had. I poke at the toast, but the whole tray smells like puki water. My tummy aches, but so does everything else. My body alternates from hurting to not feeling like it is hitched to me at all. *No—no food, I don't want any food.*

When the nurse returns, she looks at my tray and frowns. "You didn't eat anything?"

I hang my head and shake it in a *No.*

"How about if I were to put some milk on the cereal, then could you eat some?"

Once again, I shake my head *No.*

"Don't you like the food?"

I just keep shaking my head, *No.* Everything is a *NO!* I think it was at that moment that I decided if I couldn't go home, I wasn't going to eat.

The activities of the day went forward. Nothing captured my attention. The boy, the nurse, had talked about, moved into the next bed, but he'd just had an operation and slept all the time. Mummy came and read a story, but then, she left again. I was growing numb everywhere, outside of the pain at the center of my being. The world beyond that place felt like it was moving slowly, very far away . . .

On the second day, one of the other nurses came into the room saying, "I'm pretty good with children. How about this nice Jell-O! Isn't this a pretty color? Do you like red? See how it wiggles when I push it. Do you suppose there is a monster inside that makes it dance like that? Here, how about a spoonful?"

My lips are locked tight. No food! *Besides, the nurse sounds dumb. Of course, there isn't a monster inside the Jell-O! I've never seen Jell-O before, but certainly, any five-year-old knows that monsters don't live in food!*

On day number three, the doctor came into the room. "I hear you are not eating for the nurses. You know, if you don't cooperate with them, it is hard for us to do the testing we need to do. You need to eat."

Stiffly I nodded. I understood what the doctor was saying, but I hurt so much his words weren't going to change my actions. All I wanted was to go home and be with my Mummy.

"Are you going to cooperate and eat for the nurses?" the doctor asked.

I shook my head; *No!* The very thought of food was an impossibility now.

Dr. Blackmore called a nurse into the room and stood talking to her. I couldn't hear all of what he said, but it sounded like if I didn't eat, there wasn't much they could find out by keeping me in the hospital. Perhaps it was best to let me go home. A wave of sunny feelings swept over my body. *Maybe, just maybe, they would let me go.*

After the lunch arrived and was taken away, my mother appeared in the doorway. She looked a little worried, but that didn't matter. "The doctor says you can come home with me today. He says you're not eating, and he feels perhaps it would be better, if you were at home. I have your clothes here with me."

Suddenly, there was bright light in the room again, and the pain started to leave my body, all but the pains in my stomach. *I had understood the doctor. I was going home!* Mother helped me dress, even babying me by tying up my pesky shoelaces. Snowsuit on, and face wrapped in smiles, we were ready to leave.

On the way out, one of the nurses said, "Goodbye, Bitzy. You fooled me. I didn't even know you had a smile! Have fun at home with your Mommy."

I didn't understand why my mother put me lying down in the back seat of the car, for I didn't feel sick at all. But it was little bother to me—I was going home! Even lying on the seat of the car, I could tell how close we were to my house by the way the car swayed as it went around corners and by how many telephone poles we had passed. I used to count them when Daddy and I walked along this road picking blackberries. In just minutes more, I would be safe in my house again— home at last!

## Looking Through My Therapist Eyes

# Food Hospital

Reading about these events in the hospital, I feel like the women were very detached from me, functioning from roles rather than empathetic people. And this distancing only strengthened Bitzy and my feelings of emotional separation from our mother. Mother was acting from buried fears of abandonment absorbed during her birth. She failed to recognize that going to the hospital was the first time I had been away from home and did no emotional preparation. As an adult looking back, I can't believe Mother missed this fact, but I understand it happened because of her fears of somehow loosing me. An institutional setting is a vast shock to any individual let alone a child. Couple that with no experience of being separated from the family, and given the forbidding, rigid environment of a hospital, it is no wonder that the only way Bitzy or I could fight back was to forgo food.

As, the third offspring in the family—nearly an only child having siblings nine and ten years older—I was not accustomed to being dealt with like an object. At home, I was treated like a smaller person. As I read Bitzy's telling of my story, I now see the nurses unwittingly talked at me, not to me, heightening my fears and widening the gap in reality that better communication might have salvaged. Perhaps it was a phenomenon of the times—children were really to be seen and not heard in the nineteen forties.

The trauma of feeling abandoned is probably the single greatest wound. The Bitzy part of me implies this as she describes how the world recedes from her, not recognizing that she is leaving her own body. This phenomenon of leaving the body when under extreme trauma is well documented in the literature on abuse—not that I was abused in the usual sense. But the experience is the same: being subjected to overwhelming pain by an invading event and feeling helpless to stop the occurrence.

It also intrigues me that Bitzy does not mention her siblings in the hospital or upon coming home. Is there really that much separation—maybe caused by Mother being too emotionally involved with me? And if Mother was too involved, why is this?

After my mother had lost two infants, I was conceived. One baby was a stillbirth and one was a third-month miscarriage. Being pregnant with me, a difficult pregnancy, my mother may have withdrawn somewhat from the family, fearing another loss. In the process, she imbued the fetus with fears of being lost or abandoned. As my mother, Jordan, unconsciously wrestled with her complex issues of death/birth experiences, her emotional wounds are superimposed onto this new fetus's emotional memory, reinforcing her need for this child and the child's need for her.

While their mother is so preoccupied, the older children, in their pre-teen years, respond with the age-appropriate behavior of pulling away from the mother and focusing on life outside the home. I wonder if these events may have caused them to perceive Bitzy as a greater intruder—sibling rival—for their mother's affections than would have been the case if Bitzy had come without the complications of previously lost children.

The old expression, "it's not what happens to us but how we handle it," is well illustrated by this family, driven by its history and experiences. These individuals constitute neither a good family nor a bad family, but simply a family doing the best it can at the moment of events, with the developmental tools that it has on hand. A family like most of the others in this world, with parents struggling to do what they perceive, is best for their children, while blinded by their emotional handicaps!

Bitzy's Hospital in Airsville Massachusetts P.

# CHAPTER THREE

# To the Doctor's Office

IT WAS GREAT to be home! Our three-colored cat greeted me by leaning her body into my legs, lifting her back, and sliding past with a slippery move that said Rag-Shag was as glad to see me as I was to see her. I hadn't thought much about her in the hospital, I mostly wanted to get home to Mummy, but now seeing her, I loved her so much!

It didn't even bother me a lot when Mother said I had to go right upstairs to bed instead of staying down with the family to play.

But the next morning was a different story. "I have to go to school? I've been in the hospital!" I announced as loudly as I dared—my family didn't like children acting up.

"Yes. I know you don't understand, Bitzy," Mother said with some patience. "But it seems to me that if the doctor felt you shouldn't be going to school, he'd have told us not to send you. Dr. Blackmore tells us it's going to take time to find out what's wrong, so I believe you should be off to school."

I wanted to cry but knew it wouldn't get me anywhere. Feeling sad and helpless, I slowly dressed for school. In contrast to how I felt, breakfast tasted even better than supper had the night before. Suddenly, the old school bus was out front, and I was off to face the Simpson girls again. Yuck!

I tried to stay out of the way at school and just get through the day.

When I got home, Mother greeted me with a cheery smile and the thermometer in one hand. "Five minutes on the couch. The doctor wants me to take your temperature every day, morning and night, to see if your temperature goes up, down, or stays the same." After a few minutes in my mouth, Mother took the thermometer and balanced the instrument on her arm. She made a kind of frown with her face.

"What's the thermometer say, Mummy?" I ask, sensing her unhappiness with the reading, my question more an effort to change her face than to gain information.

"Well, it's elevated a bit. But that doesn't matter so much. It's what it says over a week or so that we've got to watch."

The next days followed this same pattern: the thermometer in the morning, first thing, and my great dread going off to school; the thermometer upon return from school and the frown on Mother's forehead. The frown got deeper with the passing days. After two weeks of checking temperatures, Mother called Dr. Blackmore to come to the house again. It seemed pretty stupid to me to be putting on my pajamas and getting back into bed since I'd been dressing and going to school all week.

When Dr. Blackmore got to my bedroom, he put that horrible stick into my mouth until I gagged three times. "I don't see anything in there that concerns me. It's a touch pink." He said. "Bitzy, does your throat hurt when you're at school?"

"No," I replied. A sore throat was the least of my worries at school. For me, it was more a case of trying not to daydream in class and to stay out of Carol Simpson's hands!

The doctor poked at my tummy and listened to my heart through his funny-looking, silver, tube-like thing he put in his ears. "I can't hear anything that's out of the ordinary," He said. "She's eating properly here at home?"

"Yes," Mother responded. "She seems to eat fine here. I guess she was frightened to be away from us."

"Well, I can't find anything wrong with her. But the elevated temperatures are not normal. I think it's time you took her to one of the big city doctors. Do you know one?"

"Yes," Mother answered, not saying any more.

After Dr. Blackmore left, she said to me, "I'm going to take you back to my childhood doctor in Medford, Massachusetts. He always seemed to know what was wrong with me!" I sensed that she was relieved to be going back to her city and a different doctor.

Days later, Mother said, "Bitzy, you don't have to go to school today. We're going off to see that city doctor."

From the black 1942 Chevrolet's front seat, I watched the houses change from small country houses, spaced well apart, to big three-family houses crowded in close to one another. The grassy areas disappeared, and in their place were sidewalks, buses honking, and cars pushing at each other to speed ahead. Mother finally stopped the car on the street lined with big green trees and dark brown houses three stories tall, squeezed tight together as if to hold each other up.

Inside, the doctor's waiting room seemed all brown, as well. Two other people were waiting there. Mother chose two chairs close together, and we settled down to wait. I was glad our chairs were together—I didn't want to be sitting here alone. The waiting room was a smelly old place, and I wondered why my mother thought this would help us. *It seemed as though we waited all afternoon.* Finally, the doctor, a sturdy-looking man in his mid-fifties, wearing round silver glasses and a bushy mustache, stepped from his office door and motioned us to come into his examining room.

We walked into his office, and *it was all brown, too!* Doctor things filled the room: a big roll-top oak desk covered with papers, a small dark chest with glass front doors and silver tools laid out neatly across the top, a little chair at the foot of a narrow, brown leather table in the middle of the room. There seemed to be closed doors to somewhere else, all around the room, and I wished to go out one of them. Doctor Archer showed me how to get up on the table using the little chair as he cheerfully talked to my mother about past times.

Mother was standing beside where I sat on the examination table and helped me take off my blouse and undershirt. The doctor listened to my heart with the stethoscope he wore around his neck. (Mother told me what it was later on.) Then Dr. Archer looked down my throat using a black-handled flashlight and a wooden stick. I tried to pull away from the stick in my throat and the strong smell of garlic from this red-faced man. He just made me gag again. "Only one more look," he said. "I know it hurts."

Dr. Archer turned to my mother, saying, "With just a quick inspection, I'd say she has rheumatic fever. We'll need to do blood tests, and I'd like you to see a specialist in the next town over to confirm my diagnosis. I won't be treating her myself; I'm just a family doctor, but Dr. Clark, in Winchester, is the best man I know for this sort of illness."

Mother thanked the doctor and helped me get dressed again. When we left the doctor's office that afternoon, we drove straight to my grandmother's house. Gramma Moody lived a short distance away. Grammy's place was a warm, cozy, two-story yellow house that always smelled of flowery perfume and good Sunday dinners.

My mother and grandmother did a lot of quiet talking that afternoon while I pressed the black and white piano keys on the piano in the living room. Before supper, Mother made a telephone call. When she was done, she announced, "Dr. Clark says he can see us tomorrow right after lunch. Grandmother says we should stay here tonight. That way, we don't have to make the long trip home and back tomorrow to the city." Mom seemed happier.

The next day was bright and sunny. I didn't pay much attention to where we were going on the drive to Dr. Clark's office until we got close to his office. A long, curved drive up past the right side of the new stone building was so different from the doctor's office yesterday. The area had large green trees all about, and the sunlight coming through the leaves on the trees made it look friendly, inviting.

I wasn't happy to see yet another doctor. But this man seemed interested in me. He used my name, Bitzy, and paid more attention to me than to my mother. Dr. Clark was tall with dark hair, turning gray at the sides, and he looked like I'd be able to talk easily to him. He did the same things to me as the other two doctors—the gagging stick, the thumping my chest, the cold silver circle of the stethoscope. Then, walking away from me, the doctor sat down and looked at papers on his desk. Finally, turning back to where I was still sitting on the examination table, he motioned to me to get down and come to stand in front of him. Taking both arms in his large hands, he leaned forward. "Bitzy, I've got to tell you something, and I want you to listen very carefully. I believe you have rheumatic fever. It's a very serious disease. It makes your heart work extra hard to pump your blood, so it's tired all the time."

I didn't really understand what he was saying, but his tone's seriousness, and the tightness of his hands on my arms, frightened me and got my attention.

"It's not a very bad case," he said. Then abruptly, he said, "Tell me, Bitzy, do you want to have babies when you grow up?"

I was confused by the change in his tone of voice. *Of course, I want to have babies. I want to grow up to have children just like my mother, to hold little soft bodies close to mine.* I stared at Dr. Clark, silently wondering what he was trying to say.

"If you want to have babies when you grow up, you are going to have to do just what I tell you. You do want to have babies when you are grown?"

As if we were sharing a secret, I whispered back, "Yes, Sir."

"Good! Very good! Then when you get home, you're going to have to put on your pajamas and go right to bed. Bitzy, you are going to have to stay in bed for a long, long time and do just what your mother tells you. You can't get out even to go to the bathroom. I think, if you'll rest and take the bitter-tasting sulfa drugs your mother gives you, you'll get well. That way, you'll be able to have children when you are a grown woman."

I stood quietly, searching the doctor's face for more clues about what was going to happen to me. I tried to understand what he was saying—what he wanted me to do.

"Now, Bitzy, tell me what you are going to do for me."

"I have to go home and go to bed and not get out for a long, long time so my heart can rest. If I'm good and take the bad medicine, I'll be able to have little babies when I get big."

"That's the ticket. You've got it. I think you can grow up to have a happy life if you'll be a good girl, now. Do you have any other questions?" He let my arms go from his strong hands.

Stepping back, I ask, "How do I go to the bathroom?"

"Good question, Bitzy. I'm going to teach your mother how to use a bedpan with you. It's a white, flat, dish-like ceramic pan that she can slip right under your bottom, and you can go into that. Do we have any other problems?"

"No, Sir. You're sure that I can be a mother when I get big if I'm good now?"

"Yes, honey, I'm sure of it!" Dr. Clark responded.

## Chapter Three T

# Looking Through My Therapist Eyes

# Doctor Office

BITZY'S EXPERIENCE, THEREFORE my experience, with the three different doctors in this chapter is an excellent example of what is emotionally important in the way one treats a child, any child, but especially a child who is very ill. Adults in general, but more specifically in the medical field, talk *about* the patient/child rather than *to* them. This way of speaking, in a sense, leaves the patient/child out of the loop of communication and contributes to the feelings of being somehow inferior or not quite acceptable when ill.

Doctor Clark chooses to speak directly to Bitzy, explaining the illness in the child's vernacular, telling her what will likely be ahead, and eliciting her cooperation. His skill in finding some feature of her future life that has deep meaning to Bitzy is what saves her future. The desire to recreate herself—have children—is enough to hold Bitzy totally confined in her bed for six months—a most uncommon feat for a five-year-old. Doctor Clark's talking directly to her causes her to feel a need to commit to him when he essentially asks her to promise her total future cooperation.

Bitzy was very lucky to have a mother dedicated to finding a doctor who could competently treat her daughter—that's me. Bitzy's good fortune was compounded by this Doctor Clark, who was clever enough to step into the position a father holds in a girl's life and asks her to commit to him—her future good health. Bitzy was one lucky lady, and so was I.

# CHAPTER FOUR

# Only a Monkey to Talk to

I KNEW IT WAS forty miles from Grammy's house to ours. Mother had told me one time when I'd asked *how much farther* for the third time. But this drive home from Dr. Clark's office seemed forever long. Knowing better than to ask *how much farther,* I sat in silence, watching the scenery through the car window. Mother didn't say much the whole trip. I usually am a chatty girl when I'm alone with Mom, but somehow it didn't feel happy in our car. Better to be quiet. There didn't seem to be anything to say.

When the car pulled into the driveway, it was late afternoon. The sun was already dipping behind the hills. Mother broke the silence. "Now, you remember what the doctor said. It's right up to your bedroom, put on your pajamas, and into that bed for you."

I nodded my head. I had understood most of what Dr. Clark had said to me, and I had promised him I'd be good. He'd made it seem almost like a secret between us. I wanted to make him pleased with me.

At the doorway of my bedroom, I stopped to eye my space. It was an old, over-large storage closet with a long, sloping ceiling that stopped just above my bed. I had to be careful getting out of bed not to jump right up and bang my head on the ceiling. The one window swung in from the bottom, and with it being on the east side, the room seemed dark at this moment. In front of me stood my bed, a white, steel-framed cot, and off to the right, the white bureau. The bureau had a mirror attached with ornately-carved, white arms which cradled and supported it. Mother would tilt the mirror downward so I could see almost to my feet when I was dressing. Beside my bed was a low toy chest painted light-green with a decorative decal on the top. The final touch was my old, striped rag-rug in front of the bed to keep my toes cozy on cold winter mornings. This afternoon, as I looked at this tiny simple room, dressed with old familiar things, I could have no way of knowing how this room, which now seemed to welcome me, would soon become my prison.

I rummaged around under my pillow and found my pajamas. By now, Mother was standing in the doorway, watching. I turned around to face her as she buttoned the last button on my pajama top. Something coming from my mother told me now was different than ever before. I moved to get into bed. Mother crossed to the side of the bed and pulled the covers up to my chin. She straightened the fold-over on the sheet, patted it down. "Is there anything I can get for you, Bitzy?" she asked.

"No, Mummy, I'm fine."

Mother continued to stand beside my bed. She looked very sad as if she wanted to do something more, but she just stood quiet, sort of watching me. I was beginning to feel funny. Suddenly, she turned her face from me to look out the window. When she looked back, her face seemed brighter, "Well, if you're fine, I'll go start supper."

Now I was alone. It felt a little like when I was in the hospital, only this time I could hear Mother moving about in the kitchen underneath my bedroom. In a little while, I heard the muffled voice of my older sister, PollyAnne. She must have come in from her after-school job at Wambolt's Hardware store down in the town. I could picture them, Mom and Polly, moving about the kitchen, busy setting the table and stirring things on the stove. PollyAnne often cooked right along beside my mother, salting the food on the stove after Mom had already salted it. Yuck! When the food was ready, Daddy and my older brother, Owen, would join them at the table to eat the evening meal.

Suddenly, it hit me—they'd be down there eating, talking, and laughing together while I'd be up here *all alone by myself. How was I going to get my supper?* I lay in the bed, looking up at the ceiling, trying not to think about them downstairs.

Mother interrupted my thoughts. "Here, I've brought you supper on this nice tray. It's the same supper we're having. I hope you like it." My Mother seemed as if she were trying to make conversation. She took the napkin off my tray, placing it between me and the tray, which now rested on the side of my bed. "There," she said, "anything else you need?"

I looked at the tray: meatloaf, mashed potatoes, and those pale green peas. Yuck! I hated canned peas. But then again, I didn't like beans, squash, broccoli, or most any vegetable. Chocolate pudding, now that was great for dessert! Mom had even put a few drops of milk on it and sprinkled a tiny bit of sugar over the top, just the way I liked it. Maybe supper wouldn't be so bad after all.

I didn't say anything to Mother but looked at the food. She waited for a minute as if she were going to stay to watch me eat and then excused herself and returned to the family downstairs.

Later, Mother was back to pick up the tray and get me ready for bed. I had eaten a small corner of the meatloaf, most of the mashed potatoes, about two peas, and all the chocolate pudding.

"You weren't very hungry?" Mother framed the remark as a question.

I shrugged my shoulders.

"You don't like peas?" Mother asked.

"The pudding was good!" I told her.

"I see that."

Mother set the tray on the floor and sat down on the toy box. "We need to talk for a few minutes before I get you "ready for bed," My mother said, planting her elbows on the side of my bed and leaning toward my face until she was almost nose-to-nose with me. "Do you really understand what the doctor said to you today?"

"Yeah! He said I was sick with something that made my heart tired. I have to stay in bed and rest. That way, when I get grown-up, I'll be able to have children of my own."

"Yes, Bitzy, those were the words he used, but do you understand what it means? It means you aren't to get out of bed to do *anything*, not anything! You can't get a toy that's fallen off. You can't grab for the cat when she jumps off. You can't even get up to brush your teeth or go to the bathroom yourself. Do you understand? It may be this way for a long, long time."

I nodded. What the problem was I couldn't take in except that my mother's voice was telling me that this somehow was a big deal. It seemed like an adventure to me. Besides, I wasn't going to have to go to school anymore and face that horrible-awful Carol Simpson every day. Staying in bed all day couldn't be worse!

Mother seemed satisfied with my nod. How she expected me to understand at five years old something I hadn't yet lived through seems a bit odd. But I guess she felt better having tried to get through to me. Anyhow she began getting things ready to wash my face from a basin of water placed on the side of the bed, brush my teeth and put me on the cold ceramic bedpan. Evening chores completed, Mom settled down on the green toy chest with a storybook in her hands. When she'd finished that story, I begged for another, and then another. Finally, Mom said, "Now, that's just enough. It's time to put out the lights." With her two-fingered kiss on my forehead, she left my darkened room.

The next morning started bright and cold with the sun shining through the window beside my bed. I could hear the rest of the family downstairs having breakfast and rushing around getting off to school. My sister and brother, nine and ten years older, would be heading out to high school. Suddenly, I felt very lonely. I wanted to be downstairs with the rest of them. I called as loudly as I could from my room. "Can I come down and have my breakfast?"

"No, Bitzy. We talked about that last night. I'll be up as soon as PollyAnne and Owen are off to school." Mother had left the kitchen and come to the bottom of the stairs so I could hear her answer better.

This part wasn't fun. I lay in bed, looking at the ceiling. I thought *Mother likes the others better. She's getting their breakfast first!* I pouted.

Finally, Mother stood beside the bed. "Would you like some cereal with milk on it and a bit of brown sugar?"

"No," I said. "I want bacon and eggs, and orange juice, and toast."

"My goodness," my mother responded. "Will you eat all that? You didn't eat well last night."

"That's what I want!"

"Okay," my mother said. She bent over, and opening the toy box, pulled out two coloring books and some Crayola crayons. "Here, you can busy yourself with these while I get your breakfast. But first, I have to take your temperature and record it in this little notebook." She sat on the side of the bed, having shaken down the thermometer, and put it under my tongue. "Now, don't go anywhere." Mother's light blue eyes crinkled at her joke.

I smiled back. I liked my mother's company. I liked my mother.

Breakfast was followed by the wash-up routine of the night before. Mother read me a story and then explained that she had to go about her usual housework. She said I would have to entertain myself with the coloring books.

Propping myself up on my left elbow, I began to attack the pictures in the coloring book. One done quickly, I moved to the next, and then the next. I colored every page with only one crayon, using a different color for each page. After what seemed a very long time, I called out to Mom, "Can you come and read me a story?"

"No, Honey. I can't right now. You keep busy with the coloring books. I'll read one just before lunch."

I lay back on the pillow. What to do now? I stared at the ceiling. This way of being was boring, nobody to play with, Mother busy, and four pictures are done in the coloring book. I sighed. Lying there looking at the ceiling, I thought about Carol Simpson. It was nice to dream about Carol having to go to school while I could play at home. I wondered *what's Carol doing now that she doesn't have me to punch around. I don't care if I ever see Carol again! But then I won't see any of the other kids, either. I wonder how long this is all going to take. How long will I have to stay in this bed?* Thinking about all this stuff wasn't so much fun after all, so I shifted my attention back to the ceiling.

There were thousands of little cracks in the old white plastered ceiling above my head. They twisted and crossed one another, leaving big, open spaces and busy, little marked-up spots. The paint didn't seem to cover the activity on the ceiling very well.

"How about that story before I get lunch?" Mother was standing in the doorway. I hadn't heard her coming and jumped with a start at the sound of her voice.

"I'm sorry, Honey, I didn't mean to scare you. What were you doing so intently?"

"I was looking at the cracks in the ceiling. They go all over the place. I can see all kinds of animals and people up there."

"Oh, there are?" Mother didn't seem interested in the ceiling. She was busy looking for a story to read.

Lunch was good. There was another story after lunch and then a rest period. It seemed stupid having a nap when I was in bed all day anyway. The afternoon brought more coloring in the coloring books. The day was slowing down. It seemed it would never get to be supper-time.

Mother stepped into the little room with the thermometer in her hand. "PollyAnne will be home from the hardware store soon. Maybe she'll visit with you before supper. Right now, I need to take your temperature."

It was nice smelling the crisp, cotton housedress and the vague, soft odor that belonged only to my mother. I liked having my mother sit on the side of my bed while she counted the pulse in my wrist.

"Still the same," Mother announced.

"Doesn't it go up and down?" I asked.

"Well, mostly, it seems to be up a bit. The doctor says the medication he's giving you should bring it down soon." Mother sat telling me about the housework she'd been doing all day. I wasn't really interested, but it was nice having someone in the room with me, nice not being alone.

Suddenly, there was a noise downstairs. "That must be PollyAnne," Mother said. "I'll be back in a bit. I've got to go check in with your sister and get supper started."

I was mad. I wanted my mother all to myself. It seemed like Mom wanted to be with Polly more than me. At the time, I couldn't see that I'd spent all day with my mother while my sister was away at school. It felt to me as if I was being stuffed away in this horrible little bedroom while everybody else got to do fun things downstairs! I began to cry.

I was still quietly crying when PollyAnne came to the doorway. "I've got something for you!" Polly had a big, brown bag in her hands. "Can I come in?"

"Sure." I really liked my sister a lot. I was glad she was here, but this sickness stuff made everything different. We don't get to play together often because PollyAnne is so much older and busy with grown-up things, but I at least have fun when we are together.

"What's in the bag?" I asked.

"It's for you. I saw it at work and thought you needed someone to talk to when Mom and I are too busy. Here, open it."

I took the bag, holding it out away from me, staring at the outside as if I were afraid something might jump out. Slowly, I opened the top. Instead of reaching inside, I poked my head into the bag. I was trying to be playful with my sister, feeling guilty about being jealous of her, and so put off finding out what was inside the bag. PollyAnne laughed.

"Take it out, Silly."

In the bag was something soft and brown and fuzzy. That much I could see. Putting my hand into the bag, I pulled out a stuffed monkey about a foot high. He was made of a soft, light brown, short-haired fabric that made him velvet-like to the touch. His happy face was a light tan color with the mouth molded into the broadest smile you could imagine. His painted-on eyes fairly sparkled with glee. The finishing touch was a bright red ribbon around his stocky neck.

I couldn't help it. Giggling, I hugged the monkey to my face, kissing his smiling mouth. It was love at first sight. Then I took a finger and traced along the happy, smiling mouth. With my arms extended, I held him up above my face. His long tail dangled down between his legs. "Look at that crazy tail! Can he use his tail to hang from trees?"

"He can do anything you want him to do, Bitzy. He's yours to play with any way you want. I thought you might want someone who could listen to you. It can't be much fun being stuck up here alone all day."

I hugged the monkey again. My tears were dried and gone, forgotten in the delight of a new toy.

"What are you going to call him?" PollyAnne asked.

"Monkey, of course, what else?"

"I guess that'll do. I'm glad you like Monkey. I've got to go back downstairs and help Mom finish supper. Have fun with Monkey."

When Mother brought the tray up that night, I had Monkey lying on the pillow, resting on his back right by my shoulder. He was nestled in close to my head, and we were both looking up at the ceiling. I was whispering to him, telling him about the other animals in the plaster. He seemed to really care about my thoughts.

# Looking Through My Therapist Eyes

# Monkey

Bitzy's rendition of events brings forward some intriguing ideas concerning the dynamics in her family. It is interesting to note that PollyAnne recognizes how lonely it must be for Bitzy to be shut away from her family and other children. It is her sister who provides a companion of sorts with which the child can communicate.

As Bitzy presents her mother, the woman seems to take excellent physical care of this little girl, but we see several times when the mother is unable to share her feelings. In the hospital, when Mother faces leaving her child in the hospital, she doesn't share any of her pain with Bitzy; she looks away. And again, in Bitzy's bedroom, as this mother, for the first time, tucks her child into bed knowing of the many months of confinement ahead, she is awkward to the point that Bitzy comments on her discomfort. But her mother never speaks about the suffering in her heart— something that might have, in later months, allowed Bitzy to speak about her own pain.

I understand that part of this behavior was part of the times, and the mother believed she was protecting the child from her pain, but if they had been able to go back to this topic later, I think it would have helped Bitzy and most likely me.

We have already heard the reasons why Bitzy's mother is unable to share her feelings—her history of emotional abandonment due to the circumstances around her birth. But it is tragic to note that this legacy of feelings being locked within has been passed down to Bitzy and me and I can see they are traveling along the family lines in later generations—even the cobbler's children don't have shoes. Oh, to have a Mummy who can hear me!!

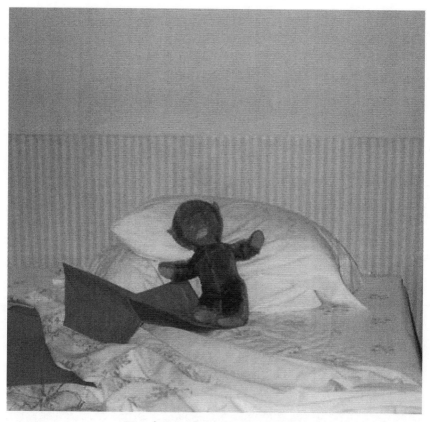

Bitzy's Monkey Companion P.

CHAPTER FIVE

# Staying Inside the Lines

**M**ONKEY BECAME MY only friend. As the days moved along, other stuffed animals came as gifts to live on my bed. But it was always Monkey that sat beside the tray each morning or whispered secrets in my ear when Mother was too busy with the washing.

Monkey got to watch when Mother brought in that horrible tasting, yellow, powdery medicine. It was hard to get down. I hated it, and sometimes I forgot I'd promised Dr. Clark that I wouldn't make a fuss. I certainly did make a fuss! "Please, don't make me take that stuff. Please, please," I'd beg. But then I'd see how upset my mother looked standing there, holding the spoonful of strawberry jam with the yucky medicine hidden inside. That picture usually shortened my carrying on. Then I'd change my tactics. If it had to be—could I have it in something sweet, or better yet, could I take it later? None of these suggestions worked with Mother. Afterward, Monkey would cuddle up close to my face and tell me how sad he was that I had to take that bad tasting stuff.

Today was Dr. Blackmore's weekly visit day. He always came up to my room with a serious doctor-like expression on his face, as if he didn't like being here. "How are you doing today?" he'd say, setting his black leather bag on the floor beside the toy box. Never waiting for an answer, he'd start getting out his terrible tongue depressor, shiny stethoscope, and flashlight. I hated that wooden depressor!

This day Mother stood in the doorway watching as Dr. Blackmore went through his routine. After listening to my heart, he pulled the stethoscope out of his ears, and hanging the instrument around his neck; he turned to speak to Mother. "I've been reading in the literature. They've got a new experimental drug out that I think might work on Bitzy. It's called penicillin. It was developed during the war for soldiers in the field struggling with an infection. We should drop the sulfa drugs and start her on this new medication right away, that is, if you want her to try it. They call it the "wonder drug." It's much more powerful than sulfa drugs. Are you interested in putting her on it?"

"Do you think it is safe enough for a child to take, Doctor?"

"Well, this early in its development, we don't know, but it seems like the best choice at the moment. You say the temperature's not gone down yet?"

"No. It hovers around 100 degrees most days."

"I think this will turn the tide. Let me order some up today."

Listening to the conversation, I prayed that whatever it was, it wouldn't taste like rotten eggs, gone bad for years and years. I hated those sulfa drugs!

That evening, the tray arrived with supper and a bottle of dark-red syrup. Mother said, "Now we've got to get a spoonful of this stuff into your mouth. How about opening up for me?"

"Does it taste terrible?"

"Oh, no, I don't think so."

*Was Mother bluffing?* I shut my eyes and opened my mouth. The spoon slipped into the hole in my face. I closed my lips. . . . It tasted like cherry cough drops!

"Hey! It tastes like candy! It tastes like candy!"

"I never thought you'd get this excited over medicine! I'm glad it tastes better. Now here, eat your supper up for me, too."

*   *   *

The days moved on very slowly, filled only with tiny things like new medicine, nicely arranged meals, stories with Mother, and an occasional visit from PollyAnne. Dr. Blackmore's house-call each Friday afternoon marked off the passing weeks. There wasn't much that I could do to play—since I couldn't get out of bed. I even had a long discussion with Mother about how much "up" I could sit. Could I just sit right up straight in bed to color, or did I have to stay propped up on one elbow as I worked? Mother voted for the one-elbow-prop, probably realizing that sitting upright in a bed was only one move away from slipping a foot out onto the floor and standing up.

"This is a dumb way to color pictures!" I declared one morning.

"I wonder if it's the position or the way you color the pictures," Mother replied.

"What do you mean? What's wrong with my pictures?"

"In school, didn't the teacher show you how to color each part of the picture with a different color?"

"No. . . ."

"Well here. Let me do one with you, and I'll show you what I mean." Mother sat down on the toy box and leaned onto my bed. She spilled the crayons out of the box, picking out a brown one. "See, Bitzy, the dog, should be colored brown, and then, you could do the little girl's dress in red. Here, you take the red crayon and color her dress while I color the dog."

I lay in the bed watching how Mother moved the crayon around the lines which formed the dog and then filled in the space with the brown color. I tried to do the same with the red crayon on the girl's dress.

"There, see how much better it looks—how colorful? If you'd color the little boy's pants blue and the tree leaves green, you'd have lots of color in the picture."

I eyed the picture. I wasn't sure I liked all the different colors. But then again, Mother seemed to think it wasn't right the way I'd done it. Maybe Mother's way was better. I closed the book and put it near the bottom of my bed. "I'll color the rest later," I said.

That afternoon, when Mother stopped by to find out if I wanted a story before supper, she found me busily coloring a picture, first with one crayon, then another. "I see you're trying my trick?"

I nodded my head.

"Want a story before supper?"

"Yup!"

The coloring books began getting steady workouts. And people supplied new books with more complicated pictures. PollyAnne came to visit one afternoon after work. "What would you like to do today, Bitzy?"

"Can you color with me in my new book?"

"Sure. Let's see which one I can do." PollyAnne flipped through the pages. "You've worked on a lot of them, I see. Didn't anybody tell you about staying inside the lines?"

"Inside the lines? What do you mean?"

"Here, I'll do one." PollyAnne picked up an orange crayon and began shading around the fat pumpkin's inner edge in the picture. "See, you kind of outline the part you want to color first, and then you shade the whole thing. That way, you don't go outside the lines. It makes the pictures look neater. Sometimes it's hard to do at first. You try."

I looked at my sister's head bent over the coloring book. PollyAnne's medium-length, reddish-brown hair smelled of fresh shampoo, pretty to my senses. It was nice having my sister here on the bed, but her words felt like the same thing Mother had said. I wasn't sure I even wanted to try my sister's suggestion. I picked up the crayon and started to outline the doghouse in the drawing. The crayon ran by itself—up the edge of the house, across the roof, out into the grassy area, and back down the other side of the house.

"See, I told you it wouldn't be easy, at first." PollyAnne didn't seem to be having any trouble coloring the little boy's shirt.

"You don't have trouble with the crayons?" I asked.

"Well, I've been doing it for a hundred years, Bitzy. You practice for a while, and you'll be able to do it, too."

I lay there watching my sister. PollyAnne made it look so easy. Maybe I'd try it when nobody was around to watch.

"I've finished my picture. Let's see yours. Oops, I've got to go help Mom with the potatoes for supper. Let's see what you've done."

"Not much. I'll do mine later. It'll be better that way."

"Whatever, Bitzy."

PollyAnne was gone, and I lay there discouraged. I couldn't make the crayon do what I wanted and what I was doing didn't seem to be right. Neither my mother nor my sister thought my way was any good. Maybe someday I'd understand.

\* \* \*

Weeks passed, and many coloring books traveled across my sickbed. I did finally learn to keep the colors inside the lines, and I did agree, once I'd learned it, the pictures did look better.

Mother had come into the room to see how I was doing.

"I can't think of anything to do," I complained.

"Well, I guess you could color."

"I've colored so many different pictures. I hate coloring! I'm so sick of staying *inside the lines!*"

"Yes. I think I know what you mean. It's a shame that the school didn't teach you how to read before you got sick! This confinement to your bed would all be so much easier if you could read to yourself. There's not much a five-year-old can do all cooped up in a bed every day and not yet able to read!"

"Yeah," I snapped back, "but I can't!"

## Looking with My Therapist Eyes

## Inside Lines

It is amazing that the adults, and semi-adults, in Bitzy's childhood felt it was necessary to teach her how to color properly but never thought about teaching her to read!

With only one outlet to stimulate Bitzy's mind—the coloring books—surprisingly, her family could not just allow her to *discover* how to color by watching them as they colored. This method of allowing discovery avoids the need to wound the child yet again, with a judgment that the work they are already doing is not satisfactory—is not *right*. This atmosphere of judging slows down anyone's ability to learn. When negative emotions are elicited, the brain and its extended learning tools shut down.

Recognizing that being able to read would lessen the entertainment burden for Mother and possibly lessen the loneliness for her daughter, it is amazing that Bitzy's mother or someone in the family did not attempt to teach me to read.

I suppose that once again, needing to avoid emotions, Bitzy's mother locked herself into a housework routine that kept her from having to be present to Bitzy's suffering. Or perhaps in a most logical sense, Mother was concerned that she would be ahead of the other children when the child returned to school and then be bored. Whatever the reasoning, Bitzy was left mostly to her own imaginational devices—in a child, a sure equation for profound loneliness, which then in adulthood leads to a yearning for intimacy while avoiding it; in a sense, practicing what one has experienced.

Bitzy's mother, my mother, had a nodding acquaintance with the teaching techniques in the mid-1940s, and she was aware that the method of the day to teach a child to read was not to teach phonics but to teach a child to sight-read; in other words, recognize by shape, size, and context what the word had to mean. My guess is that my mother, Jordan Elizabeth, raised by a mother who taught all her children to read using phonics, did not feel she was qualified to teach reading. On the other hand, I am surprised that PollyAnne didn't teach whatever method she wanted to Bitzy.

Over the years, I have learned that Bitzy's mother, my mother, tried to keep the older children away lest they pester or upset Bitzy over some issue. Because of that, my memories of my sister, PollyAnne, and brother, Owen, are almost magical; these people seemed to me to be grown up, do almost anything they wanted, and only came on occasions to visit with me. It is a very lonely experience to live in a house where there are other children, large or small, and not interact with them for whatever reason. The things we learn through years of experience.

# CHAPTER SIX

# Horses on the Ceiling

B EING SICK WITH rheumatic fever wasn't an adventure anymore. I was beginning to understand what my mother meant when she talked on the phone downstairs, telling people that I had a long term illness. Staying in bed was feeling forever long!

The coloring books were full. Monkey had heard every story I could dream up, many times over. And he was squirming under pressure to find something new about which we could talk.

The fight with Carol Simpson was a distant memory. What Carol might be doing to some other poor kid didn't cross my mind. It seemed so far from me now. Nobody came to see me except my mother, Polly, and Dr. Blackmore. I could hear my brother Owen and my father downstairs at mealtimes, but they didn't come to visit much.

Because of my bed placement in the room, I couldn't even see the fall leaves changing colors. My mother told me the days were getting shorter, but to me, they seemed endless.

My world was this bedroom. I didn't feel happy. I didn't feel sad. I didn't even feel angry any more because I couldn't get out of bed. The days were filled with the same routines.

Friday was the high point. Dr. Blackmore came in the late afternoon, seeming dark and angry. He acted that way because he cared about me and was worried that I wasn't getting better. But his loyal visit signaled the end of another week.

One particular afternoon, Mother stepped into my bedroom. "A friend of mine stopped by today asking about you. She left this new kind of book, said she thought you might enjoy looking at several of them." Mother put the books on the bed. They were thicker than books I'd seen before. The outside was covered with a bright shiny picture wrapped around the book.

"Open it up, Bitzy," Mother suggested.

As I flipped to the first page, a girl in a red cape and an old lady wearing a gray shawl popped out of the pages. I looked again. The book's pictures were cut from the page, folded in places, and designed to stand right out from the background. I turned to a new page. Here, a gray-black wolf stepped out of a forest of green trees, flashing a frightening smile while the girl held out a basket of treats toward the wolf.

"What do you think?" my mother asked.

"They look so real. It feels like you could get right into the picture."

"Want me to read the story part?" Mother asked, settling herself on the toy box with two other books in her hands.

That afternoon went quickly. When I was alone again, I held the pictures up to my eyes and pretended to be taking a place in the story's action—being a character. After many days, I found the stories didn't run like the words on the pages, but that didn't matter to me. The time in bed went faster.

Another afternoon when Mother stopped by, I had my head almost into one of the pages. "My, it looks like you love those pictures, Bitzy, but do be careful. They're delicate, and if you're not kind to them, you won't have the lovely pictures." After that, I tried to treat the pictures with greater care.

Owen stopped in to look at the new books, and I said, "Now don't pull at the pictures. Those are my best books!"

Owen looked right at me and opened the picture book wider.

"Don't do that!" I yelled. "Those are my special books!"

I don't know why older brothers are like that, but Owen just kept stretching my book. I screamed and hoped someone would come to stop him. Later, I tattled on Owen, and Mother explained that he didn't know what to do with a sick sister, so he teased me as if I was well.

Owen didn't come often, but this day I was almost glad when he left, and I could get my precious books back.

As time went by, the books became old and no longer of interest. I had memorized the stories and told them over and over again to Monkey. One tiny part of one of the flip-up characters had torn loose. Most days, the books were in my toy chest or spread across the bottom of my bed.

Over the months, I grew accustomed to being in a bed and felt lazy, sleepy, not even thinking about getting free. Life seemed serious, not hard work certainly, but serious. I didn't fight any longer inside myself about not being able to play like other children. My dream world was coming in closer and closer, and I forgot about the other children. I was slipping into a quiet place, framed by the edges of my bedroom.

The days were short and the light entering my room in the late afternoon was dim. I lay in silent loneliness staring at my ceiling. As my vision altered, the cracks came alive. A man was standing tall and beside him, a fatter man. Underneath them were wiggly-looking horses. The two began to move, and the horses started to trot, picking up speed. Perhaps someone was chasing them.

Yes, back in the distance, was a barely visible group of Indians, or were they animals? I blinked my eyes. The riders were gone. But close to where they had been running was a cluster of houses. A woman stood outside. She brushed at the sidewalk with a skinny broom. The broom wasn't clear because a crack ran across the whole village, making it look like a broken windowpane. And there, off to the left, was a big bear. He wore a red bandanna around his neck and was standing upright, moving one foot at a time around in a circle. His front paws stuck out before him. Was he dancing? He looked over his shoulder, and I knew he was dancing for me. The bear looked happy, giving me some fun. I smiled back, and the bear was gone.

In the twisted lines right over my head was a doorway, partly open. What was behind the door? If I could get the door to open . . .

"Bitzy, what are you doing here in the dark? Let me turn on a light."

Mother's voice cuts into my concentration. "I am watching the horses on the ceiling," I said.

"What horses?" my mother asks. "Let me see."

I point to the spot where the horses had been. Mother turns her head, trying to view the ceiling from my perspective.

"I don't see anything but a bunch of cracks. You say there are horses up there?"

"Yes," I respond. "There are horses, and an old woman, and Indians, and a door that goes somewhere."

"Well, I guess if it gives you something to do, there might as well be horses on the ceiling."

For an instant, my eyes fill with tears. Mother doesn't see them. She isn't excited. She doesn't understand!

Not seeing my tears in the dark, my mother goes on, "Whatever you say, Bitzy. I'll turn on the light and take your temperature. Now, move your things so I can bring up supper."

Mother doesn't see the pictures. She hardly even tried! That hurts, but no matter. I know they are there. I can see the horses!

# Looking Through My Therapist Eyes

# Ceiling Horses

Even today, my mother doesn't see the horses on my ceilings. We are two different people, but as a child, I needed her to understand my perspective, be in my world.

Two strong issues become visible in this part of Bitzy's story. She says that Owen, her older brother, seldom visits her, Owen who is close in age to PollyAnne, the oldest sibling. Bitzy sees Polly as a strong personality, outgoing, talkative, projecting a solid sense of being. Polly seems to be close to their mother—Mother's right-hand helper. This companionship sets up a pattern in which Owen, as a boy, feels he is outside the picture. He must model his behavior on what he sees from his father, a man who is physically present but emotionally removed. We will talk more about Bitzy's father in a later chapter. This isolation from the males in Bitzy's family affects her life in an acute manner—another psychological wound—causing her to yearn for men while being awkward, somewhat withdrawn, or a blatant flirt when in their company.

The other issue that Bitzy points to as she talks is the difference in personality typing between her and her mother. One of the first psychiatrists, Carl Jung, and later expanded by Myers and Briggs, explains these personality differences. Bitzy's mother would be classed as a Sensing Type, using information gained from her senses. Jung's theories explain that a Sensing Type is primarily concerned with details—the nuts and bolts of living. Most people manifest two of the four personality types as they live in the world. The first typology classification is how an individual gathers information and the second typology classification is how one processes that information. Bitzy's mother has emotional damage from her birth and childhood circumstances, causing her to suppress her expressions of deep feelings inappropriately. This damage is incorporated into the way she functions as a Feeling Type, either verbalizing emotional material in a restrained manner or with excessive emotions.

Bitzy, by contrast, has the Intuitive Type as her first function. Using Jung's typology again, she takes abstract information out of the air in an almost magical manner. This way of gathering information causes Intuitives to use their imagination creatively, seeing connections between unlike things and events, weaving this material into an abstract reality. Bitzy's second function is like her mother's, a Feeling Type, which causes her to process incoming information in terms of its emotional charge. With the feeling function prominent, one decides if things are right or wrong, good or bad, kind or unkind. In her story, Bitzy speaks about knowing that Mother doesn't want to leave Bitzy's room on the first night after returning from the Winchester doctor—this is the Intuitive at work. And if life had not damaged the Feeling function in the family, Bitzy might well have stated that she felt her mother's anguish. Children often absorb the damaged aspects of their parents. Bitzy recognizes that feeling words are not used in her family—the damaged functioning of the Feeling Type—and yet she experiences the emotions within the room. Deferring to her mother's strongest typology, Sensation, Bitzy states that she *recognizes* her mother's discomfort, which is an observation, taking in information through the eyes.

This crossing of typology between mother and child is why Bitzy's mother has no interest in the horses on her daughter's ceiling.

The mother's mind is on getting a hot supper into her child—the Sensation Type as the first function—while Bitzy is excited at the sudden recognition that she has an escape hatch from the imprisonment of her bedroom, her imagination—the Intuitive Type as the first function. Bitzy's ability to see the animals on the ceiling becomes a gift in later life. It is because of this typology cross, Bitzy feels unheard, wounded—her mother cannot understand and reflect back to Bitzy the world according to Bitzy's experience. And this crossed-type experience exists in many families, creating a lot of miscommunication and hurt feelings.

# CHAPTER SEVEN

# Thanksgiving from a Bed

With the daylight time getting shorter, my world grew into a smaller and smaller space. Everything seemed to focus around my being sick. Even my bedroom seemed to be getting smaller. I knew that couldn't be true. But sometimes, I wished it would eat me up, and then the sickness would be gone. The only part that gave me any fun was my friends on the ceiling. Mother never did see them, but she told me once that I had quite an imagination. The stuffed animals on my bed became actors in endless games I played between the animals and my few toys.

When Dr. Blackmore came on Fridays, he'd often ask if I was having pain in my knees or elbows. "Do they hurt?" he'd ask. My mother told me later these were characteristic symptoms of rheumatic fever.

"No. My knees and elbows don't hurt," I would tell the doctor. "Sometimes my arm hurts from being propped up on it all day doing things. I can't sit up, you know. The elbow only bothers when it's stuck into the bed too long. Nothing hurts—it just lies in bed all day doing nothing." My body wasn't a problem—it was useless. Only my head seemed to give me fun.

*   *   *

Halloween was a few days away. Mother never let me go trick-or-treating even when I was well. That was something only the big kids were allowed to do since most of the adventure in the mid-1940s was a matter of "tricking." Children didn't get dressed in monster costumes and go around asking for candy, as much as older youngsters would dream up wild pranks to play on each other or somebody's parent who was easy to scare.

It was Wednesday, and Halloween was on Friday this year. Right after lunch, both Mom and Dad came up to my room. (With Dad's job, he always got to come home for lunch). "You're doing so much better," Mother said. "We thought we'd give you a treat. Daddy's going to carry you down to the dining room where we've fixed up a nice day-bed for you. Would you like that?"

"I can come downstairs today?!"

"Yes. We thought you could have your nap down there while PollyAnne and Owen are in school. Then when they get home, you'd have a chance to be a part of the family until time for supper. We'd have to bring you upstairs to eat your supper. Daddy's home by then, so it would be no matter to carry you back." Mom stopped, took in a breath, and looked at me as if she wanted to see some reaction.

I was so surprised about this change that I was silent.

It had been so long since I had seen anything other than my room that for a moment, I was frightened. Daddy didn't wait for more conversation but bent down and scooped me up, I and my flower printed flannel pajamas. Mother got in the way while trying to tuck in the edges of a protective blanket she'd thrown around me. When Daddy got to the top of the stairs, he moved my body to one side to see and to make sure I and my dangling blanket would fit going down the stairway. At the bottom, he stepped to his left into our sunny dining room.

I had forgotten how nice Daddy smelled—that bit of body odor from hard work, mixed with the scent of dying leaves from his landscaping job outside. He smelled safe like when I was tiny and he'd pick me up on his lap, tucking me into a corner of his arm as he tried to read the evening newspaper. Snuggled now against his faded, blue denim shirt, I felt safe—so safe to face this change in my small world.

Daddy put me down onto the day-bed in the back-right corner of the room.

"There," Mother said, "Won't that be so much better to be down here with all the rest of us?"

Suddenly, I wanted to cry. I wished my Mother could know how great it felt to be back near the whole family again!

That afternoon, when Owen got home from school (he was fourteen and skinny but not as skinny as me), he went straight to the kitchen. In our house, the kitchen, connected by a short storage corridor, was behind the dining room where my parents had placed my daybed. I could hear almost all their conversations from my bed.

"Mom, how far away do you suppose Gavin's house is from ours?"

"I can't say. I've never had a reason to measure it. Why? Why do you want to know, Owen?"

"Oh. No matter. I just wondered."

"You aren't thinking up some trick to play on Mrs. Gavin, are you?"

There was no answer from Owen, only silence. From where I was listening, I could picture the way Owen would slightly droop his blond head so he'd be looking at the floor, not wanting to meet Mother's eyes and give away his thoughts.

"Well?" Mother's voice was sharp. "Are you hatching up a plot, Owen?"

There was still no comment from Owen.

"Whatever you do, don't make it a mean trick. You know how easily Mrs. Gavin gets frightened when her husband, John, is held up late at work."

"Maybe . . . I'll tell you about it after Halloween," Owen offered in an attempt to get on Mom's good side.

There was a moment of total silence, and then Mother made a clearing noise in her throat.

"Have you got a very long piece of string and one of those sticky rubber suction cups you use to hold your cigarette ashtray onto the old, brown chair?" Owen asked.

"Yes. I think you'll find both things in the top right hand kitchen drawer by the sink. But what exactly are you up to?"

"I can't tell you right now. I don't want you to give it away before Friday. I'll tell you later."

I could hear him move across the kitchen to the drawer. I heard it open and then close. *What was my brother planning?*

Owen was very busy for the next hour going up and down to the basement, outside onto the front porch, where he could see across the street to Gavin's house, and then back down to the cellar. I listened from the dining room. *What on earth could he be scheming?*

Shortly after all this action, PollyAnne got home from the Hardware Store. Surprised to see me downstairs, she came into the dining room and plopped down on a chair. "Hey, it must be pretty nice to be downstairs," she said as she handed me a large red Maple leaf from the tree out front. "I brought this to you because I thought you could use something bright. It's the last one that isn't all dried up."

I took the leaf and turned it over in my hands. I stroked the back of the leaf. It felt soft like human skin with the veins all sticking up.

"Did you do a lot of coloring today?" Polly asked.

Putting the leaf down, I showed her the pictures I'd completed.

"These are looking good. Don't you think so?" And with that, PollyAnne was off to the kitchen to talk to Mother.

Later, Dad came home from work. He poked his head into the dining room. "How do you like it down here?"

"This is great, Daddy!"

"When I've said hello to your mother, I'll come to take you back upstairs." He disappeared down the central hallway that led back to the kitchen.

Upstairs again, waiting for supper, I found I was tired. It was nice to be back in the safe, quiet space of my bedroom. I closed my eyes for what seemed like a moment, and then, Mother was in the doorway with the evening tray.

Friday came and went without much excitement. The only "trick" that happened to our family was a broken branch on the young tulip tree that Daddy had set out on the side-lawn six months before. Dad was furious! As the landscape instructor for the state reform school, he was very protective of all the plantings around the houses, most especially our own. "Some dumb kid was taking a shortcut across the lawn during the night and ran into that new tree in the dark. Why is it they always find the one I've just set out? You'd think a boy could walk around it instead of right through the center. I'd skin his hide if I knew who it was!"

If Owen had observed the tree's attacker, he wasn't talking. Had he seen the kid when he was spooking Gavin's house?

From my place on the daybed I could hear him change the subject. Mother had him cornered in the kitchen where she was ironing. "So do you know who got the tulip tree, Owen?"

"I wasn't with the other kids. I was busy with my prank on Gavin's place." He wasn't waiting for Mother to ask again about his buddies.

"You know that string I took?"

"Yes?"

"Well, I took the little silver thing on the suction cup from your ashtray. I tied a long string on it."

"I can just imagine what you did with it!" Mother sounded as if she'd rather not hear the outcome. But her comment didn't slow Owen in his confession.

"In the afternoon, I took my bike over to Gavin's lawn and put it in behind their front bushes, so that I could get away fast. I had to be extra careful that Mrs. Gavin didn't hear me. I climbed up on the bicycle seat and stuck the suction cup high up on the windowpane where she wouldn't see it. Then after dark, I went back, held the string in one hand and rode like lightning, across the street to our porch and tied the string to the support post."

By now, Mother had lost track of the tulip tree. "Weren't you afraid a car would come by and pull the string down?"

"Well, that was why I needed my bike over there, so I could stand on the seat and get the string high enough to clear a car."

"So, what happened?"

"I waited 'til about ten-thirty because Mr. Gavin gets home at eleven. I pulled the string, and the metal piece next to the suction cup went tap, tap, tap on the windowpane. Mrs. Gavin came running to the window and looked out. I could see her from the light of the living room lamp. I stopped, and she went back to her chair. Then I pulled the string again—tap, tap, tap on the window. She was back in an instant.

This time she put her hands up on the window as if maybe she could feel for the sound. She didn't see the string. I waited until she'd gone back to her chair. I pulled the string again. She got smart this time and shut the light before she came to the window. She looked all over the glass. I could barely see her from the light behind her in their kitchen. Then she pulled the curtains like she was mad or frightened. I guess I scared her good!"

Listening from the dining room, I could just imagine the look on Mother's face. My Mom was not above a prank or two of her own, but at the same time, bothering the neighbors was not a good idea, living in a small community like ours. "Well, I guess you got me to forget about the tulip tree, Owen," Mom said. "I hope Mrs. Gavin will still speak to me when she figures out who was making her Halloween eve for her."

Not much other excitement took place from Halloween until Thanksgiving. Being down on the daybed every afternoon made the days go faster. It was a nice change of view.

Thanksgiving dawned dark and dreary that year, 1945. Mom was busy with the turkey downstairs in the kitchen, so she had to rush with my breakfast tray. "I'll be back, but you'll have to wait a while before I can wash you up this morning. Polly and I have all the vegetables to get ready. I thought maybe you'd like fresh pajamas today to celebrate. I'll be up again in a while."

*It is going to be terrible this year. My family will all be downstairs, and I'll be up here in this tiny room by myself. Big deal! Thanksgiving turkey and gravy—alone!* I lay in the bed feeling sorry for myself. Monkey tried to be comforting, but I was into pity.

"Okay!" Mother announced from the doorway. "How about we put on those pretty new pajamas after your wash-up?"

I didn't say anything but just let her bathe my face with the warm water in the white, enamel wash pan. The fuzzy washcloth felt soft as it slid across my shoulders and under my arms. Mom handed me the towel, and then she helped me put on the new pajamas. As I was buttoning the last buttons, Mother stepped to the top of the stairs. "We're ready," she called down. Returning to the room, she said, "Daddy's going to carry you downstairs for Thanksgiving. How about that?"

As Daddy lifted me into his arms, I fought back the tears. I didn't want my parents to ask why I was crying. At the bottom of the stairs, Daddy stepped into the dining room. The sight was beautiful! The linen-covered table held a gigantic roasted turkey crispy brown and oozing with meat juice where Mother had stabbed it with a fork, testing for doneness. There were mashed white potatoes, orange squash—yuk, turnip—double yuk, small white baked onions, Dad's favorite chunky cranberry sauce, and his sweet potatoes. Beside the mashed potatoes stood the decorative yellow flower pot filled with brown gravy. Last year, for some reason, Mother had forgotten to dig out the fine china gravy boat. There had been guests at the table, and handing the flower pot to them, she'd said, "I can't seem to remember to get a proper container. Here, have some gravy for those potatoes." Today, it didn't matter. It was a comfort knowing there would be the joke about the yellow flower pot, and I would be there to hear it.

Dad put me down gently on the couch, pulling the covers up to my waist. "Now, how about a big Thanksgiving feast, little one!" he said, patting my legs before moving over to the head of the table. My Dad checked the sharpness of the carving knife. I knew from last Thanksgiving that he'd already sharpened it to a fine edge. I could tell now by the way he drew his thumb across it, ever so carefully.

The other family members began taking their places at the table. Grandmother Moody sat to Mother's left, then Aunt Agnes—she was Daddy's cousin on his mother's side—then PollyAnne. On Dad's left was Mr. Herald, the State School's blacksmith. My folks often invited him to Sunday dinners because he didn't have "any of his own in this country," they said. Next to Mr. Herald sat Owen. My place would have been between Owen and Mother. There was just a moment of shock as I saw my chair was missing. Then I remembered— I was on the daybed right behind Mother's place! What difference did it make? I was here and part of this magnificent Thanksgiving family dinner.

After Daddy carved the turkey and the others added the hot vegetables, Mother turned to her mother, saying, "Grammy, would you say the grace for us?" There was a tiny tremor in my mother's voice when she spoke. I wondered why. Maybe that was part of a family thanksgiving.

Everyone bowed their heads, and Grammy's voice spoke out strongly with its deep, steady tone, surprising for a small woman of her age. "Thank you, Lord, for another safe year and the bounteous table before us. Bless this house and family seated together. Thank you for the little girl that is getting better here among us. Bless those who are not as fortunate as we, and provide a safe way through the coming year for all. Amen."

PollyAnne motioned with her head to Mother.

"What is it, Polly?"

"We forgot the celery in the refrigerator!"

"So we did! Would you go get it, please?" Turning to everyone, Mother said, "I don't know why we always forget the celery! But it seems to happen every year." I wondered if that would become a family tradition, too.

PollyAnne reappeared with the long cut-glass dish in her hands, heaped high with bright green celery. She set it down on the table, and as if that were the signal, everyone began eating.

## Looking Through My Therapist Eyes

## Bed Thanksgiving

This chapter in Bitzy's story is the first in which we begin to see the strength of family and why she is so motivated to be *a good girl* for the doctor so that she can *have babies* when she is grown up. For all the shortcomings of this family—like most other families—they also have warmth, caring for one another and outsiders, and solid family traditions. This positive family image holds Bitzy on her course of staying confined to her bed for six long months. Some colossal feat for a five-year-old turning six!!

The trained eye also sees the beginning of the split in the psyche. The internal child is in misery with her feelings of loneliness and abandonment, the tears upon being carried downstairs. Yet, in the face of such apparent family happiness, she is suddenly happy. Children's feelings do move this quickly from one side of the aisle to the other. But the authenticity of these feelings comes when the child has voiced their true inner emotions. Bitzy has not shared her profound loneliness, as a sickbed prisoner, with a single individual outside of her monkey.

This splitting of feelings tends to hide one's real emotions by immediately turning away from pain to pursue something to make one happy, and that coping skill will dog Bitzy for years into the future. So, if we spy deeply into Bitzy, we can see she has already absorbed the Cinderella myth. This story presents the belief that if the female is good enough and works hard, a prince will rescue her and everything will be good and happy. The second myth is that of the Wizard of Oz, with his promise of the Yellow Brick Road. And in this myth, the belief is that if one can dream long and hard, is cheerful; one will automatically get the prize. These two myths are very American complexes, but ones that are hard to bring into consciousness and work through to the place of resolution.

# CHAPTER EIGHT

# Yes, There is a Santa Claus

EVEN CLOSED AWAY in my bedroom, I knew Christmas was coming. That came next after Thanksgiving. *It seems like it will never get here.* It was hard to know how fast time was moving because days just slid into oncoming days.

One day when Mother came in for the daily wash-up, she said, "Bitzy, how would you like to have your room moved around a bit? You're so close to the window now, and it must be getting cold with winter almost here. Besides, if we changed it, you might be able to see outside a bit."

I just looked at Mom. There wasn't much space in my little room. *Where could she move the bed that it would make any difference?*

"When the 'all-morning' boy gets done with his work downstairs, I'll ask him to come up here and help us move your bed." I knew Mother was referring to the State School inmate that my father sent from his work-gang each morning. The all-morning boy's job was to help Mother with the household tasks.

Daddy handpicked the best boy he had in his gang. He chose him for his trustworthiness and general cooperation. The boy only got to stay until noontime, but it was considered a reward to be pulled from the regular squad for house duty. Often Mother would send little goodies back with him to his cottage, like a piece of the family birthday cake or a slice of pie she'd made. It gave a sixteen-year-old juvenile delinquent a tiny piece of happy family life, if only for four hours each day.

"James is the present all-morning boy. He'll be free in just a few minutes," Mother said.

Soon, James was upstairs in my bedroom, pushing and shoving my bed around. "The white bureau will have to move, too!" Mother tried it first one way and then another. "You know this room doesn't leave much space for imagination," Mother said.

I was thinking differently. With the bed moved to a new spot, there'd be a whole new batch of characters to find in the ceiling cracks. I'd have a fresh new set of pictures from which to make stories for Monkey. *Something new to do!*

Finally, Mother settled on an arrangement. My bed was now at the opposite end of the room, almost directly across from the tilt-in window. The white bureau was in the cubby beside the chimney where the chimney came up from the kitchen, passing through my room on its way to the roof. That was to the left of the bed. The all-morning boy put the green toy box in place of the bed. It looked lonely left in the opposite end of the room. I wondered where Mother would sit when she read stories.

"There!" Mother announced. "It's a little top-heavy with all the furniture at one end of the room, but your sloping ceiling makes arranging furniture a real challenge." I didn't care. *It was my nest, and it was a change!*

I spent the next week looking for new ceiling friends. It was like a spy hunt, helping me keep my mind away from how long it was until Christmas. I also enjoyed seeing outside just a little, not enough to see trees and sky, but at least a chance to see the windows of my brother's room and some reflected sky. He had the room that looked out over the screened-in back porch. If my bed could have moved a touch more, I would have had a clear view of Owen's window and been able to see the pine trees across the street. Instead, I had to be contented with remembering them.

*   *   *

The house was beginning to buzz with Christmas excitement. Mom and Dad had put their heads together again with the result that I was able to come down on special afternoons to rest on the old blue couch in the living room. Today, the family was going to decorate the Christmas tree.

"Want to come down and watch us get the tree ready for Christmas?" Daddy was standing in the doorway. I couldn't believe he had to ask!

"Yeah, sure, I want to come down!"

He gathered me up, blanket and all, and we made the now-familiar trip down the stairs. This time at the bottom, turning to the right and walking across the entrance hall, Daddy stepped into the living room. It was a long, narrow room with six windows arranged in pairs around the three outside walls. A fireplace was on the fourth wall. I wondered why they never had a fire in it. No matter. My eyes caught sight of the undressed, green Christmas tree stuck in the old, wooden, cross-shaped tree stand. It smelled so good! They'd moved the blue couch to the long outside wall across from the silent fireplace, making room for the Christmas tree. The tree sat proudly in the back window, filling the room with its Christmas scent.

Dad plumped the couch pillow. "There, you can coach all the decorating from here."

That was the joke. Dad did the coaching! He always sat in his rocking chair with his newspaper open for reading. But it usually drooped in his lap as his eyes inspected where Owen, PollyAnne, and Mother were putting the decorations. Occasionally there would be a quiet, "You missed a spot over there . . . Need a decoration to the left . . . There's a hole on that side."

Mother held her irritation in until later. "Why can't he just get up and put something on the tree if he wants it there!" she'd sputter. "He faithfully brings the tree in from the yard every year, where the State School boys drop it off. He cleans it up and gets the wooden stand on it. From there, he expects the rest of us to do all the decorating!" I knew that even though Mother complained about Dad's way of tree decorating, it was still the accepted way of having Christmas.

Owen opened the box containing the tiny nativity figures. "Bitzy, where should we put the crèche this year?"

"I don't know!" I said, surprised that he asked me. Owen usually made his own decisions. But I watched as he pulled Joseph and Mary out of the yellowing tissue paper. It was nice to have been asked.

"Here, you hold Mary while I get the Kings out." He handed me the tiny figure of a kneeling woman. She was painted in a soft blue, while her under-robe was a creamy white. I wondered, *what's it like to be Mother Mary—the mother of such a special person? It must be scary to be that important.* I drew my fingers across the smooth plaster-of-Paris statue, and my thoughts wandering on. *What will it be like for me to be a mother someday? I'd like to be a mother.*

"Here, I need that now. All the other figures are up." Owen was reaching for the statue. I wanted to keep holding Mary as if she were my promise of a future. I handed the statue to my brother, not quite releasing the figure into his hand. As we both held Mary, he looked at me for a split-second with a strange look. Then taking Mary, he set her into the scene he'd made under Mother's sewing cabinet.

I was tired that evening when Daddy carried me back up to my room—it must have been all the excitement of Owen and PollyAnne around, busy with the tree. The constant tug of wishing I could take an ornament myself and put it on the Christmas tree, but not being allowed, had drained away my energy.

I lay quietly in bed, waiting for the supper tray and looking at the ceiling. Would Santa know I wanted a Jack-in-the-box for Christmas? *How does he get to know what I want, anyhow? Who tells him?*

I remembered the mailbox Mother helped me make last year out of an old used shoe box. She'd gotten some string and we'd tied it to the white, street-marker post that was at the edge of the backyard, under the giant oak tree. I'd written a letter to Santa and put it out in the box. Mother had to do most of the writing because I didn't know how yet. After it snowed, the box got all soggy and bent. I got two of the things I'd wished for, so Santa must have found the letter. *Now, how did he get to the box without my seeing him? . . . Oh, all this thinking is just too much work!* I shut my eyes.

"Ready for supper?" Mother was standing beside the bed. The food on the tray smelled really good. I was hungry!

*  *  *

There was just a week until Christmas. Owen was getting ready to go to the community Christmas party. It was the custom at the State School to have the parents of all the instructors' children put on a Christmas party at the old Shaker Meeting House which they now called the Club House. There were Disney cartoons first at the Central Building—the major administration building for the school, and then our bus driver drove the children to the Club House where a sparkling Christmas tree awaited them. Spicy smelling strings of evergreens always decorated the room. (It was my father's job to make these decorations each year with his gang of boys.) Christmas carols played on the big console record player. The women had made cookies and cake and served a sweet-tasting punch. Santa came each year to give out the gifts the mothers had purchased for each of the other children. It was like a giant family Christmas! Mom said I would have to miss it this year. I tried not to cry about it. But it wasn't fair! Owen was getting to go, and I had to stay home in this dumb bed! He'd get to see Santa Claus, and I'd miss out! I pounded the bed with my fist, and the tears came.

Through my temper tantrum, I could barely hear my mother downstairs. "Owen, are you going to the Christmas Party? I thought you might be too old this year."

"Yup, I'm going. Someone has to take the presents you have from Bitzy for the other kids. She can't be there."

"Well, I don't have to serve refreshments this year, so I could run them up in the car if you didn't want to go."

"No. I'm going. That way, you don't have to worry about them."

"Okay, Owen. Whatever you want to do."

I pounded the bed with my fist and then placed one last well-aimed punch into the bed and subsided into massive tears. I heard the door close downstairs behind my brother. I wasn't getting to go. *This world is an utterly cruel place!*

The silence in the house was deafening. Mother had driven Owen to the party and would be right back. There didn't seem to be anything to do. I lay in bed staring at the ceiling. This treatment wasn't right. There was nothing I wanted to play. *I just want to be with the other kids!*

Mother returned and started to bustle downstairs over supper. Even on Christmas party day, meals had to be gotten. I lay quietly in my bed, watching in my mind, each step my mother was taking downstairs. I was getting good at this—seeing in my head, what was going on underneath my space. Memory was a good tool!

I could pretty well tell by the sounds coming up through the floor that Mom was about ready to bring my tray upstairs.

The chairs were scraping across the floor as PollyAnne and Daddy pulled them up to the table.

Brrrrring! Brrrring! *What was that? That's the front doorbell,* I thought. *Who's ringing the doorbell at supper time?* I heard my mother's footsteps move up the front hall toward the door. Then there was laughter and muffled talking as the door swung open.

"Ho! Ho! Ho! Does a wee blond girl live here? One of my busy elves told me that a little blond girl was sick in bed in this very house! Where is she?"

I could hear the heavy boot-steps starting up the stairs. *Was it Santa Claus? Was it Santa Claus coming to visit me?*

He burst through the bedroom doorway, all red and white, big and burly with a white beard and bushy, white eyebrows. One sweeping gesture poured the contents of his green bag onto the bottom of my bed. A jumble of prettily wrapped presents tumbled over my feet.

"I believe these are for you, little one! And what else would you be wanting from Santa when I go back to the North Pole? Christmas is not far away. You need to tell me quickly. I can't stay long. I have to be getting back to my workshop and my busy elves if all you children are to have a proper Christmas! Now, what is it that you want?"

For a minute, I just stared at him. *Santa Claus was really standing in my bedroom—and at the end of my bed.* I tried to remember what I was going to write in my letter to Santa. *What was it that I wanted?* "A Jack-in-the-box, please," I said.

"A Jack-in-the-box? Well! Well! Well! We'll have to see about that when I get back to my shop. One Jack-in-the-box for Bitzy Girl.

Now you just remember that." He turned to an imaginary elf standing beside him and gestured as if the elf was expected to write the request down. I giggled a silly, happy giggle. *Imagine Santa and his elves in my bedroom!*

"Come on, open your presents. I haven't much time to stay here. I've got to get on to the others." Santa bent over and poked a finger into the wrapping paper of the package I had picked out of the pile. "Now, don't be careful! You're a child. Just rip into it quick so we can see what you got."

My fingers worked so slowly while I tried to get into the package. As the paper fell away a floppy Raggedy-Ann doll dressed in blue, with a white apron and a smartly embroidered red mouth appeared. I held her up to inspect.

"No stopping now, on to the next!" Santa commanded, handing me another package.

This one proved to be more troublesome. Mother had been standing at the far end of the room, with her arm draped around Owen's shoulder. "I'll run and get you a pair of scissors," she said, leaving the room.

When she returned, Santa was stepping back from the bed. "I've got to be going." He picked up his sack where it had fallen. "You have a good Christmas, and don't forget to have your brother put out my cookies and a carrot for the reindeer. He's a good lad, you know, your brother Owen." He waved goodbye with his big mitten-covered hand and left the room.

Mother went down to let Santa out, and Owen moved closer to the bed to help me open presents. He was there only a few minutes when Mother called, "Owen, come on down and get your supper. It's ready."

"I had cookies at the party!" he called back.

"All the same, I think you should have some real food to go with your dessert. Come on down." Owen slowly backed away from my pile of gifts, responding to my mother's words.

As I opened the rest of my presents, I could hear the family talking underneath me.

"You asked Santa to come and visit your little sister?" That was my mother's voice.

"Yup. I don't think it's fair, her having to stay home and miss all the fun. She loves Christmas, and I'm too old for Santa and that stuff."

I heard dishes clink as silverware hit plates.

Owen continued, "I think she needs to be cheered up. I told him my sister was sick in bed at home, and it would really make her happy to see him. He only hesitated a minute and then said, 'Yes, I can come after I give out the other children's gifts.'"

"You know, Owen, that was a very thoughtful thing to do for Bitzy. I'm so proud of you!"

## Looking Through My Therapist Eyes

# Santa Claus

It is interesting to note that the older children are the ones who recognize Bitzy's intense suffering caused by her being shut away from life. The family doesn't talk about their feelings or those that Bitzy must be having—at least not within her hearing—but the other children do recognize the problem. Like most good New England families, no one shares their emotional responses to events; they feel the emotions, and Owen, in his way, tries to make it better for Bitzy. He puts aside his embarrassment at *being too old to go to the party* and uses that time to talk Santa into making the trip to Bitzy's bedside. For all that Owen does not talk or visit much with Bitzy, he seems to have natural empathy and understanding for the deeper parts of his sister.

To Mother's credit, she recognizes what her son Owen has done for his sister and takes the time to praise and thank him. If you want kind behavior in your family, you must reinforce it with praise and recognition.

I wonder if this isolating of Bitzy in the household, and all the silent emotions circling around her and her illness, caused the older children to resent Bitzy. This sick child must have consumed much of their mother's attention and time, intensifying the natural sibling rivalry. With a family that cannot talk about what is happening to them, the feelings get suppressed, only to surface later in life, sometimes unbidden and with surprising ferocity.

Here I would like to share a story that I wrote in my present-day blog "My Little Bird by JMK" that illustrates just how these repressed feelings can come forward:

These attitudes displayed here between myself and my mother set me up for some unexpected backlash from my older siblings long after these days had passed. My sister PollyAnne had been married for many years and lived on a farm with her husband and four children. I was married with three children and beginning to think about a divorce. I and my children had gone to visit my sister during the summer as I played with could I handle my children alone.

PollyAnne came out of the house with a wet dishrag and asked my middle daughter, Elizabeth, to wipe off the outside wooden picnic table in preparation for a picnic. Elizabeth was about seven at the time and did her best to wipe off a table that had seen much use and abuse over the years. A little time later, PollyAnne came out to inspect. (I have to interject that Polly was a very calm, laid-back sister, and I can't ever remember her being mad when I was a child.) She let loose with a whole barrage of insults as to how well Elizabeth had cleaned the table. (I can't repeat here the words she used.) Elizabeth was crushed because she thought she had done a good job. I was stunned. I simply stood there, shocked by what had just happened.

Wisely, I didn't address the incident at the time. It was several months later, when my sister and I were talking, that I said, "I have to talk to you about a situation between us." I reported what I had seen and heard. I told her that I didn't think it was an appropriate response on her part, and then I asked the magic question: "Do you suppose you were yelling at the little sick sister who never could do anything wrong?"

PollyAnne was silent for a moment, and then she said, "Oh, I am so sorry! You're right. All I could see was the 'sweet little sister' from whom Mom told us to stay away. I couldn't even yell at her. She always had Mother's attention and got her way every time."

# CHAPTER NINE

# Sunshine in a Basket

IT SEEMED LIKE Christmas was long ago. Time moved so slowly, being a five-year-old shut away from the world with rheumatic fever. Next month would be my sixth birthday. Big deal—a birthday in bed!

"Monkey, it's too bad you had to stay up here in bed for Christmas. I couldn't believe my eyes when Daddy gave me that package wrapped in red and silver paper. Guess what was in it?

Monkey didn't say a word.

"Come on, guess! You give up? The Jack-in-the-box, of course! Santa remembered and had the elves make me a Jack-in-the-box. It has a clown head on it. He doesn't pop up too fast. It won't scare you, I promise. Want to see?"

Monkey must have agreed because Mother said she could hear all the way downstairs as the little latch released on the metal box, letting Monkey see how the Jack-in-the-box jumped out of his hiding place. Then—snappity-click—he was locked back into his box.

Under the tree, I'd also gotten a little red bulldozer with black caterpillar treads. It had to be wound up first but then would run from one end of the long living-room to the other, pushing and bumping into the furniture in its way. Of course, each furniture attack left it stranded until someone came to nudge it free. I couldn't play with this toy by myself. Owen volunteered to help. I would lie on the blue couch in the afternoon during Christmas vacation, and Owen would wind up the bulldozer, releasing it to run on the dark maroon rug. That worked well for a short while. Then I'd say, "Owen, let me have the bulldozer to run."

"Next run. You can have it on the next run."

"But it's mine. Mommy and Daddy gave it to me. It's not yours! Give it to me."

"If I give it to you, you can't chase it. I'd better keep it. I can make it run better than you can. Besides, you can hardly wind it up."

"Owen! It's mine!"

"Owen, is there some trouble there with Bitzy's toy? You know I asked you to help her play with it since she can't fetch it herself." Mother's voice came from somewhere beyond the living room.

With a mean grin on his face, Owen called back, "No problem, Mom. I wasn't getting it fast enough for Bitzy."

"You're terrible!" I whined from the couch. "Give that to me. It's mine! You can't play with it anymore."

"Okay! Okay! I'll be nice," and with that, Owen brought the bulldozer to the couch for me to wind up and release. He knew one more yell from me would bring Mom, and she'd say he couldn't play with it at all.

Knowing it wasn't wise to push his luck, Owen brought the little red bulldozer over to where I lay. While I struggled to wind it up, he stood quietly and watched as I swung my body around and released the toy onto the rug. It ran crazily around Owen's feet and then scuttled off toward Mother's brown reading chair. It settled snugly into the claw-foot of the chair, stuck for the moment. "See, I told you; you can't handle this toy."

"Yeah, but it's mine. Remember, Mom said you were just supposed to help me play with it."

Owen loosened the toy and brought it to me. The bulldozer made a few more major trips across the rug, and then both Owen and I tired of the activity. Owen went off to the kitchen, and I lay on the couch examining the little red bulldozer: ridges on its black treads, the plow on the front that moved up and down, and the tightness of the key stuck in its side that set it into motion.

* * *

January, a month of long, gray days, was colder than usual this year, or so Mother told me. The days were so dark, with not many hours of sun to shine through my tilt-in window. I wished for the time to go faster. *What will it be like to get up out of bed and walk? Will they ever let me walk again? Have I been quiet enough that I'll be able to dance when I get to high school? I'll be as big as PollyAnne then. That seems like a long, long time away. Maybe I'll have a boyfriend. Polly doesn't have one. But then PollyAnne is in school all day and working after-school at the hardware store. She is pretty busy.*

As I wandered through my thoughts, the sun broke through the clouds filling my room with bright morning sunshine. It felt so warm— so cheerful in the tiny room. Maybe it wouldn't be much longer that I'd have to lie flat in this bed. My body soaked in the edges of the bright sun's rays filtering into my space.

"Bitzy, I've got a special surprise for you today." Mother was moving around in the bathroom next to my room, drawing water in the white enameled bowl she used when she gave me a sponge bath each morning. "Your Aunt Jenny and Uncle Charles were here yesterday. Did you know that?" Uncle Charles was Mother's middle brother, and Aunt Jenny was his wife who couldn't have children. She paid special attention to me whenever I got to visit my aunt and uncle.

"Yeah, I heard you all talking downstairs. Why didn't Uncle Charles and Aunt Jenny come up to visit me?"

"They hadn't come to visit but to drop off a gift for you. Your aunt and uncle were on their way to do something else."

"Can I see the present? Can I see it right now?"

"No, Bitzy, I want to get you washed up and set for the day. Then you can see it. I also want to tell you about this gift. It's very special. Your Aunt Jenny spent a lot of time making this for you. But I'm not going to tell you anymore until you see it!"

"Aw, come on, Mom, hurry up! I want to see what it is."

Mother seemed to take twice as long to wash under my arms and put on fresh pajamas. Next, she brushed my hair, shaping it into two neat braids that kept the hair from becoming a tangled mass of blond hair scrubbed to death against a pillow. Finally, Mother was done.

"I'll go downstairs and bring it up. Be just a minute."

*She's taking so long. Why does Mom always drag everything out like this?*

"Ta-da!" Mother set a wicker laundry basket in the sun on the floor beside my bed with a flourish. The edges were all wrapped in pink, green, and white crepe paper. The handles, twisted tightly with the colored paper, were covered and tied with crepe paper bows. Colorful, curly streamers flowed from the edges of the basket, spilling onto the floor. And the basket itself was mounded high with artfully wrapped packages in different colored papers.

"This is for me? Just for me?"

"Yes. This basket is all for you. Wasn't your Aunt Jenny nice to do this?"

"Can I have the presents now?"

"Well, that's the trick to it. It's a sunshine basket. Your Aunt Jenny arranged it so that you get one present to open every day until there are no presents left. Isn't that a great idea? That way, you've got something to look forward to every day after wash-up."

As she spoke, Mother fished around in the basket, pulling out first one package, then another. Finally, she settled on one and gave it to me. "I had to look for the one with today's date on it. See, Aunt Jenny dated every package so you'd know which one you could have today." Mother flashed the date before me as she handed me a funny-shaped, flattish gift. Aunt Jenny must have known about little girls, for none of the packages had ribbons to cut or bows to untie. I tore at the tightly scotch-taped paper. Santa had taught me well. There was no careful saving of paper. Rip! Rip! And the object was out into the sunshine in the room.

"What's this?"

"Haven't you seen one of these before, Bitzy? It's a paddle with a ball attached by an elastic cord. That way, you can hit the ball, and it can't run away from you. Pretty smart idea for a girl stuck in a bed all day. Try it."

I made a feeble attempt at hitting the ball. It sagged lifelessly back onto the bed.

"Here, I'll show you. You're going to have to sit right up in bed to have space to work it. You're getting some better. I think you could do that for a few minutes." Mother held the ball and batted at it with the wide wooden paddle. The little red ball raced off into the air only to be jerked back to the paddle. Mother flexed her wrist, and the ball flew from the paddle again. "See. It just takes a little practice. You try."

I tried again. This time the ball cooperated and spun out along the elastic cord, only to be pulled back with a smack against the paddle. "See, I can do it, too!" My delight at success rang through my voice.

Mother smiled. She looked as if she was having as much fun watching me as I was having, making the ball run. Maybe the sunshine was beginning to shine into this long, horrible illness. Perhaps a happy ending was coming for all of us.

"Can I have another present?"

"No. I told you what the deal was. Your aunt marked each one so that you would have only one a day. That way, there will always be something out in front for you to look forward to."

"I know. I just wanted to see if you'd change your mind."

"You fox! I bet that's why your aunt dated them. She knew you'd want to be into all of them at once. Well, I wonder what you'll get tomorrow." With that, Mother moved the basket away from my bed, leaving it where I could look at it and dream of tomorrow's package and what new adventure it might hold.

## Looking Through My Therapist Eyes

## Basket Sunshine

Bitzy has been locked in bed, so to speak, for four months now. Depression is evident; at the same time, we see the beginnings of the child looking forward in time, an indication that the depression may start to lift. There is a growing maturity that one senses in the way Bitzy speaks about events. Also, it becomes abundantly clear that this little girl has discovered the extreme control Mother is exerting over the older children, with her spoken, or unspoken, command to them not *to upset their sick younger sister*. Is this why Owen is surprisingly quick to give up his teasing of Bitzy over the red bulldozer? This teasing is healthy in terms of keeping this child in a somewhat normal family environment.

In this chapter, Bitzy becomes aware of the power she has to manipulate the rest of her family by being *a sick person*. A talent, which I know from experience, she never loses.

We can see how this much isolation is taking its toll on our child in the fact that the only two events Bitzy chooses to talk about are a little red bulldozer and a basket full of gifts. In a month, that is not much mental stimulation. The other question, of course, is whether Bitzy is even present much of the time, or is she emotionally suspended somewhere above the events of her life?

Adults, who have been abused or have suffered from a post-traumatic event, talk about leaving their bodies, going somewhere else in the universe to avoid experiencing the intense physical and emotional pain during the abusing event. This splitting of the mental and physical aspects of the individual sets a person up to have many issues they cannot quite bring into consciousness. It is as if they wander around in the world, being only partially present to the events and circumstances of their lives. An escape hatch, if you will, but not a safe or fulfilling place in which to live.

On the Left: The Pressed Glass Cream and Sugar Bowl P.

# CHAPTER TEN

# Stepping Outside the Bed

I COULD HEAR DR. Blackmore's feet coming up the front stairs. That meant it was Friday. He'd drop his old black leather doctor's bag on the floor and make an effort at some pleasant-sounding questions. He never carefully placed his bag but rather leaned forward, swung it close to the floor, and let it settle itself with a soft thud. Today he looked almost cheerful. "Your mother tells me you've had a birthday recently."

*What is he getting at?* I wondered. "Yeah, it wasn't anything big."

"She says you're now six years old."

"Yeah. My family just had a cake for me. Mom says when I'm all well and back to school, maybe then I can have a real birthday party. She says I have to get better first."

By now, the doctor had taken out the old silver stethoscope from his bag. He wasn't taking my temperature every Friday anymore. The stethoscope felt cold against my bony chest. Dr. Blackmore sat on a little straight chair Mom had brought in, and with the little black tips of the stethoscope in his ears, he turned his head in one direction and then twisted it the opposite way, as if to better hear the tiny pounding heart. "It sounds better in there. Your mother says your temperature was normal twice this week, although not for all day. That's really good news. It shouldn't be too much longer."

*What does he mean? "It shouldn't be too much longer?"* But it didn't feel right to ask him. Sometimes he seemed frightening–his face serious, in a frown, his eyebrows scrunched up—he usually felt so distant. Today, he acted friendly, but still, I held back my question.

"Well, I guess you're done for another week. It's a better picture we're getting here. Shouldn't be too much longer, Bitzy."

Somehow, I felt I ought to be happy, but I didn't know why. Dr. Blackmore didn't usually call me by name. *Why did he do that?*

The doctor picked up his leather bag, as if it were a weary chore, and traced his steps back down the stairs. I could hear his deep, voice talking to my mother in the lower front hall, but I couldn't hear what he was saying.

My eyes wandered to the sunshine basket. What would be in the basket tomorrow? Today, Mom had pulled out a heavy, lumpy package. "Here, I believe this is the one you want. It's marked Friday, March 8, 1946." Handing the package to me, Mother stood waiting for my hands to tussle with the wrapping paper. A tiny glass pitcher popped out, immediately followed by a matching tiny glass sugar bowl.

*What is this? Some stupid glass pitcher? I want a toy!*

Mother's quickly drawn-in breathe ended with, "Oh, Bitzy . . . ," making me turn to look at her.

"Honey, that's a tiny pressed glass cream and sugar set. I can use it on your tray to hold maple syrup for pancakes and sugar for your cereal.

I turned the pitcher over in my hands, examining the dimples pressed into the sides.

Mother went on, "But really, they're lovely things, and we should take especially good care of them. When you're well and grown-up, you can have them in your own home. Someday you'll get married. Then you'll appreciate them." If Mother said they were important, I would try to like them, but a toy would have been more exciting.

That evening, when the tray arrived, Mother had filled the little glass pitcher with milk and the sugar bowl with just a bit of sugar. My favorite chocolate pudding sat at the back of the tray, again. Mother knew I liked to sprinkle sugar over the tight surface of the dark chocolate pudding and then add a touch of milk. Maybe the creamer and sugar bowl weren't such a loss.

Mother had also added a tiny glass, hardly bigger than a shot glass, next to the new creamer. It had a rusty-brown liquid in it. "What's that stuff?"

"Dr. Blackmore said you sounded so much better, but he's still concerned with your pale skin color and the temperature that goes up and down. He feels you need to eat better. I guess he wants to fatten you up a bit! Anyway, that brown stuff is a tonic to build up your appetite."

I took a sip of the brown liquid. "It's sweet!" I said, screwing up my face into a horrible grimace. "It burns! That's funny stuff—tastes good and terrible at the same time!"

"I don't know. I didn't try it. However, the doctor seems to feel it will build your desire to eat. He wants you nice and strong before he tries putting you up on those long legs. Do you realize how much you've grown while you've been in bed?"

Growing was not one of my major concerns. I didn't even know what mother was meaning. I looked under the covers at my legs. My feet stuck out a little more at the end of my pajamas, but otherwise, they looked the same to me.

"I bet you've grown two inches just lying around this winter. When it's time for you to be getting up, you will need all new clothes."

The words 'getting up' slid right by my attention. My mind was stuck back on having grown taller, maybe even two inches taller. *Perhaps I'll be as tall as Carol Simpson. Carol will have to pay more attention now that we might stand eye to eye.* In my mind, I didn't recognize that while I was growing, so was Carol. Somehow, for me, time had stopped when I crawled into bed six months ago. Like a butterfly coming out of its cocoon, I anticipated everything in the outside world to be as I had left it.

\*   \*   \*

Time had crept on into April. A week ago, Mother had gone through another room arrangement, and the bed was now back to its starting point beside the window. "With Spring here, your room's going to be getting hot some days, and that fresh breeze close to your ear should feel good."

As Mother left the room, I was playing with the red rubber ball from the ball and paddle set Aunt Jenny had given me. The ball had come off after a particularly violent round of ball batting. Sometimes, in pure fury, I'd bat at the ball as if it was my rheumatic fever, and I could beat the disease out of my body. Snap! The elastic string had broken. I hid it from my mother for a while, but then, Mom spied the little ball sitting alone on top of the blanket one day. "Had an accident with the ball and paddle?" That was all she said. I was afraid she would take the ball away now that it was free.

Rolling the ball around in my hand, I thought about the incident. I shifted the ball to the other hand and then back again. Starting the routine a second time, first the right and then . . . the ball went flying up into the air and down. Bouncing twice, it settled about four feet from my bed on the floor. Quick as a dog after a bone, I threw the covers back and scrambled towards the ball. When my feet hit the cold wood floor, I suddenly realized I was stepping outside the bed. *What if I can't walk? What if someone catches me? Can I get the ball and get back before anyone downstairs hears my footsteps?* Like a flash of summer lightning, I crossed the floor and was back into bed holding the tiny red ball—a defiant symbol of my first rebellion.

I lay still in bed listening. All I could hear was my pounding heart. Nobody came. Nobody had heard me. *I did it! I got out of bed and back without my heart stopping, or my legs breaking, or anything.* Then, I got scared. *Maybe I've just done something to hurt my heart. But it was so easy! Just two steps, and I had the ball for myself. Surely that little trip was not going to damage my heart. Should I tell Mother? No! Most definitely not!*

It was only a week later when Mother announced with the morning wash-up that she had a surprise for me. "What is it?" I asked. "What have you got for me? Is it a toy?"

"No. It's not a toy. It's something I want you to try to do for me. But first, we have to get your hair combed." Mother brushed hard at my blond hair. Was Mom mad? She seemed to be pulling more than usual. "Ouch, you're hurting."

"Oh, I'm sorry, Honey. I guess I'm a little excited."

Mother put the brush over on the white bureau. "Now, for my surprise! I told Dr. Blackmore last Friday that your temperature has been normal for a week. He thinks you are well enough to get out of bed." Mother spoke carefully, looking directly at me. "But you understand you can't just get up and run around. He believes you may have to learn to walk all over again. Mom paused as if she were measuring my understanding. "That means one step at a time, and then another step. Today we will see if you can stand up; then, tomorrow, you can take a step. Each day it will be another step." Mother was standing, looking directly into my eyes as if asking if I understood.

I met my mother's intense look. From somewhere deep inside my wise soul, I answered, "I understand, Mommy." I wasn't about to tell my mother that I had already stepped halfway across my room. *What if I broke my heart on that trip? Better to keep quiet and do things the way the doctor says. One step a day seems dumb since I already know I can walk.*

Mother pulled the covers off and stood back to let me move my legs alone. First, one leg was over the side, and then the next. The rug beside the bed felt rough to my feet with its rows of neatly woven rags pushed tightly one into the next. I'd never realized how heavy my body was. My wobbly legs stood straight, locked at the knees, and slightly tilted like a new fawn's. My ankles did indeed show well below the pajama bottoms. I played my part like an actress. "Look, Mom. I can stand up!"

"Just look at that! You're standing up for the first time in over six months. How does it feel to be out of bed?" The relief and excitement showed in Mother's voice. I guess it had been a long six months for her, too.

"Good. It feels good! I think I could take a few steps. Can I try?" I wasn't going to let on I already knew I could walk. "Oh, no, Honey. I think we need to do just as Dr. Blackmore says. We've all been working too hard getting you well to take a chance on messing things up now. Just standing for today!" Mother moved in to touch my shoulder. "Tomorrow, you can try a step. Now you'd better get yourself back into the bed before your legs say they're tired."

As I sank back into bed, I was surprised to find that Mom was right.

My legs were very tired. My body felt funny. It wasn't used to being upright. It complained with mild twitches and weak spasms through my legs. *Tomorrow! Tomorrow I can take a step, and then Wednesday I can take two steps, and Thursday . . . how long will it take? How long before they'll really let me walk?*

## Looking Through My Therapist Eyes

## Red Ball

As is so often true in life, the little red ball and its burst into freedom from the confinement of being attached to a paddle heralds Bitzy's burst from imprisonment back into life. In a sense, her unconscious defiance of going after the ball speaks to the strength of spirit needed in this next phase of her illness.

Patience in learning to do something Bitzy already knows she can do–walking again–must be maintained to benefit the adults around her. Imagine the conflict of suddenly being free to move about and yet having to hold back this exhilaration. But in her child-like wisdom, Bitzy understands that this is the way to gain her freedom.

Freedom to move and the confining demands of relationships seem to be emerging as life issues for this child. Her start into school and the adventure of dealing with other people and their demands were too much. Perhaps fortunately, Bitzy became ill and was temporarily allowed to retreat from this challenge. She gave up freedom to avoid relationships. Now freedom is reappearing, but this time our child is older and has learned valuable information about the price of not extending herself into relationships. Still, there are many more lessons ahead. And the question remains: was Bitzy afraid to go off to school, or was her mother afraid to let her go? This mother and daughter were so symbiotic that the question has yet to be answered some seventy years later.

In a recent addition to these notes, I can tell you now that we took my mother in to live with us for the last of her days, and when the death-day came, she somehow conveyed to me that I was to be somewhere else while her caretaker held her hand through those very last moments. So the question remains about this very symbiotic relationship: who was unable to face separation?

# CHAPTER ELEVEN

# First Steps Then Blood Taken

I AWOKE BRIGHT AND filled with excitement. *Today Mother and the doctor are going to let me take a whole step. Maybe Mother will let me take two or three. If I can only take one step a day, it will be forever until I can walk again!*

I lay still in bed, listening to the rain beat against the panes of glass in my window. What was it Mom had said yesterday, "April showers bring May flowers?" Well, by the sounds outside the window, there were certainly going to be many flowers come May. The wind whistled with a soft encouraging tone as it gusted into the corner between my bedroom window and Owen's. It was as if the elements were cheering me onto my feet.

Mother stepped into the room with the breakfast tray. "Are you ready for the big day, Bitzy?"

"Yeah! Can I take a step right now?"

"Oh, No! Not so fast, young lady. We've got to get some breakfast into you and wash-up, and then maybe you can try."

*Why does Mother always wait until later for everything?* I slammed my spoon into the cereal dish. *I was tired of waiting!*

Indeed, Mother waited until she had cleared the tray, scrubbed my face, combed my hair, and then she said, "Now, Bitzy let's see you take a whole step." This time I threw back the covers like a theater queen and flung my legs off the bed. The rug felt squishy beneath my feet. I'd forgotten that feeling from the day before. *One full step will take me off the rug.* I stood still. *Should I bargain for the extra steps now or start and then not be able to stop? Besides, what was a step? Do I move only one foot or both?*

I decided on the start-and-find-out method. Out went the right foot and then the left, a shift of weight on the feet, and now the right . . .

"Whoa there! We said only one step today and then another tomorrow. That is the deal."

Mother was too quick. She wasn't supposed to have noticed. I struggled to regain my balance as I drew the right foot back under me.

"This is silly! One step a day and it will take the rest of my life to walk! I know I can do it."

"Yes, I can see you can. But we need to do it the way Dr. Blackmore feels would be best. You'll be walking soon enough."

I sagged back into the bed, which was not that far away. This time the sag was not from muscle fatigue but from anger at being held back. I wanted to be well—to run and play, like other children!

The rest of the day seemed to drag. All of my attention was focused on tomorrow and being able to take two steps. Tomorrow came, as it always does, and this time I had to wait until the afternoon until I was downstairs on the couch in the living room! With slippers on my feet, I stepped strongly away from the couch. Watching my feet to see that they behaved properly, my eyes saw the swirled pattern of oak leaves buried in the maroon rug. *Maybe I can count oak leaves. No, they're too small. If I count oak leaves and only take one step each day, it will take forever to cross the living room. Best to forget about the rug and just take the second step.*

By the seventh day, I was surprised to find I wobbled as I took steps. Maybe it was because I was only allowed to take a few at a time. I didn't understand that my muscles had weakened over the six months in bed. I was longer and thinner, and things didn't seem to be in the same places where I'd left them last fall. The drive to outgrow the prison of my bedroom became intense.

The day came and went when it was fifty steps. "My goodness, you look as if you'd been walking all winter. You are really doing fine. The doctor says he feels we can stop counting steps, but you must remember you can't run, not at all, not anywhere! Only walking, and that slowly."

I was overjoyed. "Does this mean I can come back to eat at the table with the family?"

"Well, I don't think we should try that just yet. It gets confusing and busy at the table, what with PollyAnne and Owen. I'm afraid it would tire you too much. Maybe next week."

So again, I began to work toward a carrot held far out in front of me. To be back with the family for meals would feel as though I were well again.

Finally, family mealtimes came and playing for short periods on the living room floor. Then, came walking up and down the stairs to my second-floor bedroom—all these things I had longed for came and went so easily. I felt fine. Mother had to keep reminding me that I still tired easily and had to do things slowly.

\* \* \*

I was sitting on the living room rug looking at a book when my mother came walking into the room. "Bitzy, do you remember when Dr. Blackmore stopped to talk with me last Friday?"

I shook my head. It hadn't caught my attention.

"Well, we talked some about you. The doctor thinks you are doing very well. He feels it is time you were getting back to some schooling. He is recommending that I take you back into Winchester to see Dr. Clark." Mother hesitated, I guess, to see if I was listening. "Remember the nice heart specialist that saw you—the one that talked so seriously about staying in bed so you could have children when you are an adult?"

This time I nodded. I remembered Dr. Clark. He was the nice man that talked to me as if I were a grown-up. It would be fun to see him again. Suddenly, I felt vaguely frightened. It had been a long time since I'd been any distance away from my bed. I remembered the long trip.

Mother must have seen the look, for she went on.

"Next week, we will get all packed so we can stay overnight with Grammy, and I will drive you in. We'll stay the night with your grandmother and go to the doctor's the next day. That way, you won't have to deal with the long trip both ways on the same day."

I smiled. I liked my grandmother's house. Inside there were dark rooms and rooms lit with bright shafts of sunlight, especially her kitchen at breakfast time. Green plants grew here and there, mostly in the living room, and the whole house smelled of cookies baking and that vague smell of Grammy's violet-scented perfume.

My grandmother, Mary Emma, was a short woman, softly rounded everywhere, but with a strong presence that you felt the moment you were near her or when she spoke to you. Grammy's voice was never harsh—she never yelled, yet her tone was firm. She was always glad to see everyone, and when she opened the door, her joy at having company drew you right into her hug. Caught in her arms, she would squish you into her, and she felt to me like a feather pillow. Next came the soft kiss on the cheek, and then she'd hold you away from her at arm's length to see how much you'd grown since last time. We wouldn't be at Grandmother's long before she'd say, "Do you suppose, Bitzy, that you are big enough to handle my best cut glass tumbler for your milk?" She always asked the same question as she moved to the dish closet and took down the special glass, the one with the round swirl cut deep into both sides. Then she'd walk around the kitchen table, her old-lady, black lace-up shoes tapping on the linoleum floor. At the icebox, she'd pick out the round glass bottle of milk. Then she'd go back around the table to get the Aunt Jemima cookie jar full of fresh cookies. "Here, there are several kinds in there. Take as many as you want."

"Oh, no, I think not," Mother chimed in. "It's right before supper, and she'll spoil her appetite. I think two would be more than enough."

"But she's so thin! A few cookies aren't going to hurt her." With that, Grammy rattled the cookies in the jar. "If you two are going to see the doctor tomorrow, we'll need to get her fattened up by then."

I loved this gentle bantering between my mother and grandmother—it wasn't a new conversation. Sitting at the kitchen table feasting on milk and cookies, I watched as a ray of late afternoon sunlight streamed through the west window, striking the far side of the table and my Grandmother's small rocking chair.

The two women moved into the living room, leaving me to finish my cookies alone. It felt so cozy in Grammy's house. Mother always seemed happier and more relaxed here, too.

Mother went upstairs to open up the suitcase and get our things out for the night just before supper. I followed. We'd have the double bed in the guest room at the head of the stairs. Mother pushed the stuffed backrest with the arms on it aside, opening the big, squared-off, black leather suitcase on the cedar chest that stood against the wall beyond the foot of the bed.

Was the picture still there? I turned to look at where the plastered chimney came up through the room. Yes, it was. Grandmother had a gold-framed, oval picture hanging on the wall of a nineteen twenty's woman draped in gauzy white. Adoringly, the woman gazed at a baby she held in her arms. Tiny ringlet-type curls and tight finger waves framed the mother's face as she looked with love at the rosebud infant. *I want to be that kind of a mother*, I thought, as I stared at the picture once again. Somehow having that picture there made the room seem all safe and warm. It was good to be in Grandmother's house.

The next morning was a lazy morning with Grandmother cooking the bacon and eggs. It was lazy until Mother said, "Oh, my goodness. Just look at the time! Bitzy, we are going to be late for that appointment."

I didn't remember much about the trip from grandmother's to the doctor's office. When it was our turn, the doctor came to the waiting room door himself and motioned us into his room. It was bright with the sunlight of the late morning. "So, how have you been?" He spoke to me.

"Good."

"Just good? That's all? I thought you'd spent a long time in bed being quiet and resting for me."

"Oh, yes. I did that. I've been learning to walk again. Actually, I already knew, but it was Dr. Blackmore that wanted me to learn again."

Dr. Clark chuckled at my story. "It looks like you've been doing a first-rate job. Today we're going to take some of your blood to test and listen to that old ticker you have in your chest. I want to see just how good a 'rester' you've been." With that, he turned his attention toward Mother and asked me to wait outside in the waiting room for a few minutes. A nurse led me out and gave me a magazine in which to look. I didn't like being away from my mother in this strange place, and besides, what were they saying about me?

In a short while, Dr. Clark called me in to join them. "We're going to take some blood from your arm so we can have it tested. We want to see how well you've gotten. But first, I have to listen to your heart." He took the stethoscope from the top of his desk and placed the silver round of it up under my cotton knit undershirt. I jumped as the cold metal hit my chest. "I'm sorry, Honey, it gets so cold hanging around this office."

He sits on the stool in front of me, listening intently to the soft pounding of my heart. "Sounds really good. There's still a murmur in there. My guess is Bitzy will always have a slight heart murmur. We're going to continue monitoring, though. It's not unusual, but we'll have to keep track that it doesn't get any worse. Now, for the blood." The nurse walks in at that very moment with a long tube thing in her hand—a syringe. The needle sticking out the end seems as big as a pencil lead to me. This time wasn't the first time the doctors had taken blood from my arm, but this needle looks gigantic. The doctor ties the rubber cord around my upper arm. "There, now. I need you to hold your arm steady on the edge of the desk while I find a vein. You'd best not look at what I'm doing. It doesn't hurt so much that way."

He runs his large, flattish thumbs over the veins in the inside bend of my arm. Then he shifts to his right index finger and makes a second pass across the arm. He taps the flesh just above the bend and runs his two first fingers across the pale skin a third time. I look at the doctor's face. I sense something is wrong. Catching my glance, he says, "Your veins are tiny and not very exposed. There, I think we've got one. This needle will just be a prick. Now look away."

I do as I am told. When the needle hits my arm, I jump. It hurts! I bite my lip. I'm not going to be a cry-baby—the doctor shifts. Something is, indeed, wrong. I look back at the arm. The doctor has pulled the needle out and is trying a different place. This time I don't look away fast enough and see the needle, more like a drill, drive into my arm. The pain burns all the way to my shoulder blade. I bite my teeth into my lip, trying to keep the tears within. The pain is so intense I can't pull my eyes from the sight of the needle as the tube slowly fills with blood. Once again, the doctor taps above the tender inner bend of my arm and releases the rubber tubbing just a bit. The syringe is filling so slowly! *Oh, God, please hurry,* I moan inside.

Finally, the doctor withdraws the needle, placing a gauze pad over the wound, and bending my arm back toward my shoulder, saying, "You can hold the gauze in place for me. Thanks." The backward pull of the needle is worse than when he stuck the arm. Still sucking in my breath, I can no longer withhold the sob. Tears run down my face. Pressing the white pad on the painful spot with my right hand, I lean into the injured arm, swiping away the streaming tears with the back of my other arm.

"I'm so sorry, Honey. You're a real trooper! You're very brave. Most children would be screaming by now. When you jumped, I missed the vein. I had to go after it a second time. I hate this part of being a doctor. I'm sorry I had to hurt you so." The doctor seemed concerned about my suffering, making it a touch easier to stand.

It was some small comfort that the doctor was so concerned, but I felt mad at him. He'd been so nice up to this point. I could feel how upset he was at having hurt me. I felt torn between forgiving him and— not trusting him anymore.

"The worst part of all this is you're going to have to come back to see me regularly for a while. And we'll have to take blood each time. Can you understand that we don't mean to hurt you? This procedure has to be done to make sure you get completely well—get so strong that you can run and dance and do whatever you want when you're all grown up. Do you understand?

I nodded sadly. Through my pain and anger, I did understand. I wanted to like this doctor. He seemed so concerned for me. (And for your information, my mother's oldest sister, Gracie, came to work for Dr. Clark after this event, and he trained her to be his medical assistant. So on return trips, she was the one who took the blood sample, and she only pinched a little.)

## Looking Through My Therapist Eyes

# Blood Taken

Like most of us, Bitzy so longed to be out of confinement that when the events took place, they raced on by without her really taking much notice. Getting back on her feet, rejoining her family mealtimes, being able to sit up and play on the floor like a normal child all passed without notice.

Fortunately for our little girl, the day before the doctor's visit, spent in her grandmother's home, was a strong baffle for the intense physical pain she would endure at the hands of Doctor Clark the next day. The strong maternal environment in Grammy's home was a place she could fall back to when she was hurt. This place of trusting counter-balanced the horrible experience with Doctor Clark.

Because Bitzy had come directly from that support, she was better able to forgive the doctor. And it was tremendously important that the doctor spoke directly to her, explaining what he was doing and why things did not go correctly. Dr. Clark also did not hide the fact that he might have to hurt her again in the future. This honesty helped to mend the rent in their relationship. Without this type of intimacy, Bitzy might have been set up for a lifetime of distrusting authority figures.

Being unintentionally hurt for a better cause—her ultimate good health—by someone she trusted, was a large lesson, yet she could assimilate this wounding and forgive.

The other behavior to note is that Bitzy felt it was inappropriate to scream out her pain and anguish—*the good child wishing only to please others*—not wanting to embarrass her mother. From the family history, Bitzy had learned this pattern of holding even physical pain inside the body to protect other people's emotions. Bitzy's grandmother, whom we have talked about before, lost her beloved husband at a crucial time. Faced with the housing, feeding, and emotional support of five small children and an infant, she had to suppress much of her grieving. *There was just too much to do—she had to keep a stiff upper lip!* As an infant, Bitzy's mother was submerged in this unexpressed grief, causing her to believe that she too should not carry on about her own two lost children before Bitzy's birth. Our sensitive child unconsciously incorporated both of these family experiences of tremendous loss with intense emotional pain held internally. Is it any surprise that Bitzy would spend a good part of her life as an adult and a therapist, helping others uncover, understand, and release their embedded anguish? At the same time, she still has trouble releasing her own emotional/physical pain?

Our current literature is becoming abundantly clear that unresolved emotional pain, not released, can transmute into physical pain in later life. As a child, Bitzy was busy absorbing more than her share of emotional pain.

# CHAPTER TWELVE
# School After School

THE TRIP HOME from Bunker City and the doctor was uneventful. My arm, bruised in circular purple and yellow tones from where the doctor had taken blood, served as a constant reminder that even though I was no longer in bed every day, the rheumatic fever was still far from over.

The daily routine changed. Mother still helped some with getting ready, although she let me do the washing and most of my dressing. There was time up to play in the morning and a rest-nap each afternoon right after lunch. As soon as they were done eating at the table, my Dad and I would move into the living room. He had an hour for lunch-break and spent it going through the day's mail or listening to the noontime news on the old brown radio which sat beside his rocking chair on the bookcase. I would settle down on the couch for my two-hour rest.

Often as Daddy sat listening to the news, he'd nod off for a few minutes, not noticing that the radio had now shifted into the afternoon soap operas. He'd wake with a start saying, "Oh, ah, what time is it?" He'd pull out the gold pocket-watch he always carried in the tiny watch pocket of his work pants. "Quarter-to-one! I've got to be getting back to the boys." And with that, he was up and leaving the house to go back to his duties as the landscape instructor for the State School.

Each time he left, I prayed he wouldn't notice that the radio wasn't on the news anymore. Mother didn't like me listening to the Soaps. Sometimes she'd come in and turn the radio off. Today the now-familiar patter poured from the radio—'The real-life drama of Helen Trent who, when life mocks her, breaks her hopes, and dashes her against the rocks of despair, fights back bravely, successfully, to prove what so many women long to prove in their own lives, that because a woman is thirty-five or more, romance in life need not be over; that romance can begin at thirty-five." The overstated announcement ended with a dramatically romantic flare of music.

"Bitzy, are you listening to that garbage again today?"

"Yes . . ."

"How many times have I told you I don't think you're old enough to understand that rubbish, and besides, it isn't good for you."

"But it's people talking! I like to hear what's going on in their lives. It makes the nap-time go faster."

"Well, I guess that's probably true." Mother reached over and turned down the right-hand knob. "I need to talk to you for a minute."

"Remember, when we went to see Dr. Clark, and he made you sit out in the waiting room for a bit?"

"Yeah, I didn't like that much."

"Well, we were talking and trying to decide what would be the next step in your getting well and back to a normal little girl's schedule. He said he felt you could go back to school if we could make some arrangements."

I didn't hear the part about arrangements—only the part about going back to school. My heart rose in my mouth. *I have to go back to struggling with Carol Simpson every day, and all those stupid orders Teacher gives? I have to go back to those noisy, pushy kids who don't like me anyway!* "Back to school?" I asked in a very soft voice.

"Yes, back to school. You're bored here at home, and you're very much better. It's time to be getting you back to regular life."

"Oh," I said, feeling sad. "Will I have to take the bus?"

"Well, no. That's the part I have to explain to you. The State has passed a new ruling saying that every town has to provide a teacher to tutor any sick child unable to attend school. You're not strong enough yet to go into the regular classroom. I've been on the telephone with the officials and with the first-grade teacher. She says there's no way she can teach all day and then come to work with you here at the house. And at the moment, she is the only qualified teacher here in town. What she's proposing is that I drive you to school, after school, three days a week, and she will teach you alone right there in the school building. How does that sound?"

That sounded like heaven to me. *I really like to learn but I'm afraid of the other kids, and I can't seem to concentrate when they are all around. This way, I can ask the teacher questions when I don't understand, and nobody will be there to laugh at me.* It sounded like a great idea. *Now I can learn to read!*

"We're going to start this program tomorrow. After your afternoon nap, we'll get you all dressed in your school clothes, and then I'll drive you to school."

"Will you stay there with me?"

"Well, most likely I will the first day because I'm sure there are things we'll have to do here at home. You can't possibly get all the schooling you need in just two hours after school. I'm sure the teacher will have things she'll want to show me to do with you here at home."

I was satisfied with that answer. "Okay, I'll go." Mother turned up the radio again and left the room.

*Tomorrow I'll be going back to school! It won't be so scary with the other children at home.* Actually, that sounded like a nifty idea. I'd have the teacher all to myself.

I thought about Mrs. Burton. *When I was in school before, it seemed as if Mrs. Burton thought I was stupid or something. She doesn't like me. Or maybe it's because I don't get the directions right very often. Maybe she thinks I'm too quiet and shy. Teacher never liked my penmanship papers. The o's are always open, and she says she can't tell which are a's and which are o's. I sure hope it goes better this time.*

The next day, the sun was bright, and I had a hard time staying quiet on the couch for my nap. Mother had switched off the radio so I could sleep. But that wasn't too likely! I was too excited about going back to school. When the nap was finally over, Mother got me up and seemed to scrub me into a total pink before she helped me put the school clothes on. Feeling stiff and stuffed into different clothes—not much like my soft pajamas—we headed toward the village grammar school—grades one through eight.

Arriving at the side door, Mother opened the right-hand panel of the big, dark-green doors. It was spooky—so quiet in the musty-smelling building. The odor of busy children gone home, thumbed books, and dusty, discarded chalk greeted us as we moved down the long central corridor to the first-grade room at the end, on the left. Just before the classroom, I spotted the girl's lavatory that had been my refuge when things in the classroom had gotten too overwhelming. I'd go into one of the battleship-gray stalls, pull the little silver lock on the door, and just sit until Mrs. Burton called from the doorway. "Come along now! All little girls back into their seats in the classroom!"

Mother reached for the doorknob on the wooden door of the first grade. For a moment, I thought, *maybe we can just forget all this and run back home.* Then I remembered I was going to learn to read. Pulling myself together, I walked ahead of Mom into the classroom.

"My, it's good to see you again, Bitzy. You're looking very well. How do you feel?"

"I feel fine. I've been in bed all this time, you know." I spoke as if my ordeal had given me some badge of importance.

"I know. Your mother was telling me on the phone what a hard time you've been having and how cooperative you've been. Good, that part is all over. Now, I understand we're going to get down to business and teach you how to read."

*Mrs. Burton doesn't seem as bothered with me as she used to be. Maybe this isn't going to be so bad after all. She seems friendly and glad to see me.*

Placing a reddish-brown, straight-backed wooden school chair beside her desk, Mrs. Burton motioned for me to sit. She pulled out the desk extension and put a book open-faced on it. "Let's get started with the reading. Can you remember what you learned before about reading?"

I look at the book, puzzling for a moment. "This is Tom. This is Tom's dog. Look at Tom."

"That's very good, Bitzy. Are you reading that, or are you remembering?"

I'm not sure. I try to go on. The next words seem like a jumble. I struggle.

"Here, let me show you," and with that, the teacher reads the next few lines aloud. It is all new to me; what I read had been memorized from those first few days in school. *I'm going to have to start all over again! I'm so frustrated. Now that I'm here, I want just to be able to read!*

Noting the frown lines above my nose, Mrs. Burton says, "Bitzy, come on. You aren't going to give up that easily. Look, I'll show you a trick." With that, Teacher pulls a black-and-white, speckled composition notebook out of her desk drawer. "I'm going to write the words from the story into this book so you can take it home with you and read it each day at home. As I write, I want you to read aloud with me."

We sit together bent over the pull-out leaf from the desk, puzzling our way through the front few pages of the first grade primer. I don't notice my mother leaving the room.

Next, Mrs. Burton writes down four words from the story on a piece of yellow-lined paper. "Let's see how well you can copy these words. Have you forgotten your cursive writing?" I sit busily, trying to make the curves in my work look like the curves on the yellow paper. Mrs. Burton leans over to inspect. "That's looking very well, Honey. You have the o's almost closed up. Your hand is neater now. It looks much better!" *How does the teacher remember what my writing papers looked like before?*

I had no way of knowing about the hours of preparation Mrs. Burton had spent in getting ready to take on this new teaching assignment. Nor could I know about the hours that lay ahead when Mrs. Burton would copy, in beautiful hand printing, all of my lessons into the black-and-white composition books, notebooks that I got to take home to read. Teacher wrote stories upon stories in that book for me to learn. They became my school books. I didn't know anything about such things as teaching programs. What I did know was that Mrs. Burton was now warmer and encouraging and wrote these lovely books that were opening up a whole new world for me. They were my books, and now I was finally learning to read!

# Looking Through My Therapist Eyes

# After School

In this chapter, Bitzy's mother shows her strong dedication to seeing that her daughter's life becomes as normal as possible, which is imperative with young children caught in long-term illnesses. She also shows some understanding of Bitzy's suffering through unbearable isolation. And for all that, Mother doesn't think soap operas are healthy relational material for young children. Still, Mother does see the bigger picture once Bitzy herself has found a possible solution to her being separated from people.

It is amazing to note that during this period of her confinement, Bitzy's exposure to soap opera trauma and emotional angst, even though brief and fictional, may have helped support her course toward becoming a therapist in her later years. Bitzy's ear was being trained to hear what was being said and what was not being said, a most necessary tool in counseling. Because the material was fictional, she was being taught to hold the emotional distance necessary in a therapist if they would be of help to their clients. Both are good lessons for Bitzy's future profession.

Much of Bitzy's isolation taught her to make sense of her world by listening—it was her only connection to her family much of the time for six months during primetime childhood development. Her endless hours of loneliness may also have driven her to choose an adult life in which people always surround her, first by her five children and four grandchildren but also by her profession.

I do confess that I can remember lying in that upstairs bed and yelling to the Universe, "I don't ever want to be this lonely again!!"

Bitzy's First Grade Classroom During Summer Clean-up P.

# CHAPTER THIRTEEN

# Hailstorm Heat

T HE MONTHS OF May and June raced by before I even noticed they had passed. Going to school after school for three days a week made life exciting again. Free of the pressure I felt from the other children, I learned quickly with Teacher's attention. I had read all of the first primer and was almost through the second as June came to a close.

"Bitzy, you're doing so very well here with me. I'm recommending that you join your class for the second grade next September. I think you'll be up to them by then. But that means you're going to have to continue reading the composition books throughout the summer to keep up your reading skills. I'll also make up some number papers for your mother to give you and, of course, the penmanship.

"Do I have to do penmanship this summer, too?"

"Yes, if you want to be ready by September to join the other students. I think the easiest way is for you to copy the sentences from your primer onto the yellow-lined paper that I'll send home with you. I've written the cursive alphabet into the back of your first primer so you can always look there to see how to make the letters correctly. That should give you enough to do, but you've got to keep up with it."

I knew keeping up wasn't a question. Mother made sure I did all my lessons before anything else. I didn't mind. I loved to read, and the numbers weren't bad. It was the penmanship that got me down. I loved to see the smooth, carefully formed words written by Mrs.

Burton on the paper. The problem was that mine always looked wobbly
by comparison. No matter how hard I tried, they were never as perfect
as Teacher's. I'd even sit and trace over Mrs. Burton's work with my
pointer finger—just to get the feel of the curves—but still, the lines
hiccupped and trembled as I put them onto the paper. I didn't look
forward to struggling with yellow-lined paper all summer long.

The lessons were done quickly at the blue kitchen table each
morning, and then I was free to play. Afternoons still consisted of a
long nap-time on the couch in the living room or outside on the sun
porch in the warm weather. Mother didn't seem to care anymore about
my listening to soap operas. I guess she did understand when I told
her that I needed to be with other people, even if it was only people on
the radio. Or maybe she was too busy taking care of the rest of our
household.

*   *   *

In early August, a letter arrived from Grandmother inviting Mom and
me to come to Medford to stay in her house while Grandmother took a
vacation trip back to her childhood farm-home down in Lisbon, Maine.
She needed someone to keep an eye on the house and water the plants,
she said.

"That works out well for us, Bitzy. You're due for another appointment
with Dr. Clark. He wants to see you again before you go back to regular
school. That way, we can kill two birds with one stone. We'll take care
of Grandmother's house for her and get you to the doctor's, too."

I wondered quietly to myself, *who is going to take care of Daddy
while we are gone? I guess PollyAnne can cook and Owen will be
there.* Mother must have picked up my thoughts, for she said, "Now
we don't have to worry about Dad. He'll have the older ones to keep
him company. Besides, you remember he goes hunting every fall and
leaves us to take care of things. This trip to the city is like us having a
hunting trip."

It would be all right to leave Daddy under those conditions.
I then turned my attention to the doctor's visit. *Will he stick me again
with that horrible needle? Maybe he won't have to take blood. I'll ask*

*him not to.* As I thought about the whole subject, my arm tightened up. I flexed my fist and twisted the arm. Surely he wouldn't take more blood.

As it turned out, my Aunt Gracie had been hired by Dr. Clark and trained to be the office manager and the doctor's assistant. He must have known about how many children she had already raised. She took my blood, and it went very quickly; hardly more than a pinch.

Dr. Clark seemed happy with my condition. I'd put on some weight and grown almost half an inch since the last visit. "Your Mom says your first-grade teacher has recommended that you go into regular school this fall. We need to check and see if that's going to be possible. Would you like to go, Bitzy?"

I sat for a moment, thinking hard on the subject. *There were two sides to the question. On the one hand, there was the reading that I loved, but there were the kids on the other. How would they treat me? Would they even remember me?*

"Well, Bitzy?" The doctor cocked his head to one side, mimicking my expression. "What is it? Ready to go back to school?"

"Yes, Sir. I want to go to regular school."

"What is the holdup, Bitzy?"

"Well, I'm afraid of the other kids, that they won't like me or remember me."

"Maybe it will be different this time. You're older now. I don't suspect that the other children have forgotten you. Besides, you've got an adventure to tell them. I bet none of them have ever spent six months in bed!"

I wasn't sure this would be enough, but it helped that Dr. Clark cared about my fears. He must have been little once; that's why he understood. Maybe he'd been afraid of school, too. That didn't seem likely. He was so tall and important-looking now. Dr. Clark found that I was in very good shape and said he felt it would be good for me to be going back to classes with the other children. He thought I was healthy enough to keep up. He suggested that I continue the afternoon nap even when I was back in school. I felt that was a dumb idea; taking a nap after school! None of the other kids did that. They'd be going out to play, and I'd have to go to bed! Maybe Mom would forget about it by the time I was back to school.

*    *    *

All worries about returning to school faded when we returned to Grandmother's house. A telephone call came for Mother. One of her friends from high school days, Betty Smith, suggested they get together to chat and catch up on the past year's events.

"Won't that be fun, Bitzy? Betty has a son, Billy, just about your age," She said. "He'll be coming with her. I don't know what she plans to do with the girls. You and Billy can play together while Betty and I talk. You remember Billy, don't you?"

I remembered Billy. He'd come to our house with his mother and two sisters the summer before I got sick. The children had run wild in the pasture behind the house. Billy was a city boy and didn't know anything about cows in a pasture. I tried to show him how to pick handfuls of grass and offer them to the big, black-and-white Holsteins. I told him to hold his hand flat, letting the grass lay loose on the palm. As soon as the cow's big, sloppy nose got close to Billy's hand, he'd panic and throw the grass at the cow's face, making it snort. The cow would roll its head and step back, terrifying Billy even more. This behavior was terrific! Imagine a boy afraid of cows!

My mind was busy now, wondering what we could find to play at Grandmother's house. *I'll show him how to pick out a song on the old piano in the living room. Maybe he knows how to play the piano. Then we'll look at Grandmother's roses along the edge of her back garden and catch the iridescent green bugs in a jar. Billy will want to kill the bugs while I just like to catch them and watch them walking around inside the jar all over each other.*

"Best get to bed early tonight," Mother said. "You haven't had any children to play with in well over ten months. You may get tired with Billy being here." I wasn't worried about getting tired. I was so excited about having someone with whom to play.

The next day arrived hot, sticky, and humid. The sun was shining through a haze of still, heavy city air. "Hope we don't get a storm today," Mother said, as she handed me a piece of toast, heaped high with Grandmother's homegrown strawberry jam. "If that happens, you kids will be stuck in the house with nothing to do, and Betty and I won't get our chance to visit."

The weather cooperated with the sun breaking through in the early afternoon. When they arrived, I was surprised to see that Billy was much taller than last summer and that his dark brown curly hair was all tight in tiny circles on his head. I had remembered his hair was curly and that he had big brown eyes. I liked his eyes. They seemed friendly, and he'd watch me when I was talking to him. Most kids didn't listen to what I said.

"What do you want to play, Billy?"

"I don't know." He looked around at all the plants in Grandmother's living room. There wasn't much there with which we could play.

"Want to see the funny plant in Grandmother's garden?" Not being able to suggest anything else, Billy nodded his head.

"I want to talk to you children before you go anywhere." Mother took both of us by the hands and drew us to a chair where she sat down. Scrunching herself down a bit, so she was at eye level, she said, "Bitzy, you've got to remember you've been very sick and in bed for all these long months. You can't go outside and just run all over the place. You and Billy are going to have to walk, not run, as you play today. Billy, you're going to have to help Bitzy remember. She can't run and play hard, or she'll damage her heart. Now, can you children remember this?"

Both of us nodded together. Of course, we would do what Mother asked. Just to prove it, I walked in a steady, studied manner to the kitchen door and pushed it open. Billy followed like a perfect gentleman of six.

We were soon back, for a jar each so we could catch the bugs on Grandmother's roses. Next, we came back for nickels to go to the corner store for comic books. Billy was used to the city and wanted to show me comic books like the ones he had at home. I had never seen a comic book.

Mother handed out the nickels and started to caution us about crossing a city street alone. Betty broke in, "Billy knows all about city traffic. He often goes to the market to pick up things for me. They'll do fine." Mother seemed reassured by her remark and pushed the screen door open, letting us go.

After the comic books came a request for fifteen cents for ice cream cones and another trip to the corner drug store. Mother suggested we wait until after lunch for cones. Soon after lunch—and the ice cream cones—we were looking about for the next adventure. Mother called to me. "Remember you have to take an afternoon nap."

"Aw, Mom, I've got company. I can't take a nap!"

Seeing the oncoming problem, Betty suggested, "Why don't you children read your comic books."

"That's a great idea," my mother said. "I'll get two pillows and a blanket, and we'll spread it out on Grandmother's back porch. I'll pull it in far enough that the house shades you, and you two can rest there and read."

We settled down on the blanket while Mother and Betty retreated to the house. Mother told me the next day that she'd looked out to check on us only a few minutes later, and we were gone! She tried listening for us. And sure enough, she heard giggling and squealing coming from the other side of the house.

All I remember was her sneaking up on the two of us down on the grass. Billy was tickling me, and I was struggling and laughing and trying to get away.

"This behavior is not what I had in mind for a nap," my mother said. "Stop that right now! This kind of play is much too strenuous for Bitzy. If you two are going to be rough with each other, I'll have to take her inside."

We both felt guilty. We had forgotten about my heart and were just having fun. Mother led us back to the comic books and the blanket. "You have just one-half hour more to stay quiet! I'll time you by the kitchen clock and tell you when you can get up."

After about five minutes, I called through the window to Mom and Billy's mother sitting in the kitchen. "Can we get up now?"

"No, I told you I'd call you when it's time. You stay a bit longer. My mother's head disappeared from the kitchen window, but I heard her say, "If you two are good, you can have a piece of Grandmother's candy from her covered dish."

That was a reason to stay quiet. We managed to squirm around on the blanket for the rest of the half-hour. "Can we have our candy, now?"

"Yes, you can have the candy, but I don't call that much of a nap. Take it easy this afternoon in whatever you dream up to play."

There must have been something in the air, for the afternoon was growing steadily darker, and we moved from one activity to another with increasing speed. By late afternoon Mother found us racing around on the far lawn. "What are you playing, now?"

"Oh, we're playing hide and seek. Billy hides, and I find him; then I hide, and he finds me."

"But Bitzy, you're running around out here. You know you can't run! Simmer down and play something quiet."

Mother returned to the house.

I couldn't help it. We had shifted to playing tag, and Billy jumped on me when he got close enough. I started screeching and laughing all at once. When my mother came after us, she was walking toward us, and her face looked like the horrible clouds that were gathering overhead.

"What in heaven's name are you two doing?"

"We're playing tag," I told her. "Billy chases me and, then I chase him. I'm faster than he is."

"Bitzy, you're running! You know you can't run. You'll be back in bed for another six months if you don't stop this. If you children can't settle down, you'll have to come inside."

Both of us looked down at the ground to avoid her look of anger. We didn't want to stop the fun. I hadn't had a chance to play like this in over a year. We didn't mean to make her mad, but I didn't want to stop. Mother went inside by herself, but even my mother's anxious words weren't enough to get us to stop.

Shortly, Mother reappeared. "Look at you! Your face is all red, and you're sweating all over. You're even out of breath. That does it! You have to come inside, and Billy and his mother will have to go home."

My mother was angrier than I'd ever seen her get before. Now, I was really scared.

Betty and Billy gathered their things together quickly, with Betty alternately scolding Billy for leading me astray and apologizing to Mother for her son's bad behavior. Mother, in turn, assured her that I had been equally to blame and would suffer the consequences. I hung in the background, wondering what Mother was going to do to me.

When the guests were finally gone, Mother silently took me by the hand and led me upstairs to Grandmother's over-toweled bathroom. She took a washcloth, wetting it with cool water, and smoothed it across my reddened, sweaty face. "I've got to take your temperature. I'm sure you've driven it way up with your racing around. I'm ashamed of you. You know you could ruin all the time you spent in bed this winter by your forgetfulness. Now go get into bed and rest until supper."

Mother got the thermometer from Grandmother's bedroom. When she took it out of my mouth and read it, there was no misunderstanding the look on her face. My temperature had shot up with the over-exertion. "Don't you dare move until suppertime!"

I wanted to cry. *It was such fun having somebody to play with. Now Mother was terribly mad at me. Maybe I'd never get to play with anybody again.* Before I could finish my thoughts, I fell asleep.

About two hours later, Mother woke me up. She was standing beside the bed. The room was almost dark. "Honey," she said, "it's supper time, and we have a guest." My mother seemed excited and appeared to have forgotten about the afternoon events. She was focused on the person downstairs.

"Do you remember the all-morning boy we had a few years ago, Tony Morello? Oh, that's right," my mother went on, answering her question. "You'd be too small to remember him. Well, he became like part of the family. He used to play and tumble with PollyAnne and Owen before he'd go back to his cottage after helping with the housework. They just loved him!"

Mother moved closer to the door. "Come on down for supper and meet him. His family lives here in the city, and he just stopped by for a visit. You'll like him."

I was surprised at the person who stood up in the kitchen when I walked in. He wasn't a boy; he was a man dressed in an army uniform, all stiff and in that khaki color. His face was reddish all over while his short-cropped, uncontrollable, red kinky hair lay tight to his head. The flattened army cap was tucked neatly into the flap on his left shoulder.

"Hello, Bitzy. Your mother tells me you've had quite a day. I bet you had a ball."

For a moment, I felt sad. I had forgotten about the afternoon and wanted it left that way, but the tone in Tony's voice sounded as if he didn't think the afternoon's adventures were so bad.

"Now, don't get her started, Tony. She's still not totally well. Besides, supper is ready." Mother motioned toward the table, already smelling of good things. The three of us sat down to eat.

Mother asked Tony questions about his home and his time in World War II. What had he done after he left the State School? Tony talked about how hard it had been to stay straight and away from the bad kids, his old friends, in the neighborhood. Finally, it seemed easiest to get away, so he'd enlisted in the Army. As luck would have it, he was sent right out to the islands to fight with only brief training.

I watched the expressions on his face change. When he talked about the fighting, he didn't look very happy. *What is it like to be fighting?* I wondered. I knew that back home, at the State School, we lived right next to the Fort Devens Army post. I could just barely remember seeing rows of soldiers marching in formation up and down the road beside my house. Nobody had told me anything about the soldiers, so I had been frightened. Then, one day they didn't march anymore. *Where had they gone? Had they gone to fight? Who were they fighting? Were the soldiers even real, or had I imagined them? Why didn't anyone explain who they were?* My young mind wandered away, being too small to understand the conversation.

I came to as Mother brought out the lemon meringue pie Grandmother had left for us. Mother made apologies for the sticky top. She said it was because my grandmother had made the pie a few days ago. It still tasted yummy to me, and apparently, Tony felt the same way. He had three pieces, more even than Owen would have eaten. After supper, Tony helped Mother wash up and put away Grandmother's dishes while I went to the living room to plink on the piano.

It wasn't very long before Mother said, "Bitzy, it's time for bed. You've had a full day, and I think you need your rest."

"Aw, do I have to? I had a nap, and besides, we have company."

"It doesn't matter. You really overdid it today, and you'd best get to bed."

"I tell you what," Tony interrupted Mother's efforts. "You get washed up and into bed quickly, and I'll come and tell you some bedtime stories."

Bedtime ceased to be an issue. I hurried up the stairs to the bathroom and then around into the back bedroom. Mother had decided that it would be better for us to sleep on the backside of the house with the storm coming. This room had two twin beds on opposite sides of the room. I didn't feel as comfortable here. It was strange, not a room I went into often.

Tony came up and pulled a chair up beside the bed. "What would you like to hear?"

"Do you know about Little Red Riding Hood?"

"Hum, well, not exactly, but I'll give it a try. Let's see; there was a little girl about your size that had a red coat. . . ."

"No, it's a cape—a funny thing with a hood that you put your arms through holes on the front." I corrected his version of the story.

"Who's telling this story? Do you want my Little Red Riding Hood or your Little Red Riding Hood?" Tony looked a little bit angry.

I tried to decide if he was joking or annoyed. I decided he was joking and said, "Okay, you tell your story, but you know that isn't the way it happened."

Tony chuckled, "You're right, but there's a lot that happened to Little Red Riding Hood you don't know. Want to hear my version?"

"Yeah!" I realized that this was not going to be any story I'd ever heard before, and I was right. It wasn't long before Little Red Riding Hood was in a war, and guns were going off over her head, and men were getting shot. The soldiers were running everywhere, and big cannons boomed . . .

"What was that?" I whispered.

"That noise? Oh, that was some of the cannons."

"No. I mean, really, that noise outside."

"It sounds like thunder to me," Tony responded. "Where was I? Let's see, we were in a foxhole."

Cr . . . ack! Shish! Boom!

"Tony, what was that?" I was really frightened now, what with the cannon in the story and the crashing going on outside. It was hard to tell which was where.

"That's a little lightning strike. It doesn't sound too far away. Let's get back to the story."

I couldn't concentrate on Tony's voice any longer. The wind had picked up outside. It roared past the windows of the room.

"I was telling you about being in the foxhole with the guns going off over our heads—" "Tony." It was Mother's voice from the doorway. "I think you need to come quickly. There are hailstones the size of golf balls coming through the windows downstairs in the living room. They've smashed in both windows on that side, and there's glass all over the floor. We'll need to nail something up over those windows and then check the others on that side." Mother's voice had an eerie calm that frightened me.

"Can I come to see?" I asked nervously.

"Yes, I'd rather have you down with us, but you'll have to stay back on the bottom of the stairs safely away from the flying glass. Grab your blanket to wrap in and come. Put slippers on, too. I don't want you getting broken glass in your feet".

I sat on the stair next to the bottom, shivering in my blanket, not from cold but from fear. "Are we going to be all right, Mum," I called from my watch-seat.

"Sure we are Honey. We've got Tony here, and he's strong enough to get these windows covered." Mother didn't seem as anxious now that Tony was looking for cardboard to put over the windows.

There was another loud crash and the tinkle of more breaking glass. The flash of lightning lit the whole room as if it were Christmas Eve, followed by another thunderous bang. I began to whimper, "Are we going to be all right, Mummy?"

This time Tony answered as he reappeared with old cardboard boxes, a hammer, and nails stuck in the corner of his mouth. "It's nothing, just banging like guns, only you're not on a battlefield, so you can't get hurt."

Mother looked at Tony quizzically for a moment and said, "Do you think that's a wise thing to say to her now that she's so scared?" With that, there was another terrible flash and bang, which blended into the hammering noise Tony was making.

The two finished covering the living room windows and moved from that room down the hallway toward the kitchen, which also had a window on the damaged side of the house. Mother stopped at the stairs, where I was now crying loudly. She gathered me into her arms. "Bitzy, I know how scared you are. I'm scared too, but I know God is up there. I call him my father: He's never let me get hurt seriously before, so I know he'll keep us safe now."

I wasn't too sure about fathers in the sky. I wished mine was here now. I felt uncontrollable and shivery all over. My small body was shaking by itself.

Mother went on. "You exhausted yourself this afternoon with all the running around, and then Tony frightened you with his war stories, and now this. It's enough to give you a real setback. She hugged me tighter as if to comfort and receive comfort.

Tony returned from the kitchen. "That room seems fine. Only one pane is out, and there's not much glass on the floor. The storm is already quieting down. Storms like this are hard, fast, and gone. See, Bitzy, we're all fine. Want some more war stories?"

I shook my messy blond head in a most emphatic, No!

## Looking Through My Therapist Eyes

# Heat Hailstorm

It is interesting to note that during this particular episode, the energy in and around Bitzy was building to a crescendo, which broke open with the hailstorm. It started with her fear of going back to a doctor who had hurt her, escalated with the discussion of returning to school, hit a high note with all the physical exertion of playing hard for the first time after a long-term illness. Then, egged on by the wild stories of this man, Tony, a stranger to Bitzy, the energy finally exploding in a rain of crashing hailstones.

Circumstances in life often come in waves like this, and they appear uncontrollable. The question is, how do we deal with them? How do we make them work for us, not against us?

Once again, we see a mother who could have offered more comfort, but because of her own absence of childhood comfort in the face of life events, Mother chose to deal by explaining things, causing Bitzy to learn to think about, not feel her emotions. This splitting off of emotions is being taught in these very events and will be assimilated by this child as the way to deal with overwhelming life happenings. *Think*, don't *feel!!* The confusion for Bitzy is that she can physically feel her mother's terror when Mother stops to hug her.

If we were not creatures of our pasts, Bitzy's mother would have spent *all of her time* on the stairs holding her daughter and moaning, groaning, and talking about how scary it is to have all this noise going on around them. Rather than staying on her feet to orchestrate the repair of the windows, she could better have spent her time showing her daughter how to feel her feelings. This fear of the storm was a time for mirroring emotions between the two, not for another scolding for the child's bad behavior during the afternoon. Good mothers often mistakenly cover their own fears with judging words. The child is already well aware of her sins, and the reiterating of the mistake only makes the child feel more like a failure. Such a missed opportunity!

# CHAPTER FOURTEEN

# Ugly Things

W E WERE HOME again after the hailstorm, and I was so glad to be back where my father was in the house and holding his place in our family. I felt safe again. It took about a week of rest-times before Mother thought I was strong enough to be up and about without naps. I remembered my mother's comment during the hailstorm about 'a Father in the sky.' Still, I was just as glad mine was here on earth where I could touch him if I wanted, although I didn't do that as much now that I was six going on seven.

I have talked before about the all-morning-boys that came in the morning to help my mother with the house cleaning and whatever else she needed, like lifting heavy things and washing and polishing the old Shaker wooden floors. These boys used to mop the floors with a rag mop and a small amount of water. Then they'd take a chunk of wood, like what we would use in the fireplace if ours worked, and the boys would wind that piece of wood tight with cotton rags. After putting a layer of wax from the wax can onto the floor, they would get down on their knees and polish the floors with a push away of the cloth-wrapped wood, and then a pullback, and out again, from their crunched up bodies. But the best part was when the all-morning boy wrapped the dust mop with rags and told me to hop on. I had to pull my feet up tight to my bum and hold on for dear life because they would let me ride the mop all around the floors. One of them even ran with me until my mother caught him. I can only remember falling off the mop twice, and oh, how we both laughed.

This particular morning was bright and sunny. Mother cornered me in the kitchen after I'd been outside once to check on flowers in the garden. "Honey, I know you like to be out hiding in Daddy's gardens, day-dreaming underneath the forsythia bush, but you are old enough to be cleaning up your bedroom upstairs. You left pajamas on the floor and slippers, not in the closet. And I expect there may be some toys under your bed."

I hated house cleaning, but Mother was not one to be ignored, so I trudged up to the bedroom and set about picking up the things she told me to put away. While I was there, I stood and looked at myself in the white curved-arm old mirror attached to my white bureau. *Look, I am getting taller! Maybe even prettier, too?* I was indeed taller, just as Mother had said when I stepped out of my sick-bed for the first time. Then I found one of my forgotten picture books away under the bed and pulled it out. I sat on the graying rag-rug in my room and enjoyed looking at the pictures that went with the stories. It brought back memories of playing with those books when I was sick, if you could call it playing.

My bedroom was an overlarge closet on the second floor tucked under the shed part of the back of our Shaker house. The only door to my room was from the family bathroom—in other words, I had to go through the bathroom to get out of my bedroom. As I've told you before, I had a single window that swung in at the bottom. Whether it was winter or spring, Mother would move my bed beside the window or across from the window. It was a small space, but I felt so safe there.

Our all-morning boy at the time was named Marvin, and I knew he was downstairs helping my mother with whatever. But he was of no concern to me.

I had decided that I'd had enough housecleaning, and I stood up just as I heard Marvin coming up the stairs. He came into my room with some folded clothes in his arms. "Your mother told me to bring these clothes up for you to put away," he said. *That's strange,* I thought. *Mom*

*always brings up our clothes and puts them away. She wants to be sure
that everything is in the right place.*

Marvin puts the clothes on my bed and steps back. I had started to
leave the room as he was arriving so I'm now standing facing him. With
his hands empty, quick as a flash, Marvin unzips his pants and pulls
out this swollen and bright purple-pink hose. "I've got a toy here for
you to play with," he says. "Want to play with him?" I look at the pink
wrinkled "toy" which I had never seen before on any man and say the
first thing that comes into my head, "No! I don't want to play with that
ugly thing! Why would I want to play with that?" And I dash out past
him. I guess he was so surprised at what I said that he didn't try to grab
me or follow me.

I never told my mother because the whole thing seemed so stupid.
*Who would want to play with an ugly thing like that?*

## Looking Through My Therapist Eyes

# Thing Ugly

How do we know when to prepare our children for these kinds of events? In the 1950's most families didn't talk about these sexual encounters, although from my counseling experiences, they went on in almost every family. Many little girls were not as lucky as Bitzy. Somehow without being taught or prepared for an event like this, Bitzy's natural instincts kicked in, and she gave the only answer to the question that would save her from an ugly first sexual experience before she was old enough to comprehend what was happening.

She speaks of the trust that she has in her father and the fact that at home, she feels safe. Many little girls have these feelings. It is such a betrayal when the father, grandfather, older brother, uncle, neighbor, or family friend is the perpetrator of these first sexual experiences. These little girls often preserve what is left of their sense of self by going out-of-body and not being emotionally present to 'the event.' This behavior follows them into adulthood and often interferes with the normal sexual activity that takes place between husband and wife in a marital situation. These early sexual events can destroy the marriage bed.

Suppose the husband in marriage was involved in these early kinds of sexual encounters, either with a man or woman, he has trouble 'turning on sexually' until there is a similar sexual staging. The husband's behavior leaves the wife confused and wondering why she isn't enough for him. When the woman in the marriage has had these early distorted sexual experiences, she is not turned on unless the male partner is equally invasive—a set up for sexual abuse. The other outcome, if the woman is the one who was damaged by early sexual encounters, is that the woman either plays very sexually interested until she has drawn the male close to her and then during the actual sexual act, she turns off and emotionally vacates her body, leaving the male confused and disappointed. It is almost as if the woman punishes her partner for each of those early unprocessed sexual encounters.

There is so much sexuality displayed on our media in today's world that these topics are more likely to come up in family conversations. These are moments in which both the male and female child in a family get some warnings and appropriate coaching on how to stay out of these dark places. Hopefully, If the encounter is forced upon a child, the parents have given the young person strategies for getting away without being harmed. We can no longer pray that our children will know when they are in danger and get themselves free. Our whole population is so over stimulated by sexual innuendo and activity through social media that it is an increasing danger to our children.

When you are holding your little new baby and enjoying all the cooing and visual contact with your child, remember you have a lot still ahead of modeling and teaching to bring your child to where they are healthy, happy adults. So do enjoy all those happy early moments. Your children need to know that they are safe in your environment.

## CHAPTER FIFTEEN

# Back to Regular School

THERE WERE NO ill effects from my wild day at Grandmother's house, although Mother wasn't taking any chances. Upon arriving home, I spent the next few days quietly resting on the old, white, iron-framed couch on the back porch. The hot August sun crept across the foot of the couch, splashing the smooth concrete floor with bright light and shifting shadow shapes.

"This isn't fair. I don't need to stay in bed. One day playing isn't going to make me sick again. I don't want to be in bed anymore!"

"I know you don't, but we can't take the risk. You played so hard at Grandmother's I should think it would set you back at least a week. You want to be strong and ready for regular school next month, don't you?"

Mother had made her point. I didn't argue anymore but stayed quiet, watching the birds swoop down past the corner of the porch and up as if they were trying to entice me off into more rollicking summer fun. Lying still, I could hear the chatter of Starlings, gray-black iridescent birds, perched in the giant oak tree. Back fence gossips had nothing on the din coming from these conversational birds.

Late that afternoon, Mother came and sat down on the old couch beside me. "You know, week after next is when school opens. We're going to have to get you a new pair of shoes because your feet have grown so much this year. I expect you're kind of frightened to be going back. How about we get you a new dress for the first day?"

A new dress—a store-bought dress and new shoes! My mind was no longer on thoughts of what I would like to do to Mother for making me rest all day in bed. There usually wasn't extra money for store-bought dresses. Mother made most of my outer clothes, or they were redesigned creations handed down from PollyAnne's closet. I hated these. It always felt as if I was supposed to be a miniature PollyAnne, and we were about as different as sisters could be. PollyAnne was lively and social, while I was shy and day dreamy.

"Can I have a pair of those shoes with the white toes and the brown middles?"

"You mean saddle-shoes? Hum . . . they've got a lot of white on them, you know. Do you think you'll be able to keep them polished all the time?"

"Of course!" Not having any idea what was involved in keeping saddle-shoes white, I could promise anything.

"Well, you'll have to take real special care of them. It means whitening your new shoes almost every night or at least once a week. I'll have to show you how." As if Mother had talked herself through to a conclusion, she continued, "Yes, I don't see why you can't have a pair of saddle-shoes if you want, like the big girls."

The saddle shoes were the first purchase on the back-to-school shopping trip, but Mother found the dresses were all too expensive after the lay-out for the shoes. I was nearly heartbroken that there wouldn't be a new store-bought dress. I tried to keep back the tears. Having gotten the shoes, I knew it wasn't fair to push for the dress, too.

"I tell you what. We can go to the fabric store and pick out whatever color you want and a new pattern. I'm sure I can get a dress made for you before classes start. Maybe we could even find some fancy buttons to go on the front."

Mother's enthusiasm was catching. We trotted off to the fabric store to pick out the cloth and a pattern. I chose a bright-red cotton percale print with tiny yellow and pink flowers sprinkled across its surface. For buttons, Mother found little yellow flower heads, and since it was a princess-style dress, the yellow buttons could march down the front, making a showy display. By now, I had forgotten that this would again be a homemade dress. It fit perfectly—not a little large, so that I could grow into it—and I felt like a real princess on the day school started. The white saddle-shoes had only been worn enough that they no longer scrubbed up and down on my heels. Still, little crease-marks showed across the toes. My Auntie Grace, actually my Grandmother's younger sister, had heard about the big day and had sent money from Maine for a new sweater. Mother chose a dark green cardigan which made a dramatic contrast with the red and yellow dress.

The day came. I stood frozen on the front porch, not from the cool, early morning September air, but from fear. How would Carol Simpson behave? During my sickness, I'd had no contact with Carol, not even watching the Simpson kids playing in their yard. Now Carol didn't seem the slightest bit interested. She was talking with her sister Sarah, probably picking on her, although Sarah didn't seem unhappy. I walked to the end of my sidewalk to wait for the bus. The other girls, Carol, Jeannie, Sally, and the oldest sister, Mary Lee, stood exactly opposite, at the end of their sidewalk on the other side of the street.

I was surprised to see a large hunter-green utility van pull up in the street between our two groups. No one had told me that the State School had decided there were now too many children to continue transporting us in the old beach wagon. The other girls began piling in through the open back doors. I pulled myself up over the high rear bumper. The inside had two sturdy wooden benches bolted along each side of the truck. I sat down close to the door and was startled to feel the cool steel sides, frosty, through the back of my green sweater. The truck started up and went around the corner. Without windows on the sides, we children had no warning of approaching turns and lurched into one another with each twist. Everyone giggled, and Mary Ellen, one of the older girls who got on before me, called out, "You'd better hold onto the bench, or you'll get thrown on the floor."

The new dress and shoes gave me some comfort, but this rolling, bumping school bus just about took it all away before we even got to the school building. Mother had given me a note to take to the second-grade teacher and had told me to go directly into school when I got there, no lingering on the playground with the other children.

Miss Carlson met me at the outside door as if she had been watching for me. "My, it's good to see you back to school. Are you feeling all right, now?"

"Sure, I'm fine. Mom says I'll have to take a nap when I get home from school. But I don't see why. I feel great."

"Well, I'm sure Mother knows what's going to be best for you. She said she'd send a note with you on this first morning. Do you have a note for me?"

With that, I remembered the note Mother had tucked into the tin lunch box behind the peanut butter and jelly sandwich. It was such a long note I had thought that surely I wouldn't forget, but with the hassle of the new bus I'd forgotten.

Miss Carlson took the note and motioned me to put my sweater in the large walk-in coat closet behind the teacher's desk. I followed Teacher's instructions and stood in the closet doorway, wondering what I was supposed to do next. Miss Carlson was reading Mother's note and nodding to herself as if she and Mother were actually talking to one another. "Hum . . . it seems as if you've had a hard time of it this past winter. Your mother says you are free to play with the other children on the playground but that you shouldn't run around a lot. I wonder if I should speak to the other children about this. Hum . . . I think not. It's best just to see how things develop. Since you're here first, why don't you pick the desk that fits you best, and that will be your seat for this year."

Miss Carlson laid the note on her desk and gently guided me, with a hand on the back of my shoulder, to the brown desks at the opposite end of the room. I tried several and finally settled on one near the back of the room. I was poking my arms inside the desk to see if there were any old papers from last year, when the outside bell rang.

The other second graders swarmed into the room and raced toward the desks like a hive of young bees. The chatter was deafening and the bustle disturbing. "All right, children! You need to quiet down.

Has everyone found a seat for this year? Now you need to make sure the desk fits you properly—feet touching the floor and knees not bumping."

I was already overwhelmed: all this noise and confusion, not to mention the new faces. There was Dick, with the ears that stuck out, and Wayne, and Nan, Dee, and Gabby. They were all kids I knew from Sunday school. But then there were others—a pretty little red-headed girl and two boys that looked like each other.

"Children, we want to welcome Bitzy back into our classroom. You may remember she started school with you last year. She's been sick for almost a year but is now able to be back with us."

Dick turned around and gave me a stare—a mixture of deviltry and cool acknowledgement of my existence. I sat trying to figure out if that was friendly or a challenge to my being back. Nan smiled, and Dee waved a hand quickly by the edge of her desk so Teacher wouldn't see.

Maybe the kids did remember who I was. Maybe they hadn't forgotten me through all those long months. I tried to figure out what Dick's stare meant.

"All right, children, I'd like you to quiet down, fold your hands neatly on your desk, and bow your heads while we all recite the Lord's Prayer together. Then we'll have the pledge of allegiance to the flag. Bitzy, do you remember the pledge of allegiance?"

I panicked inside. What was the teacher meaning? But I nodded my head in agreement as if I knew.

"Fine, then we'll get on with the start of our day."

That first day things ran smoothly. The hours during the summer, working over the yellow-lined paper had paid off. I got a little, brightly colored school-box sticker on the top of my paper that first day—a most amazing thing after the papers I'd turned out the year before. Teacher hung my penmanship paper up over the blackboard along with many of the other children's papers. "This way, we can compare them later in the year and see how much you all have improved."

The math period didn't go as well. We worked from workbooks and started by learning which was our right hand and which our left.

Teacher explained that it was easy to remember because most people wrote with their right hands. I sat looking at my hands and then at the picture of the hands in my book. I wriggled my fingers and tried cramping them into a writing position. Sure enough, I did write with the hand shown in the book as the right hand.

Now, Teacher had us close up the workbooks and take a piece of Manila paper. We were going to make columns of numbers, setting them into the position to add. The first ones were easy. Teacher was dictating the numbers and they were all single numbers. Then she called out two number sets. "The seven of seventy-two goes to the left, and the two to the right."

I was lost! I sat holding my hands palm down on the desk, trying to remember the picture in the book. By the time I had the picture in mind, I had forgotten the number Miss Carlson had called out. Hastily, I wrote something down. Teacher had us do three sets of numbers this way—all of them a total disaster on my paper.

"Now, I want you to add up all the numbers in the different columns; then we will correct the papers together."

When we got the correcting done, I had answers very different from the teacher's. I wondered why mine was different but decided not to ask out loud. Teacher had the papers collected, and we moved on to reading.

By the time the green school van pulled up in front of my house again that first day, I didn't make a bit of fuss when Mother said, "I think you'd best take a nap before supper."

I fell asleep and had to be awakened for dinner.

The following day went almost as well, but there was still the trouble with this left-and-right-handed arithmetic. I struggled with working from the workbook and tried hard to understand the dictation. By the third day, I had a knot in my stomach, even before I got to school. This year was a little better because I was able to stay with what Miss Carlson was giving for directions, and the yellow pencil seemed to remain in its place inside my desk. But this math thing was getting worrisome and the penmanship papers were even worse.

"Bitzy, I need to see you up here at my desk."

I jumped. I'd been concentrating on putting the numbers in columns, copying from the workbook. *What is wrong?* I could tell that something was by the tone in Miss Carlson's voice. *Why do I have to walk up to Teacher's desk?* Yesterday one of the twins had gone up there, and the teacher yelled at him. Benjamin acted as if he didn't care. He didn't look at Teacher but instead looked all around the room, alternately grinning and trying to look serious. I didn't want Teacher to yell at me.

"Look at these o's on your paper. None of them are closed at the top. And the a's look the same as the o's. Now your work the first day wasn't like this. And, here, is this a two? You don't make their bottoms with straight lines; you curve them gently like this. Now you try. Try one right here where I can watch you!"

I shivered all over. I fought back the tears. This woman was not the kind, pretty, gentle-spoken woman who had welcomed me into the school building three days before. I didn't like this new person. Feverishly, I tried to make my pencil copy the curved, looped tail on the bottom of the two. It wasn't working. The tail just went straight across like the ones I'd done all summer. *What is wrong with two's with straight tails?* I tried again.

"This is definitely not satisfactory. Try it again!"

I struggled again to make a loop on the bottom of the two. Now the line quivered and twisted as it descended down and then up and around.

"Well, there's not much improvement in that one! You go back to your seat and fill this paper with o's and a's and twos that are made correctly."

I slid back into my wooden chair with the dreaded yellow paper still clutched in my hand. I didn't think I could make the letters good enough to satisfy this teacher. Dry-eyed and angry, I sat for a few minutes trying to decide what to do. I was frightened and mad and confused. I wanted to go home!

Teacher forgot about the penmanship paper because she didn't ask for it before we students left for the day. I folded the paper neatly and put it at the very back of my desk. I tried a few letters and then gave it up as an impossible task.

The next morning, when I awoke, I felt funny. Maybe I was just hungry. I had a bowl of oatmeal Daddy had left for me before he went to work. He always got up ahead of the family and made a large pot of cooked oatmeal, leaving it in the old, aluminum double-boiler for those who followed. This morning, I took the first taste. It was almost cold and felt slimy. I ate a few bites and then pushed the bowl aside. I wasn't hungry. Mother didn't say anything about the uneaten cereal. That was a blessing!

Clothes didn't seem to go on right either, and by the time I got to the school playground, I felt limp and shaky all over. I didn't tell the other children but hung by myself, waiting for the bell to ring to go into school.

Once in my seat, my stomach began to hurt. The students in the class bowed their heads for the prayer. I wished I could keep mine there. Then, up they all stood for the pledge to the flag. Next, it was to take out yesterdays' yellow papers and finish the penmanship. Oh, those dreaded two's! I put my head down on the desk. The other children got started writing. I lifted my head and looked at yesterday's work. It was hopeless. I put my head back down.

"Bitzy, are you all right?" Miss Carlson spoke from the front of the class.

I didn't stir in my seat. Maybe I could just hide, and Miss Carlson would go away. I heard the teacher's black high heels clicking on the wooden floor as she walked toward my desk.

"Honey, are you feeling all right?" Now Miss Carlson was right beside my desk. I raised my head and looked at the teacher. "Bitzy, is there something wrong?"

Oh, if I could only tell the teacher! I shook my head, and the tears started to run down my cheeks. I put my head back down onto the desk.

"What is it, Bitzy? What's wrong? Are you feeling sick?"

I just shook my crumpled head on the desk. I didn't want to look at the teacher again, and I couldn't talk.

Miss Carlson laid a hand on the back of my neck. "You seem a little feverish. I think you'd better see the school nurse. Benjamin, would you please go up to the nurse's office and bring her down here?"

I could hear Benjamin hurry off to get the nurse.

"You rest until the nurse comes. She'll tell us if you need to go home or not. Meanwhile, Class, we'll go on with the penmanship lesson."

It was a relief to have the teacher move away from my desk. I lay quietly listening to the teacher's voice giving instructions . . . if I could just go home!

There was a rustling sound as Miss Phillips, the school nurse, came into the classroom. I could hear the two women whisper to one another and then the nurse approaching my desk. I lifted my head and was greeted by the softest gray eyes I'd ever seen.

"Miss Carlson says you're not feeling very well. Do you want to come with me up to my office and tell me all about it? She touched my head in a gentle, caressing manner, encouraging me to stand.

This bulky, large, uniformed woman felt kind and soft to me. Without even knowing what I was doing, I jumped up and threw my arms around the nurse in a tremendous bear-hug of relief. Miss Phillips responded by stroking my braids. "What do you want, Bitzy?" she asked.

"I want to go home! I don't like it here." And into the large, rumbled folds of Miss Phillips's uniform, I continued, "Miss Carlson is mean, and she yells at the kids. She yelled at me yesterday. I can't make the o's like she wants, and I don't see why the two's have to have curly tails."

Miss Phillips whispered back. "School is so hard it makes you want to go home where it's easy. But you're a big girl now. I believe you can make those o's. You don't want to give up and take the easy way out. Come on with me. We'll go get a drink from the water fountain, and you can tell me the rest."

I released my grip on the nurse, and Miss Phillips ushered me out into the hallway. Once outside the classroom, I felt better. We went and got a drink, and Miss Phillips asked, "Is there more you need to tell me?"

"No," I shook my head. "My stomach hurt when I was in there with the teacher, but out here, it doesn't hurt."

"Then you don't need to go home, do you?" Miss Phillips didn't wait for my answer but went right on. "You worked so hard this year getting well. Now, you need to show us you can be as strong here at school. I know the work is hard for a second-grader, and I know Miss Carlson can be mean. Sometimes she gets in a mood. You just have to be patient with her, but she is a good teacher. Think you can go in there now and show us that good fighting spirit you had at home?"

I nodded my head. I wondered how Miss Phillips knew I'd been sick. But then, Mother seemed to know everyone in town. She must have told the nurse.

"Anything else we need to talk about?"

"No. Well, that Miss Carlson is a mean teacher."

"Yes, I know, Bitzy, but I think you can deal with her. Ready to go back inside?"

I nodded, yes. Miss Phillips took my hand and led me back to the classroom door. "Ready?"

I, looking up into the woman's warm, gray eyes, felt safe and strong. I gave Miss Phillips another big hug and opened the classroom door.

Miss Carlson greeted us from the other side of the door. "Are you all right now, Bitzy? Want to take your seat? In a minute, I can come and help with that penmanship paper."

*Now how does she know I am upset over the penmanship paper? I didn't even know it was the paper bothering me. All I have to do is play sick, and Miss Carlson is as nice as can be. Maybe school isn't going to be so bad after all!*

# Looking Through My Therapist Eyes

# Regular School

Bitzy again shows us the patterns of anxiety that often exist in a child that has been too sheltered within their own family of origin, a child possibly needed by the mother for some reason. This anxiety response is now exacerbated by having been shut away from the outer world and other children for an extended time, with a long-term illness.

The rush of energy that Bitzy feels from the other children, and the demands of the new experience, causes her to use a technique that children often display when frightened or overwhelmed: disassociation, also known as 'splitting,' or leaving her body—a sure way to exit a threatening scene. This escaping behavior creates mental confusion for her when she *re-enters*, returns to the classroom, and then doesn't hear or understand the teacher's directions. These episodes are momentary, but for Bitzy this response has been cemented into place by the long time alone in her sickbed. Her solitary confinement has heightened Bitzy's ability to move in and out of consciousness. As a child, it causes her to lose a solid connection with her environment sometimes. Still, as a therapist, later in life, it helps her to read a client better because she can access their unconscious material quickly.

Two other matters become visible in this chapter. Bitzy believes she is powerless to change the situations that surround her. This approach to living is often displayed by children who are raised in authoritative households. Because these children are never consulted about whether they want to do a particular task or how they would like to accomplish this task, their sense of personal power is not strengthened. They become compliant, *good children*. These children are easy to live with, but they have difficulty in dealing with the outside world. Although very lovingly done, the manipulation that kept Bitzy quiet in bed for six months has taken its toll—she now feels even less able to cope with obstacles in her life. We see this as she quickly puts away the writing paper when Miss Carlson criticizes her. Given her background, it is a wonder Bitzy didn't just spend that whole day *trying* to do the penmanship paper, which would have made her work even less attractive to the teacher. The central issue here is that she could not improve her work because she was initially angry, a very healthy emotional response to having been humiliated in front of her classmates. Then Bitzy, of course, represses the anger, as she has been taught to do by her family; the result is tears of helplessness and a sick stomach on the next day.

Our little girl has just stumbled upon a useful tool, at least to her child-self that often is the outgrowth of long-term illnesses; her body's ability to perceive outside events as threatening. Therefore the body response is *to get sick*. This unconscious, passive-aggressive behavior becomes her device for manipulating her world. Bitzy's recognition of this new power comes in the last line of this chapter.

We have just witnessed the makings of an adult manipulator. Now mind you, manipulation is a whole other topic and not always a bad behavior to own. The healthy version is to recognize that you use this pattern—only using manipulation when conscious of doing so, and in appropriate circumstances that will benefit all.

Bitzy's Second Grade Classroom
View Coming Back in with School Nurse P.

# Second Dialogue With the Inner Bitzy

Things seem to be rolling along for Bitzy, with her illness slipping farther and farther into the background. But I do wonder how she feels about her return to a regular classroom. Could she possibly be hiding fear behind her breezy style?

Today to keep our relationship growing, I choose to move directly to the computer from my morning meditation instead of my usual trip to the bathroom. As if my thinking can create realities, I find the mirror of my mind sliding across the computer screen, blocking out the reflection of my face.

Nothing is visible in the mirror. For a moment, I feel fear. Is Bitzy gone? Is the split in our psyche so great that she has disappeared? And then the familiar images begin to swirl forward through the mist of the mirror. I find my girl snuggled down on her bed, back in her bedroom. Her body curled around a book–no, it's the handwritten black and white composition notebook with all her precious stories inside.

Trying to break into her space, I start with, "You look kind of content, Bitzy. Is there anything we should discuss today?"

Bitzy lifts her head from the book and stares at me. She says nothing. I feel awkward as if I've interrupted her in some deep reverie. Should I push her? Maybe this is a regrouping time, and I am invasive.

"Discuss?" Bitzy finally acknowledges my presence. "What's there to discuss? I have to go back to school with all the other kids. I won't fit in. I didn't before. They won't remember who I am."

"I can't tell from your words if you're discouraged or afraid," I say, assuming my best therapeutic voice.

"Afraid . . . you don't understand–*afraid*! I've always been afraid of other kids and new situations. Now it's going to be worse because now I'm supposed to know something, like writing, and reading, and numbers, and stuff."

"Seems like you're afraid you won't measure up to some magical criteria. Who set this expectation on you?" I ask.

"You and your mother! Your mother had a dream as to who *we* were supposed to be. Don't you remember the picture she showed you when you were helping her pack up and move into the elderly housing apartments?"

I'm completely turned inside out by Bitzy's comments, for she is talking about something which happened just a few years ago–in my adult life. Trying not to make the connection, I reply, "What, what picture do you mean?"

"Stupid! You can be so dense. The gold framed one she had in the bottom of her picture box, of a little girl from 1915, backed up against a white picket fence, with her skirts blowing and her blond hair trailing in the breezes."

"Yes, I remember the picture . . . but how do you know about her showing it to me?"

Bitzy ignores my question. "That was a picture of what she wanted us to become; carefree, happy, obedient, idyllic little girls. That was a picture of what *she wanted to be. That was a picture of her missing childhood!*"

Bitzy's words, spoken aloud for the first time on this subject, make me want to vomit, or run, maybe disappear. Where had this child gained such insight? Was she telling me that all of my childhood was a gauzy haze of events wrapped around my mother's deep desire to regain *her lost childhood*? If that was true, then my life had not been my own; it had been a sham, or was it? I had been there. I participated. I adored my mother and hated this internal child that clung to me—helpless, sick, crippled, and awkward; this child that was now telling me who I was and who I had become.

Bitzy seems to read my thoughts. "I'm always with you, JessieMay or should I call you Birdie? I'm within you; I lived in the sick room, and I live in your counseling chair. I know all there is to know about you and the fact that you don't talk about any of it very much. You hide behind helping others or just being distant. Try crying *your tears* for the childhood you refused to live because you were too afraid."

Bitzy's words are sharp. All I want to do is close down this session. It is too close. My insides plead for the mirror to recede and the computer screen to come up in its place, my computer screen of the present day, with its comforting blue and green valley picture of my childhood landscapes. It doesn't happen. Bitzy is now sitting on the side of our bed, in our childhood bedroom, her sneakered feet swinging back and forth as if she feels relief or a change of energy. She smiles, and I sense it is my turn to speak.

"I know you're right, but this is all so hard to take in. Can I rest for a bit, just now?" *I feel sort of silly, for the tables seem to have turned, and it is Bitzy who is teaching me.*

In profound silence, she places her hand up to the mirror. I know what she is asking in a flash, and I lay my hand over the image of hers. Bending forward to see more clearly, I spy a tiny space still left between our hands. Bitzy flexes hers, and I feel it through my palm. She mouths the words, "I'm yours when you choose to claim me."

# CHAPTER SEVENTEEN

# To Ride a New Bicycle

HAVING DISCOVERED I had the power to get what I wanted, namely, kindness and attention, school didn't seem overwhelming. The incident with Miss Phillips, the school nurse, coming down from her office to the classroom, seemed to change Miss Carlson. From there on, she was gentle and understanding when working with me. She acted like she was afraid I might become sick and that it would be her fault. I wondered if the nurse had said something that made Miss Carlson change. Whatever, it was easier to ask questions and get help. School began to be interesting, and my work improved.

The adjustment to the kids was a whole other matter. I was shy and quiet. Growing up in a family with two almost adults and then my parents, I didn't know how to be with children my age, so I kept to myself. I guess this made the other children think I was stuck-up, for they left me alone. My out-of-school experiences with the Simpson girls were no preparation for life on a school playground.

Dee and Gabby, two girls from Sunday school, lived next to each other across from the school and played together every day. *No room for friendship there.* The third girl, Nan, was as quiet as I. Often, we'd sit side by side on the swings without talking, as if by swinging elbow to elbow, something magical would happen, and we'd become friends; at least I hoped so.

After some time of struggling to make friendships, I noticed Bobby Hall. He was a blond-haired boy about my size with laughing blue eyes. He and Dick often played together. Dick was rough and tough, while Bobby was more gentle and polite. Bobby often got the short end of things and would wander off to the sandbox to sit, pouring sand from one hand through the fingers of the other.

One day I was in the sandbox when Bobby came. I moved closer. He didn't seem to notice. I tried to pour sand through my fingers like he was doing. Bobby stared at me for a moment and then went back to pouring sand. Again, I moved closer. He continued pouring. I grabbed a handful of sand and threw it at his face. It caught both of us by surprise. Frightened, I flattened myself down into the sand, pretending to be a cat, and watched to see what he'd do next. Bobby started to his feet, and as he did, I scrambled and ran. He was after me. I ran as fast as I could, dodging between students. Bobby wove in and out along the path I'd cut. I ducked under the steel supports of the slide. He reached out to catch me. I dodged around the end of the structure, but he was coming from the other side. Smack! We collided. Recovering from the stunning quicker than I did, Bobby grabbed my arms.

"Don't ever throw sand at me again!" he yelled, shaking me as best he could.

"Yeah, who's going to stop me?" I screamed as I wriggled and broke free, running blindly toward the school. Bobby, smarting from my threat, was after me.

Looking down at the ground so as not to stumble, I lost my direction. When I looked up, I was on a collision course with the playground duty teacher. *Aw . . . oh! Too late to change!* I plowed into Mrs. Dorriety, a sturdy, older woman with gray permed hair and a constant frown. Oomph . . . it was a chilling sound as I hit the backside of this seventh-grade teacher.

*"Oh, God, what's she going to do to me?"* I thought, as a strong hand reached out, holding me tight, like a kitten that might escape. The teacher drew me around to face her. Mrs. Dorriety's silver rimmed glasses were askew on her nose, her hair ruffled. Her face, red

like burning embers, gave off waves of anger. Before I could speak, Mrs. Dorriety grabbed Bobby with her free hand. Now we three stood in a tight circle, this furious teacher glaring down at us.

"So, what do you children think you are doing out here?" She asked.

"Oh, nothing," Bobby said. "We were just running around having fun."

"It didn't feel that way to me," said Mrs. Dorriety. "And what is your name?" She asked looking at me.

"Bitzy," I mumbled, hoping she wouldn't hear.

"So, Bitzy, what do you say was the reason you ran into me?"

"We were just running around having fun," I said, trying to copy Bobby's version.

"Do you consider it fun to ram into people?"

I looked at Bobby. He was trying to hide a grin. As the teacher's rage got hotter, the laughter inside bubbled up and I tried to bring my thoughts under control. *But she looks so funny! Her glasses tilting over to one side and those great red blotches on her face . . .* I fought to keep the giggles silent.

"We didn't mean to run into you," I blurted trying to cover the rising laughter.

"Well, that's good. I'm glad you didn't plan to run me down! You both agree you were having fun?" Mrs. Dorriety asked again.

We nodded.

"Then maybe you'll find writing sentences together fun, also. You will spend the next week in your classroom, during recesses and lunchtime, writing: 'I will not run on the playground, and I will watch where I am going at all times.'"

She released us.

We shook our arms, trying to get rid of the pain where she'd been pinching. Backing away, I turned and ran toward the safety of the sandbox. Bobby was close behind. We settled low into the box, hoping the teacher might forget the whole affair. I muttered to Bobby, "God, I thought she was going to kill us!"

\* \* \*

By the time a week had passed writing, "I will not run on the
playground . . . ," Bobby and I had become good friends. Back on the
playground, things moved to shoving, and tickling, and promising
never to let old Mrs. Dorriety catch us. With Bobby as a new playmate,
Dick sometimes joined in the chase, but I didn't like what he did when
he caught me. Dick would hold onto me, pinning my arms behind my
back and not let me go when I'd had enough. He didn't play fair like
Bobby. In time, other girls joined our horseplay and I began to feel
accepted by my classmates.

*　　*　　*

Valentine's Day was coming. "Mom, can we get a Valentine card for
Bobby?"

"I guess we could. But wouldn't it be more fun to make one? Maybe,
PollyAnne would help. I think we have some red construction paper
and a few white doilies tucked away. Why don't you ask her?"

PollyAnne agreed and we two sisters settled at the oak dining room
table with our red paper, doilies, glue, and magazines spread out across
the tabletop.

"See, if you take a thin piece of paper and fold it like an accordion,
you can glue it onto the face of the card," my sister said. "Then, stick a
paper doily to the springs, and you'll have a lacy screen. Behind it you
can put a picture of a cute little girl and boy kissing."

"Bobby won't like kissing stuff," I said. "A puppy would be better."

"Oh, why?" PollyAnne asked.

"Boys think kissing is yucky."

"Whatever you want, I was only showing you how they used to make
valentines a long time ago. Pretty, huh?"

"Yeah . . ." I responded. I was busy making little springs; holding
them down, and watching them jump as I pulled my finger off. *What
freedom! Imagine if you could put things like that on your feet and bounce
wherever you wanted.* My thoughts traveled from the white springs, to
kids with their bicycles on the road in front of our house. Carol Simpson
rode up and down, racing with her next sister down in age, Jeannie.
Afternoons as I watched from my napping place, I wondered, *will I ever*

*have a bicycle—ever be able to ride free on the road? Maybe I could take it to the top of the hill and ride down past the front of our house.*

"Where are you?" Polly asked, bringing me back to the valentine cards.

"I was thinking about the kids riding their bikes outside. Do you think I'll be able to ride a bicycle?"

"Sure you can. I'll let you ride mine as soon as it gets warm outside. The seat's too high, but you can stand up on the pedals and ride standing up," PollyAnne said, sliding a piece of construction paper under two of my springs. "That way you'd have a chance to see if you can balance a bike."

"I want a bike of my own!" I said, remembering how Polly's bike was scuffed up, with chipping greenish paint and white walled tires, gray from splattered mud.

"I didn't say you could have mine. My bike is to get me back and forth to work, but you could try riding it to get the feel.

Unlike most sisters, PollyAnne was always willing to share, or to help. "Why don't you ask Mom if she and Dad can get you a bike?"

Suddenly, the valentines were replaced in my mind by how I could get a bicycle for, say . . . my birthday. That was only a couple of weeks away.

Next day, when Mother was brushing my hair for school, I came out with it. "Mom, can I have a new bicycle for my birthday?"

"What?" Mother sounded stunned. Money was tight in our family.

"You want a bicycle for your birthday? Where do you think Daddy and I can come up with that much money in so short a time?" Mother stopped brushing and looked at me.

My courage faltered—*I shouldn't have blurted it out.*

"Maybe we could find a secondhand one, but we couldn't do it by your birthday. Besides, you don't even know if you can balance on a bicycle."

"I can. I can. I know I can, already!"

Mother eyed me suspiciously. "How do you know that?"

"I just know I can ride. Then I could go anywhere, and you won't have to drive me"

"Whoa, Bitzy, you haven't been out of your sickbed for that long. First things first," my mother said. "Like, how are we going to come up with that much money?"

"I could work for it and save all my allowance."

"You'd be willing to do that?" I expect my mother didn't think I could stick to that bargain.

"I suppose if you're willing to do extra chores and save, Dad and I could see what we could find." Mother had stopped brushing, again. "First, I've got to see that you're serious about this before I speak to your father."

"I am! I'm serious!"

"Let's make up a jar marked BITZY'S BICYCLE and we'll see how much you save. If all that money goes into the jar, I think we could consider doing this, but not by birthday time."

"I can have a bicycle?" I asked. I'd expected Mother to say no, that it would strain my heart too much. So it wasn't any disappointment that I couldn't have it for my birthday.

Next week the allowance went into the jar and I began working on the chore list. On the day of my birthday, a card came from my great Auntie Grace, my Grammy's younger sister. She had no children of her own and had taken an interest in me. Mother handed me the envelope, watching me as I struggled. When I pulled the card apart, money fell onto the floor.

"What's this?" my mother asked, bending down to pick up the green paper. Mother looked shocked. "What does the card say, Bitzy?"

"I can't make it out. The writing is tiny, something about my bicycle. Can you read it to me?"

"Dear, Bitzy," my mother started. "You can not possibly understand what great pleasure I derive from receiving your lovely Christmas thank you notes. It is not often a little girl thinks of an old woman like me. Your grandmother said you were saving for a bicycle, and I thought this money might be of more use to you than it is to me. Put it with what you are earning and buy yourself an elegant new bicycle. Much love to you, your great Auntie Grace."

"Wow! How much is it?" I asked, wondering why Auntie Grace was being so helpful.

"Honey, it looks like you can have your bike this spring," my mother said, her voice quivering. "Do you realize your great aunt has sent more than half the cost of a new bicycle? You are one lucky lady!" My mother stood fingering the bills. "You're going to have to write a super thank you letter, back."

Mother let me hold the money and I clutched the card and bills, as if fearful it might escape. *I can have my bike,* I thought. *And now, I can ride free up and down out front like the other kids!*

## Looking Through My Therapist Eyes

# Ride Bicycle

This chapter shows Bitzy's tremendous need to put her illness behind her. Her first adventures into how one makes friends help point out the isolationism that was a part of her family. She either had never chosen to focus on how her family related to other people, or she was presenting life as it was for her—very few friends coming into the home, and those either to see her parents or to play with her older brother or sister. By the age of five-and-a-half, Bitzy had no social skills. The months shut away from other children heightened this problem.

We can surmise that the work ethic was very strong in this family since we know that Bitzy's sister, PollyAnne, was working a regular job, on top of going to school, by the age of fifteen. Also, if you notice, we only hear Bitzy talk about her father in terms of his work. And when Bitzy puts her mother into a scene in the story, we usually find the woman in some working situation. Was this family hiding their emotional selves behind work?

In support of the mother, we need to recognize that it must have been a strain for her to allow—no, encourage—her daughter to secure a bicycle after being so sick. At some level, she must have recognized the child's indomitable need for freedom. She could have continued the protectiveness that must have been her first choice, but she did not. And with that decision, we see the beginnings of a pattern that Bitzy's mother will display all through the book—of vacillating between being overprotective and perhaps too permissive.

One wonders if this pattern of vacillation would have existed if Bitzy's father had taken a more active role in the *hands-on parenting* of his children. This brings us to another question: Why was Bitzy's father such a shadowy person in this family? Was Bitzy's mother overbearing, dictatorial, uncompromising? Or were there issues within Bitzy's father that put him into the background of this household? We certainly know he was physically *very much in the home,* even preparing breakfast and coming home for lunches. Why was he distant, unavailable?

Bitzy's Beautiful Blue Bicycle P.

# CHAPTER EIGHTEEN

# The Men's Maternity Ward

I PUT THE MONEY from Auntie Grace's birthday card into the jar marked BITZY'S BICYCLE. The jar was looking close to full, now, stuffed with my extra chore money and my allowances. "Can we open the jar and count the money?" I asked my mother one day in early April.

"I don't see why we couldn't."

I raced to get the jar down from the shelf by the kitchen sink. Spilling the contents onto the old blue-painted table where my family ate our meals, I started to group the pennies, and then the nickels, and then the shiny dimes.

"How much do we have in there?" Mother asked.

"I don't know. I'm sorting the pennies!"

I fussed with the money while Mother stopped to watch.

"Bitzy, do you know how to count money?"

"Yes, of course I do! They teach us that in school."

I struggled a little longer with making the piles. By now, Mother had crossed the kitchen twice past the table.

"Would you like me to help with the counting, Bitzy?"

"Yeah, I get stuck a little on the dimes part."

Mother smiled.

It had never occurred to me that I didn't know how to count money. My mother took the stacks of bills I'd organized and began counting with the tens, "Ten dollars, twenty dollars, thirty dollars . . . see Honey, we start by counting the largest bills first. Why don't you get a piece of paper, and when I count out an amount, you write it down. Then we'll add up the figures together."

I was so grateful that Mother had figured out the problem without making me confess that I still didn't understand how much nickels and dimes were worth.

When we were done counting and adding, Mother said, "Bitzy, it looks as if we could get your bike any day now. Your father and I will have to look around to see what kind of a buy we can get."

"When can I have it?"

"We have to wait until it's warmed up enough for you to ride outside, but I would expect that once we've located the bicycle, you could have it most any time."

I wondered why Mom wouldn't give me a sure day but knew it was best to leave the subject alone.

It was a day late in April. I'd gotten home from school and gone into the pantry to make a peanut butter and mayonnaise-with-cinnamon-on-it sandwich. As I came out of the pantry on my way to get a glass of milk from the refrigerator, Mother called from the back porch. "Bitzy, come on out and see what's out here."

The day was damp and dreary with dark threatening clouds overhead—typical April weather. As I stepped out onto the cold porch, I saw the cream and blue, brand new girl's bicycle leaning against the porch wall.

"My bicycle! You've gotten my bicycle! It's beautiful! It's blue. My favorite color! Oh, it's so beautiful!" I ran to the bike, squatted down on the floor, and threw my arms around the cream and blue center support post. "Is it mine? Is it really all mine?"

"It's all yours, Honey, thanks to your hard work and your aunt's help. See, look at this. It even has a horn. Just press this little silver button here on the support bar."

I followed with my eyes to where Mother was pointing her finger. I pressed the button. The sudden urgent buzz made both of us jump.

"Well, I guess that's loud enough to protect you!"

I pressed the button again and again. The noise was just like the glee I felt inside.

"Enough! Enough! Bitzy, I think we know how well the horn works! Put the kick-stand down and see if you can balance on it while it's still in place."

"I can do it! I've been riding PollyAnne's bike when she lets me." I had indeed been out practicing on my sister's bike. On that bike, there was no possibility of sitting on the seat and touching the pedals, so I had to master the art of riding by standing up on the peddles all the time. It hadn't taken me long to catch on to the way you had to shift your weight as the bike tilted first to one side then the other in its progress forward.

"Can I take it out and try it?"

"I'm sorry, Honey, not today. The roads are wet, and it's still raining a little. You don't want your new bike to get all wet. Also, we don't want you skidding in the winter sand on your first time out. Maybe tomorrow it will clear up. Today, just work with it here on the back porch. Now don't ride right through the porch screening." Mother chuckled as she backed away from the bicycle, signaling my opportunity to move into ownership.

When Mother called the family for supper, I was still out on the porch polishing my already shiny new bicycle with an old cotton rag.

"Come on to supper, Bitzy. You know you can't sleep with that thing tonight." The family sitting at the table laughed at my mother's comment. But to me, it didn't matter. I finally had my bicycle.

*   *   *

My maiden voyage on the street out front of the large white saltbox was a marvelous affair. After a few momentary lurches from side to side, the bicycle came under my control and moved ahead smoothly. It was as if, like a child with a new babysitter, the bike needed to question my ability to handle this large new venture in my life.

Freedom! It fairly whistled through my hair as I rode down to the corner where the school bus turned left. I followed the familiar turn and pedaled onward past the pine trees that my father had set out many years ago with the boys in his state crew. Then it was on past the telephone poles I'd counted on my return from the hospital. Coming to the end of the street so quickly, I was frightened for half an instant— this was a long way from home! Should I turn right, which would take me farther away, or turn back and head toward home? I turned around and retraced my journey.

The next day, after school, I took the bicycle in the opposite direction. Having mastered the ride along flat ground, it was time to try the hill. Heading off to the left from the front of the house, I soon had to pedal hard; the bicycle wove and tilted left and right as I tried to climb the low hill. Terrified that I would fall off, I pushed harder at the pedals. Then I found I made more headway if I allowed the bike to move first to the left and then to the right in a crisscross pattern as we began to conquer the hill.

Perched at the top looking back, I wasn't sure I wanted to ride down. It wasn't the steepest hill in the world, but it brought memories. While I sat on the bicycle seat resting with my legs braced against the ground, my mind wandered back to Daddy's sliding on the flexible flyer down this very hill with me clinging to his back. He'd start with a few running steps, throw the sled onto the hard-packed snow and drop belly first down onto its frame. "Come on, Bitzy, jump on quick!" he'd call.

If we timed it just right, the sled would take off as if pushed by unseen forces and careen down the snow-covered hill, finally coming to rest in the flat area almost halfway to the front door of our house.

Should I risk it? All the other kids seemed to ride the hill without effort. As if I wasn't thinking, I kicked with my feet, and the bike slid beyond the crest of the hill. Like it or not, I was headed down. My knuckles gripped the handlebars, turning white as the fear quickened. The wind pulled at my braids and tugged at the collar on my shirt. My eyes smarted as I squinted into the oncoming air—no need to use any force on the pedals. Finally, the bike slowed in its descent to the point where I had to start pedaling again. I'd made it! I'd ridden the hill.

Recognizing the wisdom of quitting when ahead, I turned the corner to the right at the end of the street and rode my bicycle over the bumpy graveled drive leading to the basement of our house. Parking the bike, I ran into the inside, yelling to whomever might be there, "I did it! I did it!"

"You did what?" my mother responded from where she stood over the ironing board with the flat iron lifted in her hand. "What did you do, Bitzy?"

"I rode the big hill!"

"Does it make you feel all grown up now?"

I was surprised by my mother's comment. That was what I was feeling. I wasn't weak anymore! I wasn't sick! I was all grown up!

"Not so fast, Honey." My mother must have read my thoughts from the expression on my face. "You've got a lot more growing to do before you're all grown up. That's just one hill you've mastered."

Still, I felt that something had changed for me. Now I was more like the other kids. I wasn't afraid of the big hill, and before long, I'd be able to ride up onto the ridge above the hill to play with the other neighborhood kids. Surely, Mother could see I wasn't sick anymore.

*   *   *

My confidence grew with my growing freedom. Mother did gradually allow me to play with the other children in the upper part of the State School neighborhood—on rare occasions.

It was a beautiful late afternoon in May as I was returning from play on the street above the big hill. I'd have to pedal fast to get home before supper. Dad would have already left the assembly field where they counted the boys each night to ensure none had escaped. This assembly field was just at the base of the big hill off to the left.

Wheeling my bike around the corner at the top of the hill, I relaxed my feet, allowing my momentum to take me beyond the drop-off point of the hill and on down, down, past the steep part, to the more shallow area across from the assembly field. This riding down the hill was so easy I could hardly remember being afraid before.

Thumb! Bump! Twist! Skid! And the bike was jerking, tilting over to the left. It was going down! *My beautiful new bike! I can't hurt my beautiful new bicycle!* . . . Grind! Scrape! My knee hit the pavement, and the hand on the lower side reached out instinctively to hold the bike away from the black asphalt.

I shrieked with pain as the bicycle finally slid to a stop, with me pinned beneath it. My hand throbbed, and my lower leg was numb. No, it was stinging—actually burning. Oh, God, the pain! Normally quiet with any kind of hurt, I couldn't hold back the combined fear that I might have destroyed my bicycle and the pain of the scraped knee and torn left hand. I struggled to lift the bicycle off me and to get my legs free. *Can I stand up?—Yes, I can!*—As I lifted the bike to an upright position, the next wave of anguish escaped my lips. I looked down to see that my left knee and leg were oozing a sickly, dirt-filled, watery-like red blood. I didn't dare look at the left hand. Alternately crying and screaming in pain, using my left elbow and good right hand, I pushed the bicycle the rest of the way toward home.

The screams of pain rolled before me as I approached the old house. Mother was coming out of the front door and down the walk. "Bitzy, what in the world has happened? I could hear you all the way back in the kitchen. What's wrong?"

Between screams and sobs, I tried to tell her. "I was just riding my bike down the big hill, and everything was going so good . . . and the bike bounced up and . . . then it tilted over . . . then it went down with me under it . . . Mummy is my bike all right?"

"I don't care if it is or not! I need to take a look at you. We'll look at the bike later."

By now Dad was at the top of the front stoop with PollyAnne right behind him. It was Polly that got the family focused on what was the necessary next step. "Oh, God! Just look at that knee!"

Mother had her arm around my shoulders while Dad took the bicycle, standing it against the support post of the stair railing. "Let me take her," he said, scooping me up just as he had when he carried me up and downstairs while I'd been so sick. In three swift movements, Daddy was up the front porch steps and through the front screen door. He placed me down as if I were a feather, so gently, on the old blue couch in the living room. "Now, let's have a look at the damage."

Mother moved to the couch as Dad stepped back. "Let me see that hand," she said. I extended the bloody left hand. Mom and Dad both peered at it closely. "Looks like you'll lose that thumbnail," Dad muttered under his breath.

"Lose my nail? What's he mean?" I was terrified. "What does Daddy mean—lose my thumbnail?"

"Honey, you've scraped up this left hand badly and bruised the nail; it's turning purple. The corner has been torn loose. Sometimes when a nail has been torn up like this, the body decides the best thing is to replace it, so you shed the one you've got and grow a new one. We'll just have to wait and see."

Mother sent PollyAnne for a basin of water and some washcloths and the mercurochrome to disinfect the scraped knee.

"It's not going to hurt too much, is it?"

"Well, we have to get it cleaned, Bitzy. I'm just glad you're all right. You can stand a little pain if it's going to ensure the wound heals correctly."

There was indeed pain as Mother cleaned the knee. I tried to push Mom's hand away once and got that you-know-better-than-this look. But I couldn't help it. I whimpered and tried biting my lip. Finally, Mother was done. She decided not to cover the scraped knee but to leave it open to the air. "We'll have to watch how this goes. I think it's best to leave it open."

Dad had returned to his newspaper by now, and PollyAnne was back in the kitchen working on supper. "You'll be all right here on the couch." And with that, Mother went back to the kitchen to finish the evening preparations.

*   *   *

I didn't get much sleep that night because the knee and thumb throbbed. Mom gave me aspirin to help but, still, I couldn't have a sheet over me, and I didn't want to be uncovered—*Oh, why did this all have to happen to me?*

School the next day was difficult, trying to walk to the bus and the school. All the kids wanted to know what had happened. I had to tell the story over and over. Sometimes it seemed to help to tell it and, then, other times, it just seemed to make the knee hurt more.

Two days later, I discovered the place on my thigh where a bee had stung me recently looked funny. It was raised and gray looking, oozing this grayish sort of stuff. "Mom," I called. "What's happening to this spot?"

"Let me have a look." Mother stared at the bee sting. "Oh, this is not good! I'll have to call Dr. Blackmore. This spot looks infected. Let me see your thumb?" I stuck my thumb up where Mother could look better. As we both peered at it, I noticed the same grayish stuff oozing from the side of the torn nail. "What's that, Mom?"

"It's pus. I'm terribly afraid it's an infection, and with the rheumatic fever last year, we may be in for trouble. Let me call the doctor."

Dr. Blackmore came. He looked at both wounds and shook his head. Turning to my mother, he said, "There's no question about it. This bee sting is seriously infected. With her history, we can't take any chances. She's got to go into the hospital. The only thing that will break this is massive doses of penicillin. This infection mustn't get to the heart. Pack her things and take her right now."

"I've got to go to the hospital, again?"

"Yes, Honey. You heard the doctor. It's the only way we can beat this. You're older now, and you've been to school. It won't be as bad to be away this time. You'll see. We've worked too hard to get you well to stop now. Besides, when you're all better, you've got your new bike to come home to."

For a moment, Mother's comment diverted my attention.

"Is my bike okay?"

"Yes, Daddy looked it all over carefully before he put it in the basement. There's not a scratch on it. You did a masterful job of saving it. Too bad your body had to take such a beating against the road."

\*   \*   \*

Mother was right. The hospital wasn't as scary this time. When the nurses spoke to me, I'd talk back to them. They were nice. They put me in a room with other women in it. As I listened to the women talk, I discovered they all had children like me. Some of them had new babies. The woman next to me would hold her baby as she gave it a bottle so that I could watch the baby. This adventure wasn't so frightening.

The next morning Dr. Blackmore came into the room to look at my knee. "We're going to have to dress this. It may hurt a bit." Indeed, it did hurt as he swabbed it with something he said would keep it clean. Then he padded the wound with gauze and wrapped the whole thing with strips of gauze. "There now, that should last you two days. I'll be back then to take a look and redress it."

After the doctor left, the nurse reappeared with another hypodermic needle. This horrible-looking thing held the penicillin. They had started giving me shots in my behind the night before, right when I got to the hospital. "Do I have to have that thing again?"

"Yes, Bitzy, you're going to have to have an awful lot of these—one every four hours. You're going to have to help me by being brave."

"I don't like these needles!"

"Yes, Hon, I know. It can't be much fun. But we have to do it to get the knee all well so you can go back home."

I bit my lip and received the needle again in the thick part of my bottom. Fighting back the tears, I lay quiet in the bed.

"You are the best brave girl I've ever seen." The voice came from a young man, about twenty-four, standing at the foot of my bed. He was on crutches—the bulk of his body hung from the cross pieces as he stood.

"Who are you?" I asked.

"I'm Jerry. I live across the hall. I heard there was a pretty little girl in here getting poked in the butt all the time. Thought I'd come to see how she was making out."

"What happened to your face?" I asked the obvious question. One side of his face was all red and raw-looking, as if someone had taken a giant piece of sandpaper to it, tearing off all the white skin. It looked more like meat for meatloaf than a face.

"I was in a motorcycle accident a week ago—got my leg, my arm, and my face torn up. I was going too fast, hit some sand, and the stupid bike went over on me. I got dragged about twenty feet across the pavement. Road burn! That's what you see. I broke my leg, too."

"Gee, I'm sorry. I did the same thing. I fell off my new bicycle, scraped up my knee and almost tore my thumbnail off."

"Well, it looks like we've got something in common. Maybe we can be friends. They say friends need to have something in common. Want to be friends? I can tell you how bad it is for me, and you can tell me about what it's like for you."

A friend! I didn't have one of those. That would be fun. "Yeah, sure, we can be friends. I wish they'd stop sticking that big needle into me."

Jerry stayed and talked for a while longer, and then the nurses sent him back to his room because it was feeding time for the babies.

Two days later, Dr. Blackmore came to dress my knee. "I have to tell you—this will hurt a little." The doctor carefully cut the gauze wrapping and poked at the edge of the padding until he had a corner lose. Then, looking directly into my eyes, he grabbed the pad and ripped it from the wound in one swift movement. I screamed. He'd taken the pad off along with all the newly formed scab, which was embedded in the gauze padding.

"Why did you do that?" I sobbed.

"I'm sorry, Bitzy, but the bandage has to be changed every two days. I have to see that the infection is going away. I don't want to hurt you, but it is necessary in this case."

In the past, if the doctor hurt me and I had felt he didn't mean to, I could forgive him. But this time . . . ! This time I'd never forgive him!

I lay sniffling in my bed when Jerry came into the room. "Sounds like you need some cheering up?"

"The doctor's mean! He tore the bandage off my knee. I hate him!"

"Yeah, I know what you mean. Sometimes I hate my doctor, too."

Jerry went on to talk about what he'd been doing out on his bike when he'd had his accident. It helped to keep my mind off the throbbing of my knee.

Two days later, the whole episode with Dr. Blackmore repeated itself. I tried to be understanding, but it just seemed stupid to me, tearing off the new scab each time he dressed it. The third time when he appeared to take care of the wound, I tried to explain it was stupid to tear off the scab. The fourth time I begged him not to touch the leg, protectively covering the bandaging with my hands. Nothing worked. When the doctor left, I was hurting and felt angry and helpless. Jerry was able to comfort me with his laughter and stories.

The afternoons were better. Mother came to visit and began bringing books to read. "Bitzy do you like horses?" Mom asked.

"Yeah, sure, but I can't have one."

"That's okay. I brought one in a book. Here listen to this."

Mother opened the book and began to read about Black Beauty. I was soon absorbed by the story and a long way away from the injustice of the doctor and the pain in my knee.

It had been almost a week and a half that I'd been in the hospital going through the torture of the knee dressing, the needles poked into my bottom—or when the flesh on my buttocks became too raw, my thighs. Through all this, I'd managed to keep my spirits up. Mom's story reading was a big help. It gave me something else about which to dream.

This particular afternoon when Mother came in, I had been moved to the room across the hall. Jerry lived in this room with two other men. Mother looked surprised when I called to her from the bed. "How did you get over there?"

"Well, there was a new mother who needed my bed in the women's maternity ward, so they moved me here to the men's maternity ward. That way, I can be with Jerry all the time. He makes me laugh."

"What did you call this room?" My mother had a quizzical look on her face.

"It's the men's maternity ward. It's across the hall from the women's maternity ward."

"That's what I thought you said. That's nice." Mother chuckled. "It must be nice being near Jerry."

I had not missed the chuckle. "What's funny, Mom?"

"You are Honey. Well, not you exactly, but what you say."

"What did I say that was funny?"

"Well, maternity means being a woman and having a baby, so that's why it's called a maternity ward. Men don't have babies, so it's hard for me to believe that this is called the men's maternity ward. Just because it's across the hall from the woman's room doesn't make this a men's maternity ward."

I was stunned for half an instant as I took in my misunderstanding. "Well, to me, it is still the men's maternity ward!"

*   *   *

Altogether I spent two weeks in the hospital. The war my body waged with the infection was monumental. By the second week, the constant injections of penicillin caused the infection to break out on my fanny. "You poor babe!" said the nurse, who brought in the bright pink rubber inner tube for me to sit on. "It seems like they could come up with some other way of giving this stuff. How about a Popsicle? Would that make your bottom feel better?"

*I wondered why the nurse was offering a Popsicle. Those were for the kids at the other end of the hall who had had their tonsils out. But no matter, a Popsicle was a Popsicle.* "Sure. Can I have a grape one?" The nurse brought a grape one. I was surprised to find it really did make the sore bottom feel better.

That afternoon I had an even bigger surprise. Daddy came to the hospital with my mother. He'd taken an afternoon off from work to come and visit. This afternoon off was unheard of—my father taking time from work. I felt so warm inside and much honored. "You came just to see me?"

My father nodded his head. "I hadn't been in to see you for several evenings, so I thought I'd come today. Besides, I have something for you."

I wondered what he'd brought. He didn't do the presents in the family, Mother did. What could it be? I intently watched as he reached into the pocket of his dark-colored work pants and drew out a silver nutcracker, the kind we used at Thanksgiving. "Why don't I settle down in this chair beside the bed while your mother reads your story? She tells me you two are right in the middle of it." Dad pulled up a chair but then seemed to change his mind. He sat down right on the hospital bed, balancing himself with one foot against the polished tile floor.

The silver nutcracker was still lying on the white cover of the bed.

I wondered, *is that the present? I can't be. What would I do with a nutcracker in the hospital?* By now, Mother had rescued the one chair, pulling it around to the other side of the bed. The book flipped open all on its own to the place where we'd left Black Beauty the day before. Mother's voice quickly brought the contents of the book to life. My attention moved to the horses in the story, but still, my eyes didn't leave my Dad's hands.

He poked his hand back into his pocket. Out came something round that looked very small. He reached over and picked up the nutcracker. Cru..nch! Dad handed the contents to me. "Careful. Pick the meat out from the shell parts," he whispered below the sound of the ongoing story. His strong hands covered the cracker to muffle the sound. Cru..nch. He cracked another, handing the nut meat to me, separately this time. I grinned up at my father. It was as if we were involved in some secret right there in front of Mom. The room seemed so cozy to me, with my mother on one side and my father on the other. This togetherness didn't happen often.

Mother stopped reading. "I see Dad has you into his winter supply of hazelnuts. You know he gathered those wild last fall. I think he was keeping them for a special occasion. Taste good?"

They tasted like pure butter to me. Perhaps even better, because I was aware that Daddy didn't often share his treasure of wild hazelnuts. They were not easy to come by, and often he was only able to find a few.

"Well, I thought it was time for a treat. The doctor says they're about done with you here, and you'll soon be coming home." Dad didn't say anymore. But I could feel how much he had missed me in the very absence of his words. I hadn't realized how much I'd missed him. At home, he didn't interact much with me, or PollyAnne, or Owen—maybe more with PollyAnne—but he was always there in the background. Like a rock, he was there, making all of us feel safe. I smiled up at my father and chomped down on the next nut-meat.

*    *    *

The return home was uneventful. I got back to the routine of school and then summer vacation. The bicycle was just like Daddy had said, without even a single scratch. Getting back up on it was like trying to mount a horse, like the horses in my stories—one that has spooked and thrown you. But soon, I overcame the remembered terror of falling.

It took a couple of weeks before I could try the hill. And never again did I ride down it with the abandonment that had caused the fall in the first place. It wasn't carelessness my father reported, but rather a small pot-hole which caught my front tire, twisting the wheel out of my control and throwing me onto the road. Now, it didn't matter how it had happened; I would always be watchful from here on in my riding career.

Another trip to Winchester to the heart specialist, Dr. Clark, confirmed the stay in the hospital had contained and destroyed the massive infection. It had not caused any more damage to the heart, nor had it brought on any type of recurrence of the rheumatic fever. Mother seemed terribly relieved by the report. I felt the same as ever.

The next year passed quickly. My health constantly improved. There was the six-month check-up in Dr. Clark's office—with an X-ray, this time to look at the heart and confirm it had not changed or enlarged. The X-ray I'd had before frightened me, but being more grown-up now, I stood up, taking the cold screen on my chest without flinching. The pictures indicated that nothing had changed. I was in good health.

## Looking Through My Therapist Eyes

## Men's Maternity

In this part of the story, we see the deep tenderness that both parents have for their daughter, Bitzy, hidden behind their New England industriousness. We see it in the reaction to events, the fact that it is PollyAnne who is cool-headed enough to suggest what the next step might be to rescue her sister from the immense physical trauma just sustained. Bitzy's parents, for once, too stunned by their connection to their daughter's pain—commiserative shock—are unable to think of the first steps to repair.

In a family where the mother presents the father *as head of household*, while she controls the day-to-day events, it is encouraging to see her pushed aside momentarily, as this child's father takes command, driven by his unexpressed love for his child. Once Bitzy's father is satisfied that his daughter will survive, he drops back to his usual role in the family.

Bitzy herself speaks of her mother's ability to control her own feelings, in order to explain and comfort her child. A calming that Bitzy needed to counter the fears she was experiencing because, as a child, she did not precisely understand the terror that she was feeling from her mother, father, sister and doctor. She didn't understand all the words, nor did she understand the emotional tension underneath what her family was saying. Bitzy had to read meaning into their actions and words, something that in later years would give her an ability to be attentive as a therapist, but for now, it caused anxiety. She repressed anxiety so that she could become *the cooperative, obedient patient*—imagine having the top of your knee torn off every two days! We know there was repression of her true feelings because she remarks on how nice everyone is as she re-enters the hospital. She only mentions once her terror at the possibility of a return trip—to the place and experience that emotionally marked her for a lifetime.

When feelings are never allowed to surface, be talked about, or worked upon, they become wounds. Bitzy's largest wound is that of feeling abandoned in the face of the greater societal need—to make her well.

# CHAPTER NINETEEN
## Playing House

MY FAMILY MAKE-UP was a bit different because my mother's oldest sister, Gracie, and my mother married cousins. So those two families, the Sandlers and the Bentons, had grandparents that were siblings and then common aunts and uncles. My mother tells the story of meeting my father when she was only twelve years old. She was babysitting for Gracie's two young children. It was Patriots Day in Bunker City, and she was helping the little ones celebrate by shooting off firecrackers out on the back porch of their apartment house in Medford, Massachusetts. My mother Jordan was wearing a long white middy-blouse as she called it, and had taken this top off, turned it inside out, and laid it on the porch railing so as not to get it dirty. Here she is, standing in her underwear with a lit firecracker in her hands when my father-to-be comes up the stairs and around the corner of the porch. They both fumble with embarrassment, and my father, then twenty-six years old, says a short, "Hello," walking quickly past my mother and on into the Benton's apartment.

That following summer, after this first meeting, my father was raking hay by hand on the Sandler farm, The Walnut Shade Farm, in Lancaster, Massachusetts. He had stayed out in the sun too long and gotten a horrible case of sunstroke. His mother, my grandmother Jessie Sandler was a very heavy woman and found it difficult to climb the narrow back stairs to my father Franklin's bedroom to care for him. So she contacted my other grandmother, Mary Emma Moody, and asked if she could part with Jordan for the summer to come and be a pair of legs for "Aunt Jessie," as my family called my father's mother. (She was an aunt before she was my grandmother.) The women agreed, and my mother spent her summer on the farm taking care of my father and getting to know him in the only way he would ever have let a woman into his heart; teaching her about the plants and animals around the farm along with their habits and growth patterns. She spent every summer from then on until she was eighteen with the Sandlers.

*   *   *

I was seven years old and recovering from my bout with a massive infection due to my fall off of my bicycle. It was probably in August, for the days were steamy hot, and sunny. Uncle Charlie Benton was my Aunt Gracie's father-in-law, and he lived with them in their family home in Woburn, Massachusetts. He was also my father's uncle. My aunt was not graceful in her comments about what a bother of an older man he was to have around all the time. I'm not sure as to who was the bother!! Anyhow, the two sisters set up a system in which when Uncle Charlie was on vacation from his job at the Boston Globe, he spent his time with us. It was usually for two weeks, but some years it was longer, depending on how frazzled my aunt was at the time. To her credit, Aunt Gracie and my Uncle Philly were also trying to raise their six children.

Probably my mother gave Uncle Charlie the job of watching out for me, and she gave me the job of keeping Uncle Charlie busy. At my age and because of my long illness shut away from other children, my assortment of things to play was small.

Across from my house were the large ball fields that my father and his gang of landscaping boys had built. The front entrance to the fields consisted of open green spaces and large pine trees with a very high wrought-iron fence enclosing the fields.

I decided to walk Uncle Charlie over to the area in front of the big fence this particular day. "Uncle Charlie, would you like to have lunch with me today?"

"Yes, but just where is this event going to take place?" he responded.

"Right here, where you are standing, under the pine trees," I told him.

"That is very interesting because I don't see any walls, and I don't see a kitchen or table and chairs."

"Oh, those will come. I'll show you." And with that, I let go of his hand and started gathering up fistfuls of pine needles and placing them into rows connecting the tall pines. It wasn't long before Uncle Charlie was bending down, gathering pine needles and placing them beside my piles to mark off the rooms of our house.

After a bit, I pointed to a spot on the ground. "Uncle Charlie, you can sit here in the living room and read your newspaper while I get the lunch ready."

"Are you sure you want me to sit right here? I don't see a chair, and I don't see a newspaper?"

Being seven years old, I had no concept of the fact that I was asking this professional man to sit down on the dusty ground in his suit clothes. I cheerily responded, "Oh, there is a chair there, you just can't see it, and I have to go out and get your newspaper. I'll be back in a minute. They left your paper in the street."

Uncle Charlie did sit down, suit and all, and waited. I arrived back with two large milkweed leaves and handed them to him. "I suppose this is my newspaper. It looks a little damp."

"Well, I told you the boys threw yours onto the street."

"That explains why it is damp," he said and began flipping the milkweed leaves back and forth as if he were looking for some bit of news or a special article.

I left him sitting while I moved off into the section I saw as my kitchen and started to check the refrigerator and then the pantry to see what I needed to get at the grocery store to make for Uncle Charlie's lunch. I was about to go out our make-believe front door when Uncle Charlie called from where he was sitting, "Are you leaving me here? Where are you going?"

"Off to Jim Smith's grocery store to get what I need for your sandwich and cherry pie," I responded. (Back in those days, a grocery store was usually a one-person operation, and Jim Smith owned and ran our local food store.)

I darted out our front door and roamed the lawns outside our "house," looking for sandwich items and cherries for a pie. I came back with twigs for the sandwich meat, large maple leaves for the bread, and handfuls of chokecherries for the pie. I hurried around my kitchen and soon called to Uncle Charlie, "Lunch is ready. Please come here and sit at the table with me."

My great uncle, who must have been in his early seventies, got up and came over to where I was sitting. "Where is it you want me to be?" He asked.

"Right here next to this tree. You see, I've drawn the table in the dust."

Uncle Charlie came toward me, stopped this time, took off his suit jacket, folded it inside out, and then sat down on it. With his white shirt still on, he backed up to the pine tree.

"I think you will like the sandwich," I said to him.

He pretended to take a bite, chewed, and then said, "This is most unusual meat. Did it cost you a lot?"

"No, this meat was on sale, but if there are a few sticks in it, you can throw those away. I hope you kept room for a cherry pie."

"There is dessert? I was hoping that there would be from such a clever cook."

When it looked like Uncle Charlie was done eating his sandwich, I brought out two big oak leaves with chokecherries piled on each leaf. "Ta-da! Cherry pie!!" I said and placed the two oak leaves down on the dirt table. "Now, Uncle Charlie, you have to be careful when you eat the pie. Chokecherries are poisonous, so you can't chew them. And you need to make sure you spit the seeds out. They are the most poisonous."

"I will remember that," Uncle Charlie responded. As he approached the pie, he scooped up a handful of cherries, made like he was chewing, and then threw the berries behind him into the grass.

"Was the pie good?" I asked.

"Delicious, I must say," he responded.

"But you didn't eat the cherries," I said.

"You told me they would poison me, so I fed them to the birds. Was that alright?"

"Most all right! The birds will love them," I said, pleased with his solution.

When Uncle Charlie was done eating his pie, he stood up, reached down for his suit jacket still in the dust, and held out his hand to me. "That was a most delicious lunch. One of the best I've ever had. Now, we should be getting home."

I got up and took his hand. Somehow it felt warmer and softer to me. We started walking back across the road toward my home. Suddenly, Uncle Charlie stopped in the middle of the street. "We forgot to clean up our house. We will have to go back and straighten up." And with that, we walked back to our imaginary house, and he helped me put the walls back to where we had found them.

When we did get back to my mother, she said to Uncle Charlie, "Did you have a good time today?"

"Oh, yes, I did have a most marvelous lunch by a very creative cook, but I did as I was told and spit out the chokecherries, seeds and all, in the cherry pie."

## Looking Through My Therapist Eyes

# House Play

This story about Uncle Charlie comes almost directly out of Bitzy's many months in bed with rheumatic fever and nothing much to entertain her but her imagination. She says that she doesn't have much life experience from which to come up with activities to entertain her uncle. This belief may be the first glimpse into her believing that somehow she is limited because of her sickness. And nowhere does Bitzy recognize that she has developed a respect for and an ability to treat others as if they were her equal. This quality has allowed Bitzy in her adult life to make friends and help clients across a spectrum of differences and a vast range in ages.

Even though Bitzy doesn't understand that she probably ruined her great uncle's work suit, she treated him as if they were somehow on a level. And he responded by following her instructions— trusting her wisdom about chokecherries and her creativity. This exercise where both individuals get to know more about each other strengthens their respect for one another. It also gives Bitzy a chance to take what her Aunt Gracie gives as an opinion about what a bother this older man is, to find out that he needs loving interaction and with that he becomes more alive.

This experience with an older person helps to strengthen Bitzy's sense of herself because her uncle doesn't question what she is doing or why, he simply plays along and gives out a few well-placed compliments—something that all children need—all human beings need.

Bitzy learns firsthand that men don't generally open up and talk. Men need a vehicle, an activity through which they can begin to relate to another human being before they will share or unburden themselves of the wounds of life. Uncle Charlie doesn't open up to larger conversation, but he does soften under Bitzy's care. That softening is so important when living with a male. Their exterior lives are built on hardness and holding boundaries. At home, life should be more loving, encouraging, and softer.

# CHAPTER TWENTY
## The Military Choir Mistress

MY OLDER SISTER, PollyAnne, had told me that Mrs. James, one of the upper-grade teachers in my school, was a strict teacher. Mother said, "Well, maybe there is a reason for that. Mrs. James puts all her energy into her students because she doesn't have any children of her own."

Polly responded, "I wish she did have children!!" PollyAnne had already been through Mrs. James's class, so she knew firsthand that Mrs. James was strict. "If she catches you chewing gum, you'll have to write, 'I-will-not-chew-gum,' not for a day, but for at least a week, maybe even two weeks."

I knew I didn't have to worry. Mrs. James taught eighth grade in my grade school, and I was in fourth grade.

Not too long after this conversation, the notice came to my classroom, and the teacher read it out loud to the rest of us students. "Church choir practice is beginning, and all children in the fourth grade and up who are interested in singing are welcome to come. Practice will be in the Shakerton Untied Church starting this Thursday afternoon right after school, and you are to meet at the Parish House of the Shakerton Protestant Church."

When I got off the school bus, I ran into the house and found Mother in the kitchen. I waved my notice in front of my mother's face, of course too close for her to read it. "Can I go? Can I go?" I asked.

"I won't know until you let me hold the notice, and I can read it myself," she said as she took the paper from my flapping hand. When she finished her reading, she said, "That is a lovely idea. Do you want to go?"

I thought it was obvious that I wanted to go. "Can I, can I?" She hadn't said yes yet, and I knew that someone would have to pick me up after practice. No school bus this time!

Thursday afternoon came, and our after-school group of rag-tag, blue-collar children, walked and skipped from the schoolhouse down to the church. Our younger ones kept quiet. I thought to myself, *this is scary, going to the church without Mother or PollyAnne.*

September's late afternoon sunlight hardly lit the parish house with all of its dark wood paneling around the bottom of the hall and the windows set high above our heads made mostly of that colored, diamond-shaped wavy glass. We waited for the choir mistress. Then, whoosh, Mrs. James, affectionately known by the church members as Sally James, stood in the doorway. *I'm scared,* I thought. *All these big kids know what's going to happen! Why am I here? I have four more years before I have to face her.*

Mrs. James smiled and cooed, "Welcome back, children. Welcome, all you new young people. We are going to become the best choir in our town!"

I stared at her dark purple dress with the lace-edged, white-collar, and dipping neckline. I could see the dusky line separating her large breasts. Her dark brown salt and pepper hair rolled up off her temples, 1930's style, framing a pretty face. *She smells like flowers. I wonder what it would feel like to be hugged, disappearing into that large bosom.*

"The first thing that you young people need to learn is how to march," she said. "I want you to make a double line. Hold your hymnals up in both hands, and keep your eyes on me. Remember, one eye on the words, one eye on my face. I will show you, and then you can follow me."

She held her book open out in front, one hand cradling the back like a woman cradles a newborn's neck, and the other placed firmly on the book's face, keeping the correct page. As she marched, her chunky black heels marked a military beat in time to some drum inside her head.

Two older girls, who I'm sure had seen this demonstration many times before, whispered about her fanny sticking out behind to balance her big chest.

"Care to share?" Mrs. James asked, stopping in front of them. Her brown eyes penetrated so sharply that I felt them as I stood near with my head craned around to see what would happen. The girls ducked behind trembling hands, and one answered, "No. Mrs. James. We were just being silly."

"That is for later," she responded. "Now show me how well you can pro-*cess!*"

We marched up the hall, around in a snake pattern, across the width and back. Mrs. James had arranged the children with the smallest in front, putting me two people back. By the third round, my book drooped.

Mrs. James came and marched beside me. Tapping my book, she said, "Up! Hold it up!"

I looked up into her face and whined, "It's too heavy! I've never done this before."

Her eyes, soft like the eyes of Bambi in my storybooks at home, met mine. "I know," she said softly. "It is hard work for a little girl, but you will grow stronger. One day you will march with all the confidence in the world. I can see it in you."

* * *

I did continue with choir practice, singing each Sunday in the church sanctuary up in the choir loft at the back of the church. By now, I was a preteen with more arms and legs than anyone needs, and having put a sudden amount of weight on my skinny frame; I was having some trouble keeping everything running smoothly. Mrs. James was now my teacher. I'd reached eighth grade! PollyAnne had warned me about the poems we would have to memorize and recite every week. Still, she didn't say anything about the tedious job of copying each one off the blackboard each Monday morning into our notebooks. (Nor did she mention the wonderful stories that Mrs. James read to us last period every afternoon.)

I was having a problem with one of the words I was coping, and I raised my hand. The room was in a sort of study hall time, and Mrs. James motioned for me to come up to her desk, which was not at the front of the room but by the side in front of large windows that spanned our classroom. On the way around to Mrs. James's desk was a big old-fashioned radiator covered with brown metal and having panels at each end that swung open easily so that you could adjust the temperature. I start past the radiator between myself and Mrs. James. Somehow an elbow hits the end cap sending that large metal cover into the wall with the worst clanging complaint you have ever heard. I want to die, but keep going. When I get to Mrs. James, she looks up at me and says, "It won't be long now before all your edges smooth down, and you will find that you are a very successful person. I know. I have watched you grow for years."

Maybe it was a good thing that Mrs. James didn't have children because she gave me the strongest ego support of all of the people I have ever encounter up until I went into therapy as a young, middle-aged adult.

## Looking Through My Therapist Eyes

## Choir Mistress

This chapter is a fine example of how the older children in the family set the younger children up for fear and distrust by offering their opinions about some oncoming event. Then it becomes the younger child's issue to experience this new person or event and come to their conclusions about the Military Choir Mistress. Here I'm sharing my experience with this woman. Many children cannot assess a person themselves or fear the family repercussions if they see this person in a different light. So they take on the "family value" about that individual. This accepting family value as reality is clearly where our prejudices about people and their ethnicity, religious stance, or sexual orientation are established. It is a credit to this family that Bitzy was able to form her opinions and not be intimidated by the older siblings or parents. Thinking back, perhaps it was handy that the older children were heavily involved in their own almost-adult lives.

I knew from other conversations in the family that both Mother and my sister greatly respected this woman, so it was confusing for me first entering each situation with fear, only to find that Sally James treated me with a great deal of respect and understanding.

Looking back, Mrs. James gave me the most support for my young developing ego of any of the teachers and religious instructors that I came in contact with during my early developmental years. My mother tried, but she was also a very precise person, and as you have read, I often did not meet the mark for her. Once a child is wounded repeatedly, even to instruct, they stop believing the positive comments when they do come. The famous television personality, Dr. Phil, has said that it takes one thousand "Ata girls" to erase one, "You stupid child" or worse chastisement.

My relationship with Mrs. James developed over the years, and I continued to contact her, visiting with her in her home until the week that she died. When I was home on vacation from college, I would stop into her house and catch her up on where I was in my life. She always was delighted that I came, even to that last time, in which she struggled to recognize me. What she gave to me I will treasure for all of my life. I'm so glad that Sally James didn't have children because it gave me a place in her heart, and I knew that. For a child who grew up feeling that I was somehow damaged or a bit stupid, Mrs. James was my counterbalance.

# CHAPTER TWENTY ONE

# How to Get a Piano

ASTER CAME AS a bright and sunny day the year after I turned nine years old. I was waiting for my Easter basket to appear, but I couldn't see it anywhere in my bedroom. Usually, it was right beside my bed when I woke up. I climbed out of bed and went down to the kitchen, where I could hear some giggling going on.

"Where is my Easter basket?" I asked my mother.

She smiled and said, "Your Dad and I thought we would do something different for you this year. It is time that you learn how to take care of someone besides yourself."

"Okay," I responded. "So, do I get a basket this year?"

"Go out on the back porch. There is a box out there for you," my mother said. "Wait, I'll come with you. You may need some help."

By now, my father had joined us on the back porch. He pulled a brown cardboard box with round holes punched in the top out from under the iron cot. And then I heard it. There was lots of chirping coming from the box. "Open it." My father commanded.

As I lifted the top off the box, two fluffy, chirping, yellow chicks hopped about, wanting to get out of the box onto the cement of the porch floor. What a noise they made!

My mother, always the teacher, said, "Now, you are going to have to figure out how to take care of these baby chickens. You will need to learn what they eat, how to clean their house, maybe even what kind of a house they need."

I didn't care about all that stuff; I just wanted to hold these fluffy squeaking babies. I quickly learned that holding was a whole other matter. They were in my hands and on the floor and scuttling back under the cot on the porch.

At that point, my Dad said, "Maybe the best place to learn how to take care of chickens is from Mrs. Henry across the street. They raise chickens."

My mother chimed in with, "I'll give Mrs. Henry a telephone call and see if we can come over today or tomorrow so she can show you how you take care of your new chicks.

Across the street from our house was the big white duplex with the Gavin family on the left side and the Simpsons on the right. Next to the Gavin's was a little house with an older couple living there, and these people were Mr. and Mrs. Henry. They had a large vegetable garden, and they kept chickens out behind the garden.

I don't remember what we fed the chickens the first day or two, maybe grain that the people at the feed store had given my parents. But by Tuesday, my mother had me by the hand, and we were walking up to the Henry's back door, between the back of the house and the garage. My mother introduced me to Mrs. Henry. I'm not sure why she did this because I'm sure Mrs. Henry already knew who I was, but I can remember feeling very nervous about meeting her.

Mrs. Henry said, "I understand you have two new chickens to take care of, and your mother says you need a little training in how to manage these birds."

I nodded my head, still not sure what I was supposed to be saying at this point.

Mrs. Henry motioned for me to follow her, and we went out to their chicken yard. My mother seemed to fade out at this point.

Back home, I told Mother as much as I could remember, which probably wasn't that much, about how to care for my new birds. Unfortunately, I quickly discovered that chickens weren't cuddling animals and cuddling was the part of this adventure that I wanted the most. So as with many efforts like this, my mother did much of the care of these two birds. She did insist that I do the feeding and the water bowl but I don't remember cleaning up after them, and my father must have fixed a yard for them.

What did come out of this effort on the part of my parents was I made a new friend. Mrs. Henry invited me to come any time I wanted to her house, and she always had milk and cookies for me. She also was a quiet person who didn't talk a lot but encouraged me to talk to her, and she listened in and around doing her household chores. I came to love Mrs. Henry and spent a lot of time at her house. As time moved along, I discovered that she had a piano, and I loved music. I had already joined the children's choir in my church, and because of a very strong music program in my school, I had learned to read music in order to sing.

I soon learned that music for singing and music you played on the piano was a little different. I had to play the piano from memory. I learned to pick out Christmas carols by ear, and I played them with one or two fingers. I loved the Christmas hymn, 'Good King Wenceslas,' and would play it over and over as I was able to pick out more and more of the tune. I played 'Good King Wenceslas' even in the summer. Looking back, I can't imagine how this kind grandmotherly woman put up with the noise of my playing. She never scolded or told me to go home. Early on, she told me that I had to wash my hands before playing and close the piano cover when I was done. I believe I was pretty good with her wishes.

What grew out of this whole friendship was a growing desire to have my own piano and to learn to play it from reading the music. I even asked Mrs. Henry, "Can I have your piano? Your daughters are all grown up, and I don't see them around here anymore, so can I have your piano? You don't seem to need it."

In her patient way, she answered me, "I can't give my piano to you because it belongs to my daughter, and she would be heartbroken if I gave it away. Sometimes she does come home and would miss it. You do understand?"

I understood, but I still wanted to have hers.

Word came the following fall that the Henry's were moving to be closer to that daughter. Mr. Henry was retiring from the Industrial

School where he worked with my father, and our houses were part of the pay for their job, so if he retired, that meant that the Henrys would need to find another place to live.

I was sad that Mrs. Henry was leaving, and I understood that she was taking her piano with her.

After the fact, my mother told me that there had been a telephone call from Mrs. Henry explaining that there was a piano left in the house when they moved into their new home. And the deal was if my father could figure out how to get it to our house, I could have the piano at no cost to my parents.

All I knew at the time was it was late in the afternoon, and I was just home from school. I hear a lot of noise and confusion in our front yard, and then the front door swings open. My father is standing there with a few of the boys from his landscaping gang and an open truck behind him. Mother comes out of the kitchen and hurries through the dining room to where my father is standing. "Beth, where do you want us to put this piano?"

"The only place we have room for it is here in the front hall," my mother responded. "Put it down closer to the kitchen. Bitzy will still have room, I think, to play it there."

That Shaker house had a small vestibule as you came in the front door and started down the hallway to the back of the house, and then another small vestibule at the end of the hall, allowing for a door from the living room, the porch, the dining room, and from the kitchen to all merge into this area. My piano was going to sit just as the long hall became part of this back vestibule.

I could hardly contain myself; in fact, I did a bit of dancing around as the gang of young men struggled to get the piano off the truck, up onto the front porch, over the lip of the front door, and down the hall to where it would sit for ten years. As they pushed and groaned, I sang, "I'm getting my piano! I'm getting my piano! I'm getting my piano!" Where it had come from was of no concern to me at the time.

It didn't take long for me to figure out that I needed piano lessons, now that I had the piano. I went to my mother. "I need piano lessons, and I know you and Dad don't have any money for that. But I do want them just the same."

My mother smiled and responded, "I knew this would be the next problem. I may have a solution for us. But I need a promise from you before I do anything."

"What? What do you mean?"

"Well, over the years, I've seen you want a lot of things, and then when you get them, you lose interest quickly, and you forget that you wanted that thing or event. I need you to promise that if I can set up lessons for you that you will practice the piano faithfully for a long period of time."

"I promise! I promise!

"Promise what?" my mother asked.

"That I will stick with the piano lessons and practice faithfully. I promise."

A few days later, when I got home from school, my mother found me in the pantry making my sandwich. "I have made arrangements with Mrs. Perry for her to give you piano lessons for free. Do you know who she is and where she lives?"

"Oh, yes, I know who she is. She has red hair, and she's often at the Christmas Parties. She lives up high on the hill in the duplex on the other side from the Patterson's, right in front of Daddy's community garden."

"You are correct, and she does know about our deal of you working hard at your piano lessons. That is the only reason she is willing to give them to you for no money. Now, she will see you next Monday. I'll drive you that day, but after that, you will have to walk all the way from here to her house. Can you manage that?

"Of course, I'll do anything to get my lessons."

My mother smiled. "Well, we will see about that."

## Looking Through My Therapist Eyes

# Piano

It seems strange to start introducing a new character with an Easter basket, but that is the way I got to know Mrs. Henry. Yes, I was aware of the Henrys as I was allowed to play all around the neighborhood, but I didn't actually "know" Mrs. Henry until after the chickens.

Like so many other parents, my parents were trying to teach me a new lesson and give me some fun at the same time. Well, I soon discovered that "chicks," as they grow, become chickens and have little or no interest in being confined and cuddled. It would help if you remembered that I lacked a whole half-year of socialization with humans, other than my family members. Interest in taking care of something, when I had just been in a sense smothered with "being taken care of," left me selfish and wanting everything to come to me. Chickens had no concerns about those kinds of needs, and I soon lost interest in caring for them.

I can tell you here that the chickens got well taken care of because after Mrs. Henry taught me how to handle the chickens, my parents wound up having to ask her if she would mind adding my two to her coop. She said they were of a different breed from her birds, but she felt they should get along together. And so I got freed from those horrible pecking, scratching, useless pets.

Now that I was comfortable with Mrs. Henry, she took the place of my grandmother, who lived so far away. I only got to see Grammy on holidays. Mrs. Henry was very different from my grandmother because she was relaxed about letting a child experiment and learn independently. How she survived my incessant picking out a well-known tune on her piano, I will never be able to fathom except that she was uncommonly patient.

Mrs. Henry's gift of the old piano from the new house set me onto a path that has been a cornerstone of my life. Music has always been my "go-to" place when the emotional pain or frustration about something has been more that I could handle. I still have a piano and will take it to my one-bedroom apartment because other things can be set aside but not my piano.

I can tell you here where I'm not constrained by the story's time frame, that it was very painful for me when it became appropriate to move my mother out of the house my father and mother built when I was seventeen. It became necessary to get rid of my old piano, which had sat in that basement for nearly fifty years, patiently waiting for me to come and collect it. And it was my now deceased husband, Sy, who said, "The only way we can get it out is to destroy it." My heart cracked a bit as he waited for my answer. "It is time," I said. "She has lost her ability to hold a pitch and she is full of dust and mildew. There is no other way." But I didn't stay in the basement as he broke that piano into manageable pieces. He was the only person I could allow to do that job because he understood how much it meant to me.

And so it is with life that we have to move on to whatever is our next phase, hoping there are not too many old scars, dust, and mildew.

# CHAPTER TWENTY TWO
## Increase in Family

I WAS NINE YEARS old, and two major events happened that year. One was the official ending of my fight with rheumatic fever, and the second was that my mother had a baby!

On our last visit into the city, Dr. Clark said, "You know I don't feel the need to conduct your six-month check-ups any longer, and I'm recommending a pair of young doctors in your area finish the job."

Sometime in the spring, we went to a clinic a couple of towns away, actually in the city of Fitzburg, Massachusetts. Everything about the clinic seemed wide open, not like Dr. Clark's warm, sunny office.

This clinic was more like a cafeteria—one large space, dimly lit, with several examining tables set up. There were privacy curtains, but no one had pulled them around our area. The nurse indicated I should sit upon the metal examining table, take off my blouse, and wait for the doctor. When the doctor got to us, he spoke briefly to my mother. Then, he took ahold of my undershirt and tugged it off over my head without even saying hello to me. He started to listen to my heart with his stethoscope, but his partner called to him, and they disappeared across the clinic behind a curtain.

I sat shivering, my chest uncovered for everyone to see. Efforts to hide myself with my arms drew Mother's attention. "What's wrong, Honey?" she asked. "Are you cold?" And then, sensing the real problem, she reached for my jacket on the foot of the table and covered my shoulders, drawing the jacket over my newly developing breasts.

We waited in silence. When the doctor returned, he looked at the jacket and asked, "Is it cold in here? I told them to turn up the heat."

My mother smiled, nodded, and said, "I think it's more a case of it being too exposed for a young woman just beginning to develop. This clinic is very public!"

The doctor appeared perplexed but went on with his examination. After another chest X-ray, he announced that I was completely cured. He found only a slight murmur in the heart, not an unusual outcome with rheumatic fever, and felt that I would never have to return to his clinic.

That was great news because I never intended to go back there, where they treated you like a piece of furniture! I wasn't a child anymore, and I didn't like the way the doctors acted. So, this monumental period in my life passed without ceremony into that shadowy place of memory.

*   *   *

The other event was not so quiet. My sister, PollyAnne, was due home from college for a weekend visit. Stepping inside the front door, she set down both suitcases, and uninhibited by two years of college, said, "Will you look at that! Two-ton Annie!"

I was behind my mother as we hustled down the hall to greet my sister, so I didn't hear Polly's greeting. But I sensed that my mother's spirit momentarily winced and sagged. Both women laughed, hugged, and danced around the front hall in re-connective joy.

Later, when PollyAnne had returned to college, Mother and I were doing dishes in the kitchen. "You know," my mother said, "I think your sister may be right. I've gained a lot of weight these last months, but I thought it was because I missed her. What do you think?" She didn't wait for my opinion. "I think I'd best go see Dr. Archer, in case there might be something wrong."

Upon returning from the doctor's, Mother was quiet. Since Mother had returned to her doctor in Medford, Massachusetts, for the appointment, we were also visiting my grandmother. I noticed my mother's silence, but her health was not a great concern to me as a nine-year-old. It wasn't until the next morning when I was waking, that she touched my arm as we lay together in Grammy's guestroom bed. "I'm going to have a baby, Bitzy."

Not awake yet, I turned toward her and mumbled, "Huh?"

"We're going to have a new baby in the family. That's why PollyAnne said I was getting fat."

Her words didn't register, except some vague recognition of her lack of excitement about the whole affair.

"What do you mean we're going to have a baby?" I asked.

"You remember when PollyAnne called me fat . . .

"No, I didn't hear her say that," I said, cutting my mother short.

"You remember when she came home . . ." my mother's voice trailed.

By now, my brain was catching up. "Wow! We're going to have a baby! I'll have a little sister or brother to boss around?"

"Well, you know it's a long, long time before this baby will be someone with whom you can play. It takes time for them to grow into children."

My mother's reserve about an event that seemed so wonderful in my eyes began to trouble me. "What's wrong, Mom?" I asked.

"Nothing is wrong," she responded. "It's that your Daddy is getting older. He's fourteen years my senior, and I am not getting any younger. This baby is going to be twenty years younger than PollyAnne and Owen. They could be its parents! I do hope your Dad and me are strong enough and have the energy to give this child all the love and attention it will need."

Not understanding how aging would even factor into such a marvelous event, I offered my best suggestion. "I'm getting a lot older now, so I can help you lots with the new baby."

My mother rolled toward me, reaching out to pat my cheek. "You are such a dear. Yes, I know you will want to help me, but babies are a lot more hard work than you realize!"

Somehow my mother's mood had shifted, and things felt as if they were going to be brighter, maybe even joyful!

Copeland was due just after Thanksgiving, but he didn't arrive. By Christmas, he hadn't come. Dr. Blackmore told my mother at her check-up that he wasn't happy because this meant he would be drinking water at his New Year's Eve celebration! She tells the story, now, with some glee, but at the time, I expect she didn't find it comforting.

Copeland managed to ruin the doctor's party; in fact, he was the first baby born in the new year for our community. The local newspaper did a feature article, with a picture on the front page of Mother and my baby brother.

On the evening of Copeland's birth, Dad returning from the hospital, burst through the back door into our kitchen. "It's a boy!" he yelled to my grandmother. "It's another boy!" This type of outburst was not like my father, who measured his words, picking ones that would tell the least and afford him the most emotional protection. Not so, this evening! Dad was as thrilled about his new baby as my mother had been reserved.

Later, I asked Grammy why Daddy seemed so happy with the baby being a boy.

"Oh, Honey, it's nothing for you to trouble your head over. You must remember that your father grew up on a farm. Running a big herd of milk cows required a lot of strong arms and backs. Most farmers were delighted to have another son, who would grow up to help them take care of the family business."

My grandmother spun around to look at me. "You do understand, don't you?"

I nodded my head. It did make some sense, but since Daddy didn't have a farm to run anymore, it seemed to me that he didn't need to be so happy about a baby boy.

* * *

My parents decided to call my little brother Copeland, after a favorite great-aunt on my father's side, Copeland being the family name. My mother felt it was only fair since they had named my older brother after her father. I thought it was a long name to put on anything that pink and tiny.

He didn't stay pink and small for long. My mother's comment about babies taking a long time to grow up didn't seem true. In no time, he was walking and not walking, depending upon what was in his way.

And then, he was babbling and acting as if we all knew about which he was talking.

Even being eighteen years older, Owen had insisted that when the baby was old enough to leave my parent's room, Copeland would come and share Owen's bedroom. I thought this was strange because Owen was off at college most of the time, but Mother bought them matching twin beds. The mirror in Owen's room with cheeky-looking girl decals at the top soon gained Winnie-the-Pooh decals at the bottom.

On this particular day, Owen was home from college. He had collapsed onto the back porch stairs after chasing the baby around the yard. When he came inside, Owen told us that while he was resting and Copeland was still toddling about, they both heard a loud thwack . . . thwack . . . thwack noise overhead. Looking up and not thinking the toddler would understand, Owen asked, "What's that, Baby Brother?"

"Copper, Copper," Copeland said, turning in a circle, backward, while looking up into the sky.

"I didn't think he'd know what a helicopter was," Owen said. "He's such a little guy. But there must be a lot of helicopters flying overhead, with Fort Devens airport on the other side of town."

Owen was right. None of us recognized that as a baby in a grown-up family, Coppy caught on to many things we didn't even know about which we'd talked. And, of course, his name stuck to him like a freshly licked lollipop. He was no longer the baby—he was Coppy!

*   *   *

Coppy must have been about eighteen months old, and both my sister, PollyAnne and brother, Owen, were home for a few days from college. We were all sitting in the living room with its maroon wall-to-wall carpet of simulated oak leaves. The conversation was vigorous when Coppy decided that he wanted to be part of the action, and he started to walk across the carpet. Now walk at eighteen months means a good bit of wobble for some children, but he was pretty steady. He was laughing, and so were we, when he suddenly decided to up the show and he picked both feet up at once. Coppy landed flat on his back, but that didn't stop him, and we were now laughing hilariously at his antics. He got up, turned around, and started back the way he had come, but now he was so excited that he couldn't remember which foot went before the other, and he again wound up picking both feet up at once and landing on his back. Still, he didn't seem bothered by our laughter, but I think about then my mother moved in and scooped him up, lest he hurt himself with his behavior. We younger children, Coppy and I, often felt that we weren't quite part of the family and would do almost anything to be full-fledged members.

*   *   *

It must have been a year or two before Coppy's birth when the whole family was sitting at the cobalt blue, wooden kitchen table. (At a much younger age, PollyAnne and Owen had painted the table and the 1950's wooden kitchen chairs in their choice of color as a gift to my mother.) We each had our places. Dad was at the head of the table, and Owen sat to his left. I sat next to Owen to his left, tucked in beside the refrigerator. Mother sat to my left at the other end of the table from my Dad. PollyAnne sat alone on the opposite side of the table from Owen and me. When Coppy did join us, he was in his carriage beside PollyAnne. The seating arrangement is important to this story. At that point in this event, I was still the "baby," and so I got the only glass of milk at the table. The older people got water.

The conversation is vigorous this evening, and I'm silent, listening. At some point, when there is a lull, I decide to make a summation of what I'd heard or something of that sort. While I am talking, Owen reaches over, takes my milk and drinks most of it, and then places his water glass where my milk had been. When I am done talking, I reach for my milk, and the table explodes in laughter—they have all been waiting for this moment, not paying any attention to what I was saying. I ask in my most enraged voice, "Who drank my milk?!!" There is a lot more laughter. Now I'm very angry at my brother because I've caught on to the water glass and its owner. I accuse him, and there is more laughter. I walked away from this scene knowing that what I had to say was unimportant, and I felt like I was being told that I was stupid. Why my mother didn't intervene, I do not know, but she didn't. And unlike my little brother, who probably was too young to process his event, I shut down my ability to speak up in groups of people because of the intense pain I experienced from this incident.

*   *   *

Coppy's birth into our family was a significant event for me, then, and still is, for it marked the end of feeling isolated and alone in this family with two older siblings, nearly grown. The nine-year age difference between my younger brother and me didn't seem to affect the fact that I considered he belonged to *my* family, the second family in our home.

# Looking Through My Therapist Eyes

## Family Increase

Interestingly, Bitzy tags the ending of her illness with the birth of her baby brother. The fact that the baby is a boy calls up an issue that is vague throughout her story, but it greatly impacts Bitzy's developing sense of self, and her place in the family and society. There is an overvaluation of the male in this household. The message is glossed over by Grandmother's explanation of why Bitzy's father is so excited when the fourth child is a son. It is also a fact that might not be immediately apparent since Bitzy's father takes a retiring role in his family; that emotional absence leads Mother to verbalize her interpretations of her husband's behaviors and thoughts—a setup for misrepresentation.

This method of family communication creates a dance between the histories of Bitzy's parents. Her mother, Jordan, who did not know her father because of his early death, projects her beliefs about what a father should be onto her husband. Franklin, Bitzy's father, the second living son in his family of origin, felt so overlooked by an alcoholic father and a bitter mother that he finds it safer to let his wife do the talking and go unrecognized. Both these patterns of absence put an overvaluation on the missing energy—that of the male.

Then to add to this family's concept of the valuation of men and women in a family, Mary Emma Gould Moody, Bitzy's maternal grandmother, was left at the age of twelve to remain on the family farm to help her father, Thomas Jordan Gould raise the next two children. At the same time, his wife, Hannah Elizabeth Gould sued her husband for a divorce–something unheard of in that generation! Once free of the household, Hannah set about becoming the communities' visiting nurse. To Hannah's credit, she took the three youngest children with her but would often take them into sick-house situations. My instincts tell me that it left my grandmother with some very bitter thoughts about her mother even though it is recorded in the family stories that her father was a difficult man.

These felt impulses were not conscious for Bitzy, but they had their impact. We see some sibling rivalry in her wonderment at why Daddy needed a boy when he didn't have a farm, but she feels more than the infringement of a new child; she feels the greater valuation the family places on the male. How can she measure up? She already feels not quite "right" and unheard in the daily family routines.

When we place this recognition of male overvaluation on top of feeling forgotten during her fight with rheumatic fever, we have the basis for a destructive behavior pattern in our girl, which will emerge later. This pattern plays out with her perception that she is not of the "right sex," and therefore needs to possess a man of her own, at any cost.

We end this chapter with an explanation for why Bitzy feels that Coppy is her family. The pain Bitzy felt when her family made fun of her contribution to the conversation marks a turning point in her trust of her older siblings. The event was meant as whole-hearted family fun–the ribbing that goes on in families–but because of her illness, Bitzy already felt that she was inferior and an outsider in the family. As she states, she doesn't know why her mother didn't rescue her in the table situation as she had rescued Coppy.

# CHAPTER TWENTY THREE

## Setting the Dream

WHEN I TURNED ten years old in the spring of that year, a letter came to my mother. It was from her oldest brother, Ralph Moody, who lived out on the west coast. "Just wanted to let you know my first book has been accepted for publication by a New York publisher. I'm coming east to wrap up some of the details on the contract. Would you people be open to a visit? It's been an awful lot of years since I've seen you, Little Sis!" There was no question about it. The family would make time for a visit. Mother went into a flurry of preparation.

*Why is Mother being so silly*, I thought. *She not only has cleaned the whole house, but she's also now up on a chair washing the windows.* "Mom, why is Uncle Ralph so important?" It seemed like a reasonable question.

"Important? Bitzy, he was my big brother when I was growing up! You know my father died just before I was born, so Ralph was the headman in our household. He's a lot older than I. Ralph was already off to work when I can remember. He didn't get to finish school but went to work to bring in income for the family. Your grandmother washed clothes for the families around Bunker City so she could feed all six of us. Ralph was ashamed his mother took in other peoples' dirty laundry, so instead of helping, as the others did, he got a job in Bunker City. The part I remember best was him bringing home penny-candy for me when he got his paycheck."

Mother's attention drifted, caught in memories of a time I couldn't even imagine. Penny-candy didn't seem like such a big deal! This man must be somebody pretty special, though, if Mother was washing the windows!

*   *   *

I stood on the school playground. The sun, striking hard-packed dirt in the yard, reflected brightly, creating an early June glow around my feet. It was morning recess time for the fourth graders. Excitement ran all through me. I'd brought my note to the teacher that morning. Mother had written to Miss Rich asking that I be excused from classes when my uncle arrived. They would be picking me up in his car. He was coming from California where he lived, to do business in New York, and Mother wanted me to meet him. Miss Rich nodded, saying it would be fine.

Unaware of the yelling and scuffling of my classmates, I sat on the swing set intently watching the road which ran along the side of the playground. *Was that his car?* It didn't look familiar. The car rolled to a lazy stop. I stood up, eying the car for a moment. *Should I go closer?* Finally, reassured that the person on the passenger side was my mother, I ran toward the car with the same excited feeling I'd had on Christmas morning. Stopping abruptly beside the driver's door, I surveyed the man sitting behind the wheel. He was of medium height with a full head of gray hair slicked straight back, sun-drenched skin, and sparkling blue eyes squinted from early years in the out-of-doors. He flashed a friendly grin and reached his arm out the window, calling, "Come on Girly. Come give your old uncle a big hug."

With reservation, I stared at this man about whom my mother was so excited. He looked different than I'd imagined. I thought he'd be old-looking and fat, but he was still thin and handsome. He fairly sparkled all over, and he seemed so sure of himself, not like Mother's other two brothers who were quiet with a New England reserve. My natural shyness and feminine instincts said *caution*—he was still a stranger. Mother motioned it was all right to approach the car. Noting my protective concern, Uncle Ralph drew back his arm and waited for me to make the next move. The pressure off, I stepped forward, he opened the car door, and I threw my arms around him in a big bear hug. From somewhere above my head, I heard my uncle say, "I like a wise woman like that!"

Much of Uncle Ralph's visit was a blur. It all happened so fast. I was only ten and too young to understand his talk about publishers. The conversation rambled around Ralph's restaurant business and his family on the West Coast. I did tune-in when he said, "I'd rather Mother not see any of the galley's of this book until it's in print. She won't like parts of it. No need to have her finger in the pie before it's done."

Mother chuckled. "Ralph, we know better. It's a tricky piece of work; you write about our father, and her husband. She's bound to have a different slant on the story." I knew they were right. Grandmother would want a say in anything that talked about her family to the public.

During most of my uncle's visit, I sat on the old blue couch, snuggled just under Uncle Ralph's arm or on the floor by his feet. Somehow, intuitively, little girl and older man developed a fascination with one another without much conversation between us. The visit lasted only three days; then, this marvelously exciting man disappeared back into the world from which he had come.

Life returned to its usual routine. I had almost forgotten my uncle's visit. When I was coming in from playing one summer afternoon, Mother called from the kitchen. "Bitzy, there's a letter for you on the table."

Letters didn't usually come for me. At ten, I wasn't much of a correspondent. I picked up the business-sized manila envelope, crisp and weighty with Uncle Ralph's home address pressed neatly onto the upper left corner. Eagerly I tore into the envelope. Delighted with this special attention, I sat down on the floor to puzzle out the message. I understood the thank you part for a splendid visit, but the rest of it needed Mother's help. Uncle Ralph's bold handwriting was hard to read. That night I put the letter on the floor just under the edge of my bed, where it rested for the entire summer.

Two weeks later, I was standing in the kitchen doorway with a quizzical look on my face. "What are you doing, Honey?" Mother asked her hands in the sink full of dishes. "You look like you're struggling with a big problem."

"I want to send Uncle Ralph a poem I just wrote in my head, but if I don't hurry and write it down, I'll forget it."

Mother dried her hands and went to the desk in the dining room, returning with pieces of white typing paper and a pencil. "Here. If you have trouble with any of the big words, call me. He'll be so pleased to hear from you." I dropped to the kitchen floor, paper and pencil in hand. Nothing broke my concentration as I wrote. Mother returned to the dishes.

Later, Mother went over the poetic masterpiece, helping me with the spelling. It was about the beautiful old oak tree in the backyard and how much I loved it. The rest of the letter told Uncle Ralph how I'd been frightened when I first met him and then how much I'd grown to like him. I also told him I wanted to be a writer just like him when I grew up. We sealed up the letter and then mailed it out.

Many weeks passed before I heard from Uncle Ralph. He'd been busy with his work, something about business contracts, but he wanted me to know how much he'd liked the poem. "Bitzy, that was truly a lovely poem. I could see the old oak tree—just about reach right out and touch it. There's no question. You're going to be a writer. Someday you may even beat me out!"

"That is nice." But Mother had a cautionary look about her smile, a cue to me to hold down my glee. "It was a lovely poem, Honey. I'm glad he liked it."

*   *   *

There were letters back and forth between Uncle Ralph and me over the next two years. In the late spring, a letter came. "I'm planning another trip to the East Coast. My first book, *Little Britches,* is at the top of the New York bestseller list, and I have to come east to negotiate with the publishers on the second book. Bitzy, would you and your family be open to another visit?"

The great day arrived. I had gotten little sleep the night before, planning all the things I'd tell my uncle when he got here. As with all great family gatherings, I became only a small force in the movement of events, again spending my time snuggled close to my uncle listening to his animated conversation. Finally, a break came. Looking at me, Uncle Ralph said in his theatrical style, "It's time for me and this gal here to go for a trip to get us an ice cream sundae. Bitzy, can you show me where to go?" *Could I?! The way things were going, I thought we'd never get a chance to talk alone. Now, he was taking me out on a mini-date by myself!*

We made the short trip to the little ice cream bar in the center of town without any conversation. I felt tongue-tied. Ralph got out, ran around the car, and opened the door for me. I was in my glory. *Would the world see what a lovely, healthy young lady I was becoming?*

We went inside to find a booth and order up the treats. I had never had a sundae before, but I wasn't about to say so. Sitting in the unfamiliar environment of the chrome and plastic, early 1950's diner, I fussed with the menu.

Uncle Ralph broke the awkward silence. "How about a nice big butterscotch sundae?"

That sounded like a good way out. I nodded. "That will be fine."

The sundaes arrived, his hot fudge and mine butterscotch. We both dug in with child-like abandon. Uncle Ralph stopped eating for a moment. "You know, I'm not yet sure what I want this second book to cover. I feel silly about it. It seems like I should have that all decided before I meet with the publishers."

I was trying to listen, but I'd developed this long string of butterscotch sauce suspended between my spoon and my dish. I rolled the string around the spoon and pulled. It just stretched. The more I rolled, the more it stretched! I eyed the dilemma with dismay. *How am I going to get this gooey mess into my mouth? Maybe he won't notice.*

Uncle Ralph caught sight of my predicament. He stopped talking. Laughingly, he took his spoon and the extra spoon the waitress had left on the table and cut through the butterscotch strand in the center, relieving its hold on the dish. I stuffed the sticky mass into my mouth. It tasted so good—so sweet! Laying the spoons on the tabletop, Uncle Ralph went on, "I think the next book needs to pick up the family story after my father died. I plan to take them back East from Denver and show what our lives were like in Bunker City without a father's support."

I reached for another mouthful—and the whole silly scene repeated itself! My face flushed. *I feel so stupid* I moaned inside. *I can't even eat a sundae without making a fool of myself. This scene isn't the way I want him to remember me. What do I do?*

Once again, Uncle Ralph picked up the spoons and rescued me. When it happened the third time, he just chuckled. "Well, it looks like I'm just gonna have to sit here and help you eat that dern thing cause it doesn't appear like it's gonna let you eat it by yourself!"

Somehow the laughter in his voice reassured me that he thought the situation, not me, to be funny. I finally gave up being embarrassed and laughing together; he patiently sat, cutting each bite while I munched happily.

After the sundaes, we continued to sit and talk. Uncle Ralph finished his discussion on the contents of his next book and then asked me about school. What was of interest to me? He listened quietly to my sadness at the fact that my first school friend, Bobby Hall, had moved away that year. He patted my free hand.

"I know it hurts right now, but you're such a pretty girl, trust me, there will be other Bobbies come into your life." Somehow, it felt better when he said it than when Mother had said it. Finally, Ralph talked about his oldest son, Charlie, and his new job out in California. I could hear the pride in his voice. I wondered if my dad would feel that way about me someday.

Riding back home in the car, we were silent, but this was different. It was no longer strained. I had had a chance to talk and be heard. As the third child in a nearly all grown-up family, I often felt no one cared much what I thought. Somehow, Uncle Ralph had picked up on this. He treated me as an equal, asking my opinions and encouraging my interests.

The next years saw many letters move back and forth across the United States between myself and my Uncle Ralph. I heard about the new books as bits and pieces came into his mind, *Man of the Family,*

*The Fields of Home*, and later, *Mary Emma and Company*. He asked questions about my friends, my progress on the piano, school work, and my growing interest in boys. *Someday*, I vowed, *I'm going to write the way he does.*

## Looking Through My Therapist Eyes

# Dream

Bitzy hasn't talked much about her father before in her story. For most young women, the father is a very important person in a women's development and her progression out of the home into the world at large. In our present-day psychological understanding, the mother's role in child-rearing is to provide a safe nest where the child can learn about themselves–their strengths, their weaknesses–become comfortable in their own skin, essentially ego development. Later the father begins to take over, showing the child how to survive in the world outside the home.

As Bitzy tells her story, it seems that she pulls her Uncle Ralph in somewhat to play the role that her father might have assumed if he was not struggling with his emotional damage.

Our father in this story, Franklin Sandler, has appeared mostly in the background. Bitzy tells us that he is her great Oak tree–she does this in the poem that she sent to her Uncle Ralph about the great oak tree in her backyard. He is tall and carrying his green vitality well above the heads of his loved ones! I'm not sure she meant to tell all that in her analogy. And of course, you need his history, at this point, because there are reasons for his way of being in this family.

Bitzy's father, Franklin, was the fourth child in his family of origin. The first son, Robbie, died at the age of five from rheumatic fever, a fact that haunted her parents all through Bitzy's struggle with her own bout of this illness.

The older sister, Bitzy's Aunt Bertha, played the role of protector and solace-giver for Franklin, who felt as the younger son that he was not favored by his mother, like Carver, the brown-haired, brown-eyed oldest son. Bitzy's mother tells of when Franklin had gotten up early in the morning, returning later, with a big basket of cowslips, a spring delicacy for farm families. He put the basket on the floor beside where his mother sat. She looked up and commented, "Oh, that is nice, dear."

As Bitzy's father passed back through the kitchen, he confided to Bitzy's mother, "If that had been my brother, she would have jumped up and hugged him!"

Franklin held onto this wounding all of his life, which tells us that he was unusually sensitive, not unlike Bitzy, herself. When the mother is not available to her child, she teaches him that it is unsafe to share one's emotions; they won't be recognized, mirrored, or returned. We have our first viewing of one of many points in this man's emotional shutdown.

Franklin's father, Franklin Lily Sandler, had a large farm to run, a big herd of dairy cows to tend, much open farmland, and a dairy that provided milk for the town where Bitzy grew up. It had the potential for being a very successful business, except that Franklin's father was an alcoholic. This addiction meant that the two boys were pressed into more and more responsibility for running and maintaining the farm as soon as they were old enough. They became adults before they were ever children!

Then there were the hard times when the money had been gathered together to pay taxes and their father, as head-of-household, took it to town via the bar. When he returned, the boys knew that it was they who would scramble to make up this crucial loss.

All these events create an environment in which a growing child, even if they have had a childhood, would not trust adults or, for that matter—any other people. When faced with this dilemma, the child learns to close down the bruised emotional side, causing it to be buried internally.

When this young person is given the opportunity outside the home to communicate and interact, they often retreat into themselves where they feel safest. This retreat was where Bitzy's father spent much of his emotional time, locked away inside, feeling much but expressing little.

Both of the early women in Franklin's life, his sister and mother, died suddenly of illness as he was becoming an adult, a fact which may have contributed to his mistrust of women and his tendency to give the emotional care of his nuclear family over to his wife.

In this man's life, the crowning insult came when his father decided to turn the farm over to the older son, Carver, giving Franklin only severance pay. The story goes that the older brother ran Bitzy's father off the property with a butcher knife. This act left Franklin, a young man with a new wife and expected child, to find a home and start a new profession. It was no wonder that Bitzy's father often seemed more involved in his work than he was with his family's growth. And this factor helps to explain why Bitzy could be manipulated into staying quiet in bed for six months for the doctor (a surrogate father) on the promise that she would have a home, family, and the intimacy she craved, as an adult. Her parent's history sets up her tremendous need to find a loving, expressive partner, who will teach her the things lacking in her background.

Once again, the wounds of the father and mother—emotional baggage—are visited upon the children even unto the seventh generation!!

# CHAPTER TWENTY FOUR

# My Soul Dog: Patches

M Y FAMILY BELIEVED that each family member should be a working part of the whole, and so we had chores to perform each day or week depending on the chore. We were given an allowance for these jobs to teach us how to handle our small amount of money. With my sister and brother away at college, they were beyond household chores and were expected to have paying jobs when they could fit this in around going to school.

Mother decided that my chores were to make all the beds in the household before I went off to school each day. In the evening, I was to help her with the dishes by drying them as she washed them in the black iron sink. (When I was younger, we would speak the parts and act out the events in familiar fairy tales as we worked together.) My big chore for the week was to help her change the linens on the beds upstairs and then dry-mop that second floor of the house, which consisted of the bedrooms and the only bathroom in the house. (During this era, I don't remember my mother ever using a vacuum as we do today.) This floor mopping took place every Saturday morning. I could not go out to play on Saturday until my chores were done and inspected by Mother.

On this particular day, I did my mopping and then called my mother for her inspection. I expect I was about eight years old at the time. When she came to inspect, she blew up at me. "These floors don't appear to have seen the bottom side of a dust mop! Didn't you pay attention to what you were doing? There! Sit on my pine chest and watch. I will show you how a floor is supposed to be mopped!!" Crushed, I crawled up on the dark-stained, plain, pine blanket-chest and watched my mother. She took the mop and started in one corner of the room, moving the mop as if she were painting a floor, into every corner and around any large pieces of furniture. I thought I had done the same thing, but maybe not. I left that inspection feeling like a failure. (And to this day, I have to vacuum my floors *myself* to ensure that they will pass Mother's inspection.)

*     *     *

Time moves on, and this was again on a Saturday morning. I was busy mopping my upstairs rooms. It is raining outside, but my mop had become covered with dirt and dust. I will have to go outside to shake it vigorously on the back steps. I'm not happy about the rain, but it is falling lightly at the moment. I'm outside shaking my mop when I see a dog with patches of black and white fur shivering out under the clothesline. I call the dog to come, and the dog tucks its head down as if it is ashamed. Then I realize I'm holding what must look like a stick to the dog. I put my mop down flat on the backstairs and move towards the dog just a bit. I call again. This time the dog comes running. I pat this rain-soaked animal and then sit down on the concrete stairs in the rain and put my arms around the dog's neck. This black and white dog snuggles in close to my body, I expect, because it has been wet, cold, and afraid for some time.

The next thing I hear is my mother opening the screen door to the porch just behind where we are sitting. "When you didn't come back," my mother said, "I came to find you. What do you have there?"

"It's a dog, Mom. A very cold and lonely dog, and it loves me already."

"Well, I don't know about the loving already part, but I can see it has been through some hard times and must be very hungry."

"Mom, can we keep the dog, please, please?"

"The first thing we need to do is to get some food and water into the dog. See if the dog will follow you up onto the porch? We can feed the animal out here." My mother went to raid the refrigerator and came back with some hamburger, a few cut-up carrots, and a low bowl of water. I had no trouble getting the dog to follow me up onto the porch where we fed it.

By now, my mother must have been thinking, and she said, "You know I'm not the one to say whether you can keep the dog or not. You are going to have to ask your father. It is almost lunchtime and a line-up for his boys. You can take the dog to meet him. But don't ask Dad about keeping the dog until he's had a chance to eat his food."

With Mother's help, I found a short rope and tied it around the dog's neck. We started toward where my father would be standing as the officials at the school counted the boys in his landscaping gang. I stood across the street watching, so anxious to show Dad my new dog. But I did remember that my mother always told us not to pester Dad about going swimming until he had eaten supper, and this would be the same.

I knew that my father loved dogs, and when he was in his teen years, his beloved Gypsy, a cow-herding collie, had been poisoned as she walked to the railroad station to meet my father returning from his high school classes in Fitzburg. Mother had told all of we children that he would not let any of us have a dog because of this horrible loss—it would be too painful for him. This wounding meant that I had to be very careful as I approached him about keeping my dog.

He greeted us in his usual understated way. "I see you have a friend with you. All wet like that, she looks pretty beaten up."

"Yeah," I said, trying to match his understated manner and play my cards right. "The dog was on the back steps when I went out to shake my dry-mop this morning."

"She looks friendly enough," my Dad said, and I wondered how my father knew the dog was a girl dog.

"Mom says she thinks the dog is a stray." I was fighting to think of things to say that wouldn't bring up keeping the dog.

"I would guess that she is a soldier's dog. You know when they get orders to ship out of Fort Devens, they will often open the door and let their dog go. The cruelest thing you can do to any animal!"

I nodded my head to keep from saying the wrong thing, but fortunately, we were almost home and that important lunch.

I ate lunch with my Dad, but I have no idea what we ate. I was so intent on my mission that I watched every move he made, almost every bite he took. After the meal, he pushed back his chair and went into the living room to sit in his rocking chair, look at the mail, and listen to the noon-time news on the radio. I sat on the tiny wooden stool that Owen had made in high school wood-working class and waited. The dog followed us into the living room and sat down right beside my father's legs as if she knew what would come next. Having looked at the mail, my father reached down and ran his hands through the fur on her back and sides. Then he slid forward in his chair, and using both hands to grip her head; he opened her mouth to look at her teeth.

"What are you doing to her?" I asked for it looked like a very unfriendly way to get acquainted with a dog.

"It's okay," my Dad said. "The best way to find out the age of an animal is to look at their teeth. I'd say she is young, maybe two years old."

"Oh, I thought you were hurting her, and I knew you wouldn't do that. Can we keep her? Can we keep her, please, please?" There, it was finally out!

My dad looked at me with one of the most loving glances I can remember and said, "You will have to post signs saying that we have her, and then we have to wait for two weeks, but if no one claims her, we can keep her."

By now, my mother had crept up to stand just behind my father's rocking chair. She smiled at me as if we had just pulled off a great feat. "What are you going to call her?" my mother asked.

"Remember the book you used to read to me when I was sick? The one where the little girl found scraps of cloth in a clothes basket and stitched them all together to find out that she had just created a live dog. I'm going to call her Patches."

They say that a rescued dog always remembers and holds dear the person who rescues them, and it was indeed true with Patches. It was a bit of a toss-up as to whether she was more attached to me and our walks in the woods or my father and his hunting trips.

\* \* \*

Patches made no protest as my father checked her out as if she knew this examination was going to take place, and we found over time that she was just so happy to have a home that she was very quiet, cooperative, and loving to everyone. I adored her, and as I moved through my junior high and early high school years, I was still struggling with making and keeping relationships. I couldn't understand the social games that the girls played with each other. All I wanted was a trusted person and friend with whom I could share life's adventures. I did develop two such friends, Jodie and Bev. But at the end of the school day, I would be looking forward to my peanut butter and jelly sandwich, or was it cinnamon and mayonnaise? If Mom were at home, I'd share some of my day with her, and then it was off for a walk with my beloved Patches.

When I was a little girl, after I got well from the rheumatic fever, my father used to take me on Saturday afternoon walks through the woods of the State School. I learned where the blueberry swamp was, where the Shakers had made their settlement of buildings, and where they held their outside gatherings on "Holy Hill." I even learned where Dad found his hazelnuts. I was warned about going to the dump, but I knew that Owen went there when he was younger to chase rats. And there was the caution about staying away from the Nashua River, which ran behind the State School property right behind the athletic fields that my father and his boys helped build. There was a huge drop off from the state land down to the river. It was not a safe place for a girl and her dog.

In a sense, Patches took over the job that Monkey had done for me when I was isolated and fearful, sick in bed with rheumatic fever. Only this time, there was interaction, and I learned a lot about communication with a dog and taking care of an animal. She was my lifeline during those pre-adolescent and early adolescent years.

There is more to the story of Patches, but that will have to wait for a later book, or you may get some more stories about her from my blog, My Little Bird by JMK.

## Looking Through My Therapist Eyes

# Patches

It is amazing as I look back from my nearly eighty years to see how I carried this veiled place in my soul of loneliness and depression. This chapter is where Bitzy reveals her true emotional attitude and how isolated she perceives herself, even free of illness, in a home where she is loved and cared for but so sensitive that she still feels alone. I believe many children go through these feelings at pre-adolescence and adolescence, and they have few tools to combat these feelings. As I listen closely to my grown daughters tell of those years in their lives, I pick up the same undertone and wonder if this is inherited or a particular growth period in the journey from childhood to adulthood.

The other issue that stands out to me is that Bitzy used a stuffed monkey as a companion when she was ill, and then as a teen, she pulls in a dog to take on this same role in her life. Maybe this is just a dependent personality emerging. Or was it created by Mother's need to see herself as a successful mother and therefore held Bitzy too close to her emotionally?

Looking back at my life, I believe that I divorced and chose a second husband, Sy Kessler, to help fill this same hole in my journey. Hard to admit in public, but I do believe this to be true. If you have read my first book, *A Bird and the Dragon: Their Love*

*Story: A Memoir,* you will see that Sy did fill this void in my life. And now it is time to find a new way to mend this empty place in the soul.

Because I have lived so many years, I can tell you that I still have dogs to help with this issue. At the moment, they are both Cavalier King Charles dogs, an expensive luxury of my older years, one breed that gives their souls and their lives over to snuggling you and being there when you need them physically or emotionally. They make great therapy dogs for my clients and me.

Bitzy's Dog Patches After Hunting with Her Father

# CHAPTER TWENTY FIVE
# "Drops" Can Make Money

THE NEED TO have a job or work in our family was very strong, and you can see that it had its roots back with my grandparents or farther back. It was almost as if we didn't believe that having fun and being silly were alright, although my mother did have British humor, and my Dad was a slapstick man. Thank goodness for PollyAnne, for she was the party lady, but that is for the next book. Still, this event starts with PollyAnne and me.

It must have been in August before I turned eleven, and I was lazing on the old iron couch on the back porch. Polly came out and sat on the edge of the couch, somewhat like her visits when I was in a sickbed. "Have you thought about getting a job?" she asked.

"No! Of course not! I'm only ten."

"You know you could go up to Davis's Apple Orchard and pick up dropped apples. A lot of little kids do that after school."

"But I think I'm still too little," I responded.

"You're not too little to pick up 'drops,'" PollyAnne replied. "You are going to have to get a job at some point to help Mom and Dad with your college education. They can't put all of us through college if we don't help."

I knew Polly was talking about work because she was already working during the apple picking season at Davis's orchard doing that in and around her hardware store job.

I don't remember what I said next, but it must not have been what Polly wanted to hear, and she soon left me to do something else.

*   *   *

I was back in school, and the leaves were beginning to fall, but I kept thinking about what PollyAnne had said to me. She thought I should get a job. Her suggestion troubled me for several days, and then one recess time Nan and I were back on the swing set, and I said to Nan, "Why don't we go up to Davis's orchard and see if we can get a job picking up dropped apples?"

She looked at me like I was out of my mind and then said, "Aren't we too young? And besides, I'd have to ask my parents first."

"PollyAnne says that some of the other kids are only ten, and we're going to be eleven in the winter, or at least I am."

Nan did speak to her parents, and they said it was alright. So the following afternoon at the end of school, we walked up the hill to the apple orchard next to the large playground of our school. We told the person there that we wanted a job picking up apples. They handed us a cardboard box and pointed to the trees that needed cleaning. As I remember, the man in charge said, "Remember, don't put any rotten apples in the box, and if you eat any, we'll subtract it from your pay." (How he would know if we ate any apples I couldn't figure out, but I didn't trouble myself long with that thought.)

We got our box full and turned it in just in time to get picked up and driven home by my mother. The next day was the same routine. Then on Friday afternoon, when I got home, PollyAnne approached me again. "You know they will be sorting and packing apples in the barn tomorrow, and you get better pay for that work. If you want, you could go in with me and help pack apple boxes." (Remember, nothing in those days was automated.)

PollyAnne made a picnic lunch for us and had me awake way too early in the morning so that I could go with her to work. I can remember that it was so cold that our breath showed bluish-white as we breathed because both barn doors were wide open. We sat on bales of hay in the center corridor of the barn as we sorted the apples into wooden delivery boxes. My sister gave me her sweater at one point and later left me there while she talked to her friend Hattie, the daughter of the orchard owner. I can remember being bone-chilling cold and feeling lost and forgotten, just as I had when I was sick. I never did go back to pack apples again, but Nan and I picked up drops the following week.

At the end of that week, it was time for us to get our first pay. Nan and I got our paychecks in little envelopes and retreated from the barn to the school swing set to see what we had gotten for pay. When I pulled out my check, it was for 3.00 dollars. "Hey, Nan, I got 3.00 dollars in my check. What did you get? The same?" I asked as I twirled around, holding up my check in the air for everyone to see. I was making it into a big deal, and of course, it was a big deal for a girl not quite eleven years old.

Nan sat on her swing and quietly pulled her check out of her envelope to look at it. I watched Nan and didn't notice at first that a boy was approaching where we sat on the swings. I didn't know him, but I did know he was a big brother to a boy closer to our age. As Nan sat looking at her check, David walked up very close to her and grabbed the check. He ran off a little way and held the check up high, waving it in the air so that if we went for it, we couldn't reach it. Nan sat on the swing, stunned, I assume, by his actions. I, on the other hand, was furious at what he was doing to my friend, so I charged right up to him and said, "Give me Nan's check now, or I'll beat you to a bloody pulp, you bully!" David stood way taller than me, but I guess it was my tone of voice or something because he did one more victory spin around and handed the check back to me.

\* \* \*

Now the funniest part of this event is that when we move forward in time, beyond the scope of this book, I am attending the tenth high school class reunion. I have gathered with the girls that I knew in high school. I was not a basketball player, but I hung with the team a lot because my best friend Sylvia played on the team, and the girl, Laura that took piano lessons with me, was also part of the team. These were the girls I was talking to when a young man walks up to our group and snuggles in beside Laura. She, in turn, gestures toward him and says to me, "This is Charlie Bronson, my husband." I reach out to shake his hand, and he says, "Yes, I know who you are. You forced my older brother to return a check if I remember correctly. I'm surprised he gave it up."

I have no idea how at the Bronson family table, they told this story. I just was so glad I didn't have to "beat him to a bloody pulp," if I even knew what that meant at the time.

\* \* \*

Hattie Davis was one of my sister's best friends in high school, and they visited back and forth between families. I suppose there were sleepovers, although that term seems to belong to a later era. Polly was a good sister and let me hang with them when it was appropriate, so I felt a bit like Hattie was my friend, too.

One evening Hattie had stayed for supper and was sitting at our dining room table. We didn't usually have dinner in the dining room, but Hattie made one more person than we had chairs in the kitchen. Mom brought out a plate of cookies for dessert. Hattie looked at the plate of cookies and said, "Oh, yum, cookies!"

In her best hostess manner, my mother said, "Hattie, do you like cookies?"

"Oh, yes, I do. At home, when the plate comes out, I pick up about four cookies and lick each one I want and then put them back, so everyone knows which cookies are mine."

My mother looked horrified but said, "Well, you don't have to do that here. We'll let you have the first choice. How about that?!"

## Looking Through My Therapist Eyes

# Make Money

Today I never see a plate of cookies come out for dessert, but I think of Hattie and what fun it would be to lick all of the cookies that I wanted on the plate.

This chapter starts with the family's work ethic and ends with the light hearted cookie story—a quality that seemed to be missing in this family. My older siblings talk of fun and foolishness, but I remember very little of that. Doing meaningful work was such an issue for my family as it is with many old New England families. Maybe it is because our roots were anchored in farms and farming. That was a very hard way of life, and you didn't live for very long if you didn't work diligently.

I've shared parts of my grandmother, Mary Emma Moody's life. Her life was definitely a life of hard work, even to the point where she had a garden in the back yard of her suburban home, which she tended into her early nineties. Maybe because I was named for her, I carry this message in my veins.

So coming out of this family, I started saving for college while I was still a child, and in high school, I avoided admitting that I didn't know how to play basketball by saying I couldn't be on the team because I had to work and save for my college education. I did work for years as a tailor in a dry cleaning establishment, but those stories are for the next book. I wonder if this "working" was a pattern of avoidance of social activities, which I learned from my family while living in my childhood home.

To this day, I have to watch that I don't turn down too many social engagements because I am "too busy working" at something. Oh, the seriousness of this family and my life! Or is some of this phenomenon fueled by the feelings left over from my fight with rheumatic fever at the age of five? Many children are left after long-term illnesses with the belief that they are somehow inferior and must work extra hard to prove they are as strong physically and as powerful emotionally as those who have not been wounded early in life.

This book does not answer these questions but is written more to help individuals look at their roots and become conscious of some of the life events that help or hinder them in their later life.

Big Sister PollyAnne, Baby Brother Coppy, and Bitzy

# CHAPTER TWENTY SIX
# Books, Letters, and Boys

I T MUST HAVE been the year we picked apples, and I was in fifth grade. The teacher of that class, Mrs. Crosby, enjoyed reading to our students in reward for good work. On this particular day, she had finished the book she had been reading to us. When she spoke the last words, she closed the book with a bit of a "thwap" and said, "Now this book is finished. Did you enjoy the story?" Of course, we all responded like good children knowing that if we were enthusiastic about her reading, we would get more stories; and what child of any age doesn't like to sit dreamily listening to someone else tell or read the story?

Mrs. Crosby didn't miss the game and said, "So does anyone in the class have a suggestion for another book we can read?"

Without even thinking, I blurted out, "Yes, you could read my Uncle Ralph's book, *Little Britches*. You know it has been on the New York Times bestseller list for a while."

Mrs. Crosby looked at me like she was seeing me for the first time. "You say you have an uncle who has written a book?"

"Yes, my mother's oldest brother, Ralph Moody, has written a book about him and his family growing up out in Colorado. My mother is mentioned just at the end."

"Do you have a copy of the book at home that you could bring in so that I can see if it is appropriate to read to our students?"

"Oh, yes. We have a couple of books. I'll ask Mom if I can bring one in," I said.

And so it began that Mrs. Crosby would read a chapter or a part of a chapter from my Uncle Ralph's book each day at the ending of our work-time. Because the book dealt with children and Uncle Ralph's relationship with his father, it held my fellow students' attention. (Not to mention that it is a well written-book and still is available to purchase.)

But we students didn't get off easy with the dreamy sitting and listening to a story being read. We then had our English lesson on writing letters. Mrs. Crosby announced as she was close to finishing the book that the polite thing to do would be to write letters to Mr. Moody. Of course, there were groans from my classmates, but we did all sit and learn how to write a thank you letter, with an introduction, commas, spelling, and closing salutation.

I'm not sure, for it was a long time ago, but I believe my uncle wrote a note back to each child, and he certainly wrote a letter to the whole class saying how pleased he was that we were having his book read to us in class and he so appreciated our letters of thanks.

You can imagine how proud I walked for most of that year in school. I was related to a well-known author, and the other students had enjoyed the book. (In later years, the book became a "reader" for students in seventh and eighth grade English classes.)

And this book also helped my social place on the playground that year. I first made friends with Jodie, the girl in third grade, as we ran the local playground collie dog back and forth across the field. She was sometimes in our school and sometimes in Athol with her mother. So at the time when she was away, I became closer to another girl named Bev. Her parents owned a small house in town not far away from the school, and we could walk to her house.

Bev was Catholic as opposed to my being a Protestant, and so we attended different churches. I spent overnights sometimes with Bev, and then I would attend Mass in the morning with her. I was so impressed with the differences in the way people worshipped in her church. I remember the family running around trying to find a handkerchief or a little hat that I could wear because I couldn't go into her church without having my hair covered; something about women's hair being a distraction to the men.

We also spent some of our Saturday afternoons, after I did my chores, riding the bus from our town, Shakerton, up to Fitzburg. That city had a roller skating rink, and Bev was a good skater, with the delightful body shape of an athletic young woman. She had all the pretty little short skirts and white roller skates. I was so jealous because my mother did make skirts for me, but they were definitely not in the same class with Bev's purchased outfits, nor as short. And it was here at the roller skating rink that I began to recognize boys for the first time. They flocked around Bev like she was a jar of honey while I tried to stumble along on those confining boots that I could hardly stand up on, let alone skate with someone. The joys and awkwardness of becoming a pre-teen and teenager!

The other thing about Bev was that she could sing. I joined my church choir when I was a fourth-grader, and I met the Military Choir Mistress, my church choir director. I also loved to sing, and in a sense, I had already been in training for five years because when this story takes place, Bev and I were starting into eighth grade. Mrs. James, the teacher for that classroom, and also the lady I fondly called my Military Choir Mistress, had a piano in her classroom. I wanted to be a big-name singer, but I was wise enough to know that my voice was not strong and was better used as a fill-in voice in a choir. So having this dream for myself, I played it out by asking Bev if she wanted to have a chance to practice her singing. "Of course I want to practice. I want to get so good that I can become a part of my cousin's band."

The next day I went to Mrs. James during lunchtime while she was busy correcting papers and eating a sandwich at her desk. "Mrs. James, Bev hasn't got a piano at home and no one to play for her while she practices her singing. She wants to become a big singing star. Can we use your piano here in the classroom?"

Mrs. James looked at me so intently with her brown eyes that it felt like her eyes would drill holes into my body. "When were you planning on doing this work on the piano?" she asked.

"I was thinking that we could come in after school each day and I'd play the piano while she sang."

"The two of you would not touch anything else in the room because I don't want to stay after school just so that I can keep an eye on you?"

"Oh, we wouldn't touch anything else, and we'd close down the piano and close the door when we left the room."

"I think if you girls can remember to do all that, I can trust you to use my piano. And I do hope that Bev becomes a big star."

"Oh, thank you so much. We won't touch anything else."

"That is good because I'm placing a lot of trust in you."

I was so delighted with the teacher's trust in us and the fact that I would get a chance to help out my friend. I was also proud that I had gotten up the courage to talk to Mrs. James. It helped that I already knew her from my church choir.

I don't remember how many days we worked on this project because I quickly learned that playing piano for my pleasure and my piano lessons was very different than accompanying a budding singer.

The story does go on but is beyond the scope of this book. Bev did get to sing with her cousin's band and did that successfully during our high school years.

I will close this chapter with a story about Jodie, the other close girlfriend in grade school. I said she had to spend her time between a mother in one town and a father in our town. The summer before Nan and I picked up apples; I was chumming with Jodie. I could ride my bicycle down to the village where most of my school friends lived. Jodie lived across the street from the school, and sometimes we'd sneak over to her house at lunch time to play with the new kittens, but today, I was going to help Jodie walk the small horse, or maybe you would call it a pony around the farmyard. She had gotten a job at the farm across the street from Davis's Apple Orchard, leading their pony around so that it would get enough exercise. I'm not sure if the animal needed this attention or the family saw that Jodie needed a little pocket money.

It was mid-morning, and I pulled my bike up to the open barn door and leaned it against the door jam. I could see that Jodie already had the pony out and was leading it around with a halter and rope. The animal was not very tall but just tall enough to make you recognize it might be a force to respect.

I called to Jodie, "Hi, am I too late?

"No," she responded. "I've been walking the pony for a few minutes. I let him have a roll in the grass and now he's very happy. Want to take a ride on him?"

"Is it okay for us to ride him?" I ask. "After all, this is a job, and you are making money for it."

"Sure it's alright."

"Great," I respond. "Where's the saddle?"

"Oh, I never use a saddle when I ride him. You have to get close to his side and just jump up. He'll stand still for you."

It sounded pretty easy. I took a couple of running steps and aimed for the pony's back. I connected, almost sat up for a moment, and the next thing I knew, I circled right around the pony's back and stomach and landed flat on my back between his feet. He didn't move.

Looking up from under the pony's stomach, I said to Jodie, "What happened?"

She is standing there holding the reins in her hand with her legs crossed, laughing so hard she can't answer me for a moment. When she finally calms herself, Jodie says, "The pony had just rolled in the grass picking up all the morning dew on his fur coat. It was like he'd just had a bath, and when you landed on his back, he was greased and waiting for you!"

I couldn't help laughing with her, once I rolled out from between the pony's legs. I don't know why the pony didn't move with all of our commotion, but I'm so glad he didn't. And that brings my horse riding adventures to a close.

Fast forward: I love the look of horses, and I love to watch them race. I've even been known to win a bet or two, but I have stayed clear of dew-soaked ponies.

## Looking Through My Therapist Eyes

# Pony

Chapter twenty-six is the first chapter in which we begin to see a fairly normal pre-teen and growing teenager with all those age related issues. Mother seems to be left in the background as she should be at this point, and Bitzy's friends are becoming more important than family. Are the wounds of long-term illness completed? I know because I lived this life that Bitzy appears to be "normal," whatever that means, but inside she lacks the confidence to do many things, even at eighth grade age, not considering that she could become a singing star.

The fact that Bitzy was willing to try to ride Jodie's job pony was a large step forward in her emotional growth. And the fact that Bitzy fell off was probably a good thing because it was one of the first times that she was forced to take herself and her abilities with a bit of lightness, here even laughing with Jodie at her measurable pony riding skills.

Bitzy in personality is like her father, Franklin, and tends to look at life with a serious face just as he did. The social awkwardness of Bitzy's family of origin may have been inherited, but her older siblings don't show so much of this inability to move smoothly through social situations. Did her mother's needs bind Bitzy emotionally too close? Maybe the long-term illness taking place just as Bitzy starts into the greater world of sociability has hobbled her in terms of confidence, sureness of purpose, and ease at working with larger groups of people. It is time to check back to the mirror and see if the "inner child" can do more to heal this split in my adult psychology.

Mother Jordon, Brother Coppy, Patches, and Bitzy age 13

# CHAPTER TWENTY SEVEN

# Final Dialogue with the Inner Bitzy

BITZY SEEMS so far away from her illness of rheumatic fever that it feels like it might be senseless to continue our dialogues, and yet, I wonder if her emotions match what she is showing on the outside. Her story sounds happy and filled with the everyday events of growing into a young woman.

Before my morning writing session, I've finished my usual meditation and sit poised before the computer. Do I want to connect with this child? I could open my eyes, and there would be a monitor screen before me. Why do I hesitate? What am I afraid of finding out? Squeezing my eyes tighter, inside my mind, I see a streak of golden light. *Follow the light*, my intuition says. *Where's it going to lead?*

I don't wish to accept what I see. The light ends at the mirror, and as I search inside for my little girl, I don't see her but rather hear her voice. Looking up, I find she is sitting on the very top of the mirror, or should I say computer monitor, legs crossed and dangling, elbow on knee, her left arm upturned with chin resting in the curve of her hand. *I don't know . . . !*

"Bitzy, what in heavens name are you doing sitting on my computer monitor?"

"Put your hand out," she responds.

I do as I'm told, having decided that I don't understand any of this kind of reality.

"No, not that way," Bitzy says sharply. "Turn it over, palm side up, so that I can get down."

Again, I do as she instructs, and this miniature child of about twelve years of age steps lightly into my cupped hand. She feels like a feather or a blade of field grass. *What should I do with her?*

Bitzy reads my mind. "You could close your hand and squeeze the life out of me like you've been doing all these years."

"I'm sorry," I say. "I had no idea. You know, I've read all this stuff over the years about the inner child thing, and it hasn't made a connection for me." As I make my confession, I wonder why I'm saying this to a little creature standing in the curvature of my hand.

"You don't have to tell me. I've been inside you, screaming to get out, and you go along shutting down everything that belongs to me."

"I guess I haven't been a very good steward," I say to quiet my feelings of guilt. "But you know you are a remarkably tiny thing. It's no wonder I've overlooked you."

"You haven't overlooked—you've crossed me off; caput... silent... unable to get comfort for my pain, or recognition for my talents, my voice, or even a sense of who I am."

"I am really sorry, Bitzy," I say, beginning to connect with her frustration. *I could even get angry with myself for the way she says I've treated her, yet, I continue to feel stupid, talking to this child that looks like me, standing in my left hand. She is fascinating!*

"You think I'm small, but I'm so big that I've kept you bunged up for years and years!"

"Bitzy, where did you get that word *bunged*? People haven't used that word for years. Just recently, the young people have picked it up again. How could you know you're only twelve years old?"

"Oh, no! You've got it wrong," Bitzy says. "I'm part of your soul energy, and I've been with you through all of the time, ancient and future. I've been around for every lifetime, whether you remember them or not."

"No! No way," I respond. "I would have felt you before this."

Bitzy continues, appearing not to have heard me. "Sometimes I'm a boy, sometimes a girl, but I hold those aspects of yourself that you can't cope with or accept. You put the pain down in the dark corners of your being along with your biggest talents."

I can't resist, and to tweak her, I retort, "I don't have many talents!"

"See, that's the story you've put out in this lifetime, and worse yet, you've blamed it on me. Haven't you always thought you weren't very smart?"

I'm caught short by her direct question. "Yes, I've thought I was a little lacking in intellectual capacity."

"You've always passed it off onto me, but it wasn't me; it was your unwillingness to let your various emotional parts live."

"You're talking about repression," I say, trying to put her concepts into a vernacular I understand.

"Repression, my foot! It's more like pure strangulation! You do understand that you've never been able to paint, or write, or get to those creative things you've been planning to do because you haven't allowed me to become a conscious part of yourself."

"But I've been afraid of the pain—black, despairing pain that comes from your side of the mirror. I know it's going to be there, so I shut it away tight behind some door, and if I open the door just a crack . . . No, I can't let it out—it's all I can do to keep it locked up."

"Just my point," my little friend responds.

Overwhelmed by a surge of emotions, I look away from the source of the voice.

"Please, don't look away. Recognize me! Do you realize that I'm on your side of the mirror for the first time? You're holding me in your hand, and you haven't collapsed?"

*She's right! I don't seem to feel any pain in my chest —none in my stomach, and little anywhere else, for that matter.* "So what you're telling me is that if I had been able to voice my fear, pain, anger, and frustration when I was sick, I might have gotten on faster in my life, with fewer mistakes."

"Hey, I don't want to go into mistakes right now. They're not mistakes but rather learning detours . . . But that's a whole other topic for discussion."

This creature is intriguing. I want to touch this girl, stroke her tiny head, consume her like I would a new kitten, but I'm afraid my touch will be overpowering, maybe crush her. She seems so complete yet fragile.

"I heard that! Go ahead. Touch me. Finally, get a feel of who I am. I've got to develop out here on the conscious side of things, and the only way that can happen is for you to see me in every detail and then give me the energy to expand into your size and shape."

"This is weird, Bitzy," I say. Then, I feel embarrassed for being so blunt.

"It's far weirder for you to be wandering around in your conscious reality with little knowledge or respect for that inner part of yourself that has been in so much pain and fear, feeling abandoned all these years."

"I've known you were there, sort of," I say defensively.

"Okay, touch me. —When was the last time you went to any friend with your suffering? You hide behind your service to others, your counseling skills . . ."

"That's enough! I'll touch you!" I put my index finger out and move it gingerly toward her blond head. *It's just like mine! As I connect with the recent short-cut hair, soft, then harder as my finger contacts the scalp.* She doesn't flinch or move. And the sense of ecstatic joy that runs through my arm and into my heart sets my whole body vibrating.

"That felt nice," Bitzy whispers. "Can you touch my back?"

By now, two other fingers join the first exploratory finger. This tiny girl's back feels soft to my touch. This creature seems tender to me, exquisite in composition, delicate, but oh, so strong of spirit. And just as I'm about to withdraw my hand, her whole countenance takes on a golden glow, radiating out into a halo of light around her. I sit in reverence, astounded by the light. "What's this?" I ask, my voice hardly more than air moving in and out of my mouth.

"You know who I am," Bitzy responds softly. "You've seen who I really am for the first time! You people in the trade have a fancy name for me."

"Yeah," I mumble, still caught in exquisite recognition. "I know your name . . . you're the Divine Inner Child."

"Whatever! Fancy name or not, I don't want to be stuck behind that mirror. And I want to grow up to full size. Once you touched my back, I knew that even if I have to go back behind the mirror some of the time, you will come to get me again. I want to live beside you, interacting in your daily life. Only when I become conscious can I be constructive for you."

"Ever since I saw you that first time in the mirror, I've wanted to feel you, hold you, love you, and give you space and voice."

"And so you have, my giant friend. Now, put me up on the computer, for I've got to slide behind my mirror. You're not ready for me to spend all my time with you. My job is to move back and forth—from your unconscious existence to your conscious mind. This past refusal to claim me—devalue me—is why I can't help you create the things you want to create. Give me life, JessieMay, and we can soar the world together!"

# CHAPTER TWENTY EIGHT
## The Red Car

ECAUSE I WAS getting a little older, I began to graduate from walking Patches through the woods to riding my bicycle to places that I wanted to explore. The state had decided to improve Route 2 in Massachusetts, an east/west commercial route, and their proposal placed the new road through the backwoods of the Industrial School, only a short walking or bike riding distance from my home. As work began on the road, my father and I would walk down to watch the construction. I asked, "Dad, why are they putting the road behind our house? Isn't there a Route 2 in Shakerton Center, on the other side of town?"

"Sometimes, they want to take the curves out of the road that farmers put there when they were driving their cows to pasture. There was a roadway on the other side of town, built a long time ago, but before that road, a commercial road ran east and west from Bunker City to the western part of Massachusetts. It was just to the south side of my old farm, the Walnut Shade Farm. They used logs jammed tight together side by side in the low spots to get teams of horses or oxen through the swampy areas. They called it the corduroy road."

"Why don't they just redo that road?" I asked.

"I'm not sure. The state officials may want to put the new road where it will bring people into newly developing communities. More and more people want to work in Bunker City, but they don't want to live in a city."

I answered his explanation with an, "Oh."

By now, we were close to the slowly developing site, and I saw machines with wheels that looked as tall as half my house. "Dad, have you ever seen anything so big?"

"No. When we were building things, we used oxen or farm horses. I've seen men repairing roads in Shakerton with regular trucks but not with any machines this large."

"Look over there." My father was pointing to the beginning of a bridge they were building. "That is going to be fun to watch going up," Dad said.

About then, he signaled me that it was time to start back to our house. And as we walked, my Dad said, "This is not a place for a little girl to go to by herself. You can see how big the trucks are that the men are using. They might not see a child. Don't come here without me."

"Okay, I won't."

*   *   *

I promised my father, but then I wanted to see how they were building the road, so I began walking Patches down to the worksite. The men built a small shack at the spot where our side road, with all the pines on it, met the new road. As the weather got cold, they would take their breaks at or in that shack. I didn't go down to that spot in the cold weather. It wasn't any fun walking Patches in the cold air.

But spring came, and I was back watching the progress on the road. I got to talking to one of the men and then with another. One asked me, "So, where do you come from?"

"I live up the street. My dad brought me down here when you were all just getting started on the road. And boy, are some of those machines big!"

"I bet you'd like to ride on one of those one day?"

"Oh, no. Those machines are way too high up in the air for me. How do the men get up into them?" I asked.

"They climb up on the tire treads until they get to the body of the machine, and then there are places for their feet."

"That would be way too scary for me!"

And it was at about that point that the man said to me, "My name is Nick. What is your name?

"I'm Bitzy," I replied.

"I think that name fits you," he responded.

"I guess I drive by your house a lot if you live up the road from here. I drive that bright red car over there with the convertible top. Sharp car, right?"

I nodded. It was a very sharp-looking car.

"It's almost supper time," I told him. "I've got to get home."

I began regularly going to visit with the men, especially Nick.

He was a good-looking man, younger than my Dad but about the same height, with curly brown hair and brown eyes. As the weather got hotter, he was often outside the shack shirtless. He was muscular and well-tanned.

I began watching for his red car as it would go past my house. I didn't wave, and he didn't wave to me, but I think he knew I was watching. I began looking from the school bus to see if the red car was in town as we drove from the school to my house.

One day soon after school was out for the summer, Mother pulled me aside. "Bitzy, you have been going down to that building site a lot, and it is not a good place for a little girl like you. I would rather that you found somewhere else to play. Do you understand me?"

I nodded my head because I heard her words, but it didn't mean much to me.

It had to be early in August because, again, the day was very hot, and this time I decided to take my bike down to the job site. The cool air from riding would feel good on my face. As I was pulling into the spot near the shack, I saw Nick pulling out in his car. He had his window rolled down, and he was shirtless, again. He slowed the car as he got beside me and stopped. "I came down to see you," I said.

"That's too bad because I was just heading out. It's quitting time."

Nick's arm was resting on the open window, and quick as a flash, he grabbed the handlebar of my bike.

"What are you doing?!!" I asked as I tried to pull the bike away.

"I thought you might like to take a little ride with me. Come on."

I don't know why, but I pull my bike backward a little and then wrench the handle bars over to one side. One more violent twist the other way, and I am free. Quick as I can mount my bike, I start pedaling and pedal that bike as hard as possible. Nick had to put his car back into gear to get rolling. That gives me lead time. I have never pumped a bike so fast ever again as I fight to get ahead of his car and closer to my home. Nick is pulling up behind me; I turn into my driveway and ride the bike clear to the cellar door far away from the street.

Inside, I am in hysterics, shaking and crying. I drop the bike to the ground and run for the porch door. I get inside, and I don't look back to see where Nick may be, but head straight to the dining room and flop down on the Honey Bargain, the love seat in that room. I curl up in a ball as if that would protect me from whatever might be coming.

Of course, Nick didn't follow me, but the scent of his hand is still on my bare arm. I cry as quietly as possible because I don't want any of my family to find me. It wasn't long before my mother comes to me. "Oh, Honey! What just happened to you?" she asked.

"I was down at the shack by the new road they are building. I was talking to Nick, the man with the red car. He was leaving work and when I pulled up beside his car, he grabbed the handlebar of my bike. He wanted me to go for a ride with him, but I wrenched my bike away and pedaled home as fast as I could. Mom, what was he going to do to me?"

"We are just blessed that you were able to get away. Now you know why your Dad and I told you never to go there alone. Those men are not to be trusted with little girls."

"Please, please don't tell Daddy. I promised him I wouldn't go down alone."

"Honey, I must tell him—he is your father. But I don't think he is going to do anything to you. It appears that you have already learned a very large lesson in life. We don't need to punish you any farther." She patted my back which I still had toward her. "You just stay here until you are ready to come out. Supper is ready, but you may want a few minutes before you join us."

No one said anything that evening, and I have no idea what I ate at that meal. I had indeed learned a very important lesson: to be alert, to not go alone where there are a group of men working, and that I had the instincts and strength to take care of myself. Oh, yes, and to not trust men in red convertibles.

## Looking Through My Therapist Eyes

## Red Car

Parents don't look forward usually to the teenage years because they know their children will be going through hormonal changes, and their personalities will be more difficult to live with for a time. I can remember sitting with my own therapist at one point and complaining about how my children were lying to me. Linda was quiet for a moment, and then she said, "How is your child going to learn about all the things you have set down as rules if they don't lie to you and break them?" I was taken aback in my chair. I had never thought about life in that light. We make rules to protect our children but the teenage years are about pushing the boundaries and finding out what is on the other side of the protective walls of "home."

This refusal to heed her parent's directions was Bitzy's first real rebellion. She heard her father's warning and promised in her mind not to go to the forbidden spot—a lot of men building a road. Of course, with her father's traditional approach, that the mother teaches all the sexuality to her children, he only mentioned the danger of the big machines—the earthmovers.

Bitzy also heard her mother's warning, but with no explanation for why it was not a safe place, Bitzy was willing to risk it—push the boundaries to find out. Although, since I was the one wandering down in that area, I have to admit that it was the lore of people to talk to and have to listen to me that was probably the strongest draw. A fascination with boys and men was beginning to creep into my yearnings, but this was so subtle—these stirrings—that I was hardly aware.

Once again, Bitzy was a very lucky young woman because Nick could have overtaken her easily, for he was certainly strong enough to hold the bicycle, but he didn't. The scare that she experienced from his actions and her response was all unconscious because I don't remember that my mother ever really warned me to stay away from strange men. And for me, it was a blessing that Mother recognized when I shared my fright that I had learned what I needed to learn. Of course, once again, she didn't explain why I needed to be afraid and what would have happened to me. She avoided all the subject of sexuality and how and when it plays out between men and women. If you ever get to the third book in this series, you will find out how I got my explanation.

The lesson in this chapter, I believe, is that parents need to be able to talk to their children before the problem of active sexuality starts and to work with the language that is appropriate for the child's age. If the child is not ready or not interested, they won't pay attention or remember your words. These days, the schools run programs and films on this topic, but sexuality is not a book subject. Sexuality is a person-to-person subject, and it is most healthful when it is taught through the family or elaborated on by the family. Don't be fooled by, "Aw, that stuff, Mom!!"

# CHAPTER TWENTY NINE
## Here's to the Older Man

I WAS DREADING GOING back to school this year. I'd be going into the seventh grade. That meant having Miss Dorriety as a teacher. Miss Dorriety was the playground supervisor I'd run into when I was in second grade, chasing Bobby Hall from the sandbox. The other kids said Miss Dorriety was mean and never changed her clothes. I wasn't inclined to believe all the things the kids said, but still, I could remember how mad Miss Dorriety had looked when I plowed into her.

I talked to myself on the way to school in the new yellow school bus. (The State School had given up driving the children, so the town sent one of their long, yellow and black buses to pick up the State School children.) *Maybe if I'm quiet and just do my studies, she won't notice me, and she'll leave me alone. I don't have trouble with the school work anymore. I won't need much help from her. I'll just pick a desk at the back of the room so she can't see me very well. That should be safe enough.*

When the first-morning bell rang, I headed for a back seat. Sliding into the chair, I looked around to see who would be my neighbors. They were all boys! There were six boys: Dick, Wayne, Raymond Lansky, Billy, Bruce, and another Raymond—Raymond Laporte, a student, held back from last year. How had this happened? All these boys weren't what I'd planned. There would surely be trouble with so many boys in one spot. I wouldn't have anybody to whom I could talk.

*Maybe I should change my seat. No. If I do that, I'll have to sit in the empty seat right in front of Miss Dorriety. Oh, well, I guess I'll have to make the best of it.*

"Class, welcome to the seventh grade! I know you've heard that I'm a hard teacher, but you will find, if you do your work properly, on time, and speak politely to me and your classmates, you will have no trouble in the seventh grade. Now let's have the pledge of allegiance to the flag."

Instead of getting up quietly, some of the boys scuffed their feet on the floor as they slid out from their seats.

"Boys, is there a problem back there?"

"No, Miss Dorriety," Dick answered in a sickly sweet tone.

Raymond looked across at Billy, and the two of them snickered. *Oh, no,* I thought. *It's already started. Dick is such a smart-aleck. He'll get us all in trouble.* I knew Dick was intelligent, a leader, and he seemed to keep the other boys in a pack under his control. Dick sat right across from me.

"Cut it out, Dick," I growled softly.

"Why?"

"You're going to get us all in trouble."

"So, what's the problem, Miss Goodie-goodie?"

"I don't want to stay after school because of some dumb thing you've done!"

"Aw, dry up. You're just a scaredy-cat. Teacher's pet!"

"Is there a problem back there? I hear voices," the teacher broke in. We sat in utter silence.

"Was someone talking back there?"

Dick and I tried not to look at each other. It would be a dead give-away. The teacher's attention moved back to the blackboard where she was writing the day's date. Raymond Lansky ducked his head so he could see along the row of students and shook his pointer finger in my direction, laughing as he did it.

*Oh, this definitely is not good. Maybe I should ask to move up front.* But at this point, the teacher was busy telling the students what subjects we would be covering for the year. The room was relatively attentive. Perhaps it wouldn't be too bad. But it had certainly gotten off to a poor start.

Dick had changed after Bobby Hall left two years ago. Back then, they'd been best buddies. And now Dick didn't have a friend who was as quick-witted as he, except maybe Wayne, but Dick pushed Wayne around. Dick was restless and rough. He'd put his attention to mischief instead of light-hearted fun. I wished Bobby hadn't moved away, but his father had gotten a better job. I missed Bobby.

The rest of the school day went a little better. There was some nonsense among the boys in the afternoon. Miss Dorriety came and stood in the middle of the group with her hands planted on her hips. The gray wool skirt she was wearing pulled tightly across her backside, revealing where her girdle ended. I faced this vision as Miss Dorriety stood confronting the disruptive boys. The kids were right. She did wear a girdle! I chuckled to myself. It was as if for an instant I could see into this grumpy old teacher—see a part of her private life. The boys were really giving her a rough time!

The next day went much the same way. But this time, it wasn't Dick acting up. It was the older boy, Raymond Laporte—a year older and taller than the other boys. He was of French Canadian stock with a smoldering temper and not enough interest in school. Lolling in his chair, he stuck his feet out under the front of his desk into the aisle. Miss Dorriety almost tripped over them during the morning.

"Raymond, let's not get off to a bad start this year. You keep your feet under your desk, and things will go better between us."

I was surprised to hear Raymond Laporte mouth back. The other boys teased and cut up, but they generally weren't rude to the teachers. I forgot that Miss Dorriety and Raymond had already spent a year together and were not looking forward to another.

By the third day, Raymond Laporte started beating his pencil on the desk whenever the teacher stopped talking. If that didn't get a rise, he'd switch to his scratch pen, which was crafted of harder wood and made a greater distraction.

"Raymond, are you making noise again?"

"Oh, no! Not me, Miss Dorriety," he lied.

She went back to the work she was doing, and he started again. Dick sat in front of Raymond Laporte and off to one side. He waved his hands in the air like a conductor of the symphony orchestra in accompaniment to Raymond's pencil drumming. As soon as Miss Dorriety looked up, everything stopped. The boys improvised in perfect time with her head movements. She'd look down, and the boys would start again. It was hard to keep from laughing out loud. Surely the teacher could recognize what was going on?

Finally, by late afternoon, Miss Dorriety had had enough. "Raymond, I don't know what you are up to, but I want it stopped! The only thing that worked last year was to put you right in front of my desk. Raymond Laporte, move your stuff down here and take this desk." The teacher tapped with her index finger, her nail grating on the desktop in front of her. This student desk abutted her larger desk. It was as if by making a physical desk-to-desk connection with Raymond, she might have a chance at controlling him.

"Now, Bitzy I want you to move your things right down here behind Raymond."

"Me?" I was stunned. "I have to move my things, too? I didn't do anything, Miss Dorriety! I wasn't even laughing. That's not fair!"

I was amazed as I heard the words rolling out of my mouth. I didn't usually speak up, and I certainly had never spoken back to a teacher. It must be the bad example from the boys.

"Why do I have to move, Miss Dorriety? I can be good."

"Do what I say, Bitzy. I want you down here in front of me."

I pulled my books out of the desk, gathered up the papers on the top, and grabbed my pen and pencils. I stamped to my new desk and flung the books down.

"Bitzy!" The teacher's voice was sharp.

I jumped. *This defensiveness wasn't my usual style. Why was I making a fuss? If I were down front, I'd be out of the mischief of the boys. Maybe there I could concentrate better.* It was hard not to watch all the antics the boys were going through, trying to upset Miss Dorriety.

I settled myself into the new desk, put my books away, and found a place for the yellow pencils—those pesky yellow pencils.

The next morning I sat down at my new, gouged up, old wooden school desk. It had an ink well. *That was strange. Each student was issued an old-fashioned black ink pen, the scratch type, but not given any ink. Maybe we are going to write with them sometime in the future. Most of the time, we use yellow pencils.*

My musings were interrupted by a soft-sounding male voice. "The other kids call me Ray, not Raymond. You can call me Ray. The teacher put you down here, you know, to keep me quiet. But I don't mind. You're pretty."

Pretty! Nobody had ever said that to me other than my mother or Uncle Ralph. It sounded nice, even nicer than when Mom said it.

"Yeah, so what?"

"I was givin' you a compliment, stupid!"

"That's nice, but now you don't have to call me names."

"I wasn't. You were just actin' stupid."

I thought for a moment. *Ray is right about my actions. But I don't know how to talk to a boy about things. My brother Owen is all grown up. He's gone to high school, prep school, college, and now is in the Army. Jackie, the Gavin's son, who is two years younger than me, is my only male playmate. He lives in the double house beside the Simpson girls. Jackie is off to Parochial school and playing football. He doesn't want to talk to me anymore—all my girl stuff.*

"So what if I was!" I regrouped from my thoughts.

"I see I'm gonna have to teach you a lot."

Just then, the teacher called the class to attention. I looked up to see a young, pretty woman who looked even younger than my sister PollyAnne—(Polly, who was married now, living in another town in Massachusetts.) Aw . . . Oh! *This setup is going to be trouble. These boys were so rough on Miss Dorriety she didn't even come in today! She didn't even make it through the first week! Now they've put this poor young substitute teacher in her place.*

The boys must have thought the same thing. The scuffling feet began at the back of the room before the teacher had a chance to lead us in the Lord's Prayer. "What are you boys trying to do?" The new teacher whined through her nose. *Oh, she's lost it already*, I thought. *Any fool can see what they're trying to do!*

The rest of the day was utter chaos—pencils flying, spitballs sticking to desks and peoples' faces; one even hit the teacher, but she just whined on.

"I feel sorry for that dumb substitute," I said to Ray.

"Ya, they're givin' her a rough time. Watch. I can do better. Miss, Miss . . . what did you say your name was? Have you ever eaten frog's legs?"

The teacher looked stunned—a legitimate question from a student that somehow didn't sound legitimate. She opened her mouth to answer, but Ray didn't wait.

"I'll bring ya some tomorrow. My uncle and I are goin' froggin' tonight. We'll get some for ya. I can bring 'em to you tomorrow—frog and all."

I slapped Ray on the back shoulder. "Cut it out! She's already in enough of a mess with the other kids. Leave her alone."

"Why should I leave her alone? Because *you* say so? You want me to leave her alone? Then just ask nice."

"Leave her alone, Ray!"

"That's not nice! . . . But for you, I'll do it." He was still looking at the confused teacher who hadn't a clue about what to say back.

Ray was true to his word. He left the poor substitute alone. Most of the rest of the day, he talked or pestered me, stuffing bits of white paper into my unused ink-well until they stuck out the top like a floppy, folded white handkerchief. Once, he pushed my desk back with his chair. When I reached across my desk to pick it up and move it back into position, he rammed his chair back, catching and pinching my fingers.

"Ouch! You're a pain in the butt!" I yelled at Ray as I rushed the two squashed fingers into my mouth. "You're a big bully!" There was so much chaos going on in the room no one even noticed our exchange.

"Oh! Geez! I'm sorry. I didn't mean to hurt you. Really, I'm sorry. Let me have a look." Ray reached over and took my hand in his. Softly, he stroked the two damaged fingers. "Honest, I didn't mean to catch ya fingers." He sounded sorry, really kind, and concerned. I looked at the hand that held mine. It was long and slender, with finger joints enlarged from popping the knuckles, his French/Canadian skin far darker than mine. Our hands looked funny together—mine so white and his, a soft, tanned brown. I looked up into his face focusing on and seeing him for the first time. Ray's face was long and narrow with intense, smallish brown eyes set above sharp, high cheekbones. His ears stuck out slightly, the top of his head covered with curly brown hair. He was actually cute. Well, cute didn't fit because he looked older than the other boys. My heart skipped a beat. *That was a funny feeling!*

Ray was saying something I didn't quite hear. He was still gently holding my hand in his. Where was the teacher? I pulled out of my fog. "What did you say, Ray?"

"I asked if you'd wanna go to the movies with me this Saturday. We could take the bus to Leominster 'n see a show up there."

"Of course not! My mother wouldn't let me go out on a date with anybody. I'm too young."

Ray looked crushed. Then he tried again. "We could take another couple, so's it wouldn't be a date. It'd be a double-date."

"Oh, I'm sure she wouldn't let me go." I didn't even have to think about it. Mother always wanted to know everything about what friends I did have, and I didn't think Mom would approve a date, not even a double-date, especially not with this boy!

The bell rang just at that moment, and I was relieved. I didn't like the sad look on Ray's face. I hadn't meant to hurt him. Going somewhere with him might be fun. But, surely, I was much too young. The children bustled off toward the buses like young sheep, and I was headed home.

When I reached my house, I went straight for the kitchen and a big peanut butter sandwich. I was standing in the pantry, slathering butter on one side of the bread, when PollyAnne and my mother came down from upstairs. They'd been settling Polly into her old bedroom. Bud, PollyAnne's new husband, was in the Navy, and sent to Norfolk, Virginia, for his basic training. Polly was going to stay with the family until he got back.

"Have a good day in school today?" PollyAnne's question was bright sounding as if she were pushing herself to be happy.

"It was okay, sort of mixed up. We had a substitute teacher."

"Oh, what happened to Miss Dorriety?" Mother seemed mildly curious.

"I think the boys did such a job on her this first week that she decided not to come in today. They gave us a lady right out of college as a substitute. The boys are making mincemeat out of her."

"That's a shame." Mother's attention was already moving back to PollyAnne.

"Can I go to the movies with Ray?" I thought I'd just slip it in around the peanut butter in my mouth. Surely, Mother would say no . . . but just in case.

Mother looked at PollyAnne as if wanting a second opinion. "Who's Ray, Bitzy?"

"He's the boy about whom I told you. The one Miss Dorriety made me sit behind yesterday. He says she wants me there to keep him quiet."

"Didn't you say he had been held back from last year?"

"Yeah. I think Ray was out of school a lot and missed getting all his work done. He said we could make it a double-date. He wants us to take the bus up to Leominster and go to a movie up there."

"How do you plan to get from here to the bus?"

"You'd drive us, of course."

"So I'd get to meet this young man at that time?" Mother framed it half as a statement and half as a question.

"Yeah. So can I go, please?"

"This would be during the daytime?"

"Yes, of course. We can't go until Saturday."

Looking back at PollyAnne, as if checking her opinion on the matter, Mother responded, "I guess if the two of you are willing to make it a double-date and I drive you to the bus, you can go."

"I can go? I really can go?" I couldn't believe my ears. Never in my wildest dreams had I expected Mother would say yes. It must have been because PollyAnne was standing right there. Mother didn't want to look too old-fashioned, like an old meanie. For a moment, I was a tiny bit scared. I'd never ridden without Bev on the bus, let alone gone out on a date with a boy!

The next day was the last day of that week of school. When I told Ray about what Mother had said, he looked victorious. I moved into practicality. "So who are we going to get to go with us? None of my friends are allowed to go out with boys yet. They don't have any boyfriends."

"Well, I don't really have any friends either. Everybody your mother would let us go out with is here in this room. She wouldn't like the other kids I hang around with."

I knew he was right. Even the older boy in our class, Eddie that Ray hung with sometimes was bad news. He was a kid who walked on the edge between being just a kid like the rest of us and heading for juvenile detention school.

Eventually, I talked Jodie, my best friend, into going with Ray's trouble-making friend, Eddie. We did have fun, but it was all so new that I was tense most of the time. Ray found it cost more money than he could easily get his hands on, so we didn't go to the movies again that year. Instead, Ray started walking the two miles to my house every Sunday afternoon, even in a bad snowstorm.

Together we listened to records, made cookies in the kitchen, did a puzzle, or kissed on the love seat in the dining room where nobody could easily see us. In the spring, Mother and Dad took us on a family picnic to a spot up in New Hampshire. We'd been going together the whole school year. Nobody else in the class was dating anybody. It was nice having a steady boyfriend, but it also made me feel older and somewhat isolated from the other kids. I spent most of my time with Ray or Jodie. Was this what it was like to be grown-up?

## Looking Through My Therapist Eyes

# Older Man

This chapter seems like the report of what many a precocious child of twelve or thirteen, living in a small town in the early 1950s, might be doing. Even the beginning adolescent rebellion that Bitzy brushes aside as a poor example of behavior from the boys in her class is very normal for a young lady of this age. In fact, this behavior is a bit refreshing, having watched the restricted life that has been Bitzy's existence up to this point; restricted by illness and overly protective parental attitudes.

So, it is almost frightening and a bit confusing to Bitzy when her mother suddenly changes style and allows her a behavior that is really beyond her social development. One wonders if Bitzy's mother was feeling that she might be judged by her, now, more worldly, older daughter. The other possibility is that having worked so closely with Bitzy during her illness, Mother too is fooled by the dualism that has overtaken Bitzy's way of being in the world. Internally Bitzy is many years older than her chronological age. At the same time, externally, she is somewhat socially immature—both stances, a result of a long period of isolation during a critical social developmental stage in Bitzy's life.

A third possibility is that Bitzy and her mother are in a symbiotic relationship in which the mother is overly invested in this planned, wanted child. This over-investment will cause Bitzy's mother to unconsciously encourage her daughter into adventures that would replace missing events in the mother's life. More precisely stated, the mother often lives her life through her daughter's experiences.

If this last conjecture is the correct one, Bitzy's mother is unconsciously afraid that she will lose the child's affection if she doesn't give permission. This event would be intolerably painful to the mother. Why one child in a family elicits this type of response in a parent, while not all of the children do, is still a mystery. (Later training tells me some of this comes from past life experiences with the same people). Children choose particular roles to play in their family of origin, and it seems as if each member of the family has the script, responding from that programming. An example of this type of response is that the older children in Bitzy's family do not break through the isolation that the parents set up around Bitzy, for her protection, during her days of rheumatic fever. The emotional outcome is that the older children experience Bitzy as a little princess.

Those of us who believe in repeated lives wonder if these may be issues brought forward from a previous life to be repeated, worked on, or solved in the present lifetime. These complex underground relationships between parents and children certainly give food for thought.

Background: The Gavin and Simpson Duplex
To Right:  Bitzy's Home
Foreground: Bitzy's Older Man

# CHAPTER THIRTY

# Sharp Endings

I T WAS LATE in the school year of my stay in eighth grade. One Sunday afternoon after Ray had gone home, Mother called me from her desk in the dining room. "Bitzy, would you please come here. I need to talk to you for a moment."

*What could Mother want me for now?* I dutifully walked toward the front of the house and my mother's little office space in the left corner of the dining room. Mother now had a job as the town's news reporter for the area newspaper. She'd made part of the dining room into her office.

"Yeah, what do you want?"

"I'm not sure how to tell you this, but I'm getting more and more concerned about your relationship with Ray. He's too old for you. He knows a lot more about living than you do."

"So what if he does?"

"Well, I'm just afraid he'll lead you into something you can't handle."

"Something I can't handle—what do you mean?"

"You were sitting in his lap this afternoon facing him, and I don't ever want you to do that again! You don't know what you're doing."

"What do you mean? What's wrong with sitting in his lap?"

"Just, don't ever do that again with a boy!"

"Why? You're not fair. Ray is nice to me. He's kind and gentle. He does fun things like when he brought all those fireworks for us to light off last Fourth of July."

"I know. I know. You've had fun with Ray. You're flattered that this boy is paying attention to you, but he's not the right kind of boy for you. You're getting in over your head. I'm afraid something will happen."

"Nothing is going to happen, Mom!"

"I know you think that, but you don't know the power of your own body. That's why I have to say you can't see Ray anymore."

"I can't see him anymore! Why? What have I done? That's not right, Mom. You can't mean that!"

"I'm sorry, Bitzy, but I do mean it. You're to call him up tomorrow and tell him you can't see him any longer. If you must, blame it on me, but you are not to see him again!"

"This isn't right! You're all wrong! You can't do this to us!"

"I may be wrong. All the same, you still have to call Ray. I'm sorry you're being hurt in this process, but this has to end."

I could feel my eyes flare with anger at my mother. The rage of a now-healthy body poured from every cell . . . But years of experience and the tone in Mother's voice told me I would not win this fight. Defiantly, I stamped my foot, turned, and raced toward my bedroom. Calling back from the stairs the worst threat I could muster, "I'll never forgive you for this!"

I mounted the last stair and slammed my bedroom door behind me. "I hate her! I hate her! I hate her!" I screamed into the pillow at the head of my bed. "She can't do this to us. She has no right! I love him, and he loves me. I'll just run away!" I sobbed into the faithful old pillow until my eyes were swollen to a sticky pink mass. The thoughts of not seeing Ray anymore brought back all the aloneness of those years of sickness. Never again did I want to be shut away, not free to move, to play, or have friends. The thoughts of losing Ray seemed more than I could stand.

I didn't come down to supper that night. The next morning I emerged from my room dressed for school. Down in the kitchen, I was thankful that Daddy was the only one up. He wouldn't ask any questions about my swollen face. Mother would have told him. I was sure of that, but he would just silently go about getting my bowl of hot cereal, pouring me orange juice, and then he'd flick the bunch of keys he carried on his belt. This gesture, his quiet way of telling me he was sorry for what I was suffering and that he had to leave to go to work.

When Mother came down, I was finishing the milk in the bottom of the cereal bowl. I kept my head down.

"Good morning, Bitzy."

I didn't move or reply. The silence in the room was painful. I got up and put my bowl in the sink. As I moved to the dining room where my books were stacked ready for school, Mother called after me. "You will tell him today?"

Alone in the cold dining room where the love seat stood, I dutifully nodded my head. I would tell him, but I would hate my mother for the rest of my life!

School was terrible that day. I tried to stay away from Ray. Fortunately, he was busy with Eddie at lunchtime. They were setting plans for some fishing that evening. I was grateful. I didn't want to talk with Ray, for I'd blurt it all out and start crying right there in school. I knew that telling Ray would go better over the telephone. As the class started moving around and preparing to go home, Ray pushed toward me from his desk. "Call you tonight?" he mouthed over the heads of the other students, just as he had on most of all the other afternoons. "Be home?"

Sullenly, I nodded my head, yes. Fortunately, Ray was too intent on getting out of school and home to the fishing poles actually to take in the look on my face. I knew he'd call about half an hour after we both got home. I hoped somehow the phone would self-destruct, and he wouldn't be able to get through. That would be the only way around it. He never forgot to call!

Ray did call. And his response to my dismissal was loud threats of murder to my mother and other obscene suggestions.

"This isn't the end of the world, Ray. We'll still see each other in school." It felt like a lie.

Finally, he quieted down. And then the grief came. "What will I do without you? You're the best thing that's ever happened to me. I'd probably not be in school anymore without you!"

I wasn't sure which was easier to handle—his rage or his pain. It was all I could do not to tell him I'd go against my mother and continue to see him. But somehow, I knew I couldn't carry it out.

We cried together, and finally, Ray said, "I can't stand this anymore. I've got to go fishing! I'll always love you, forever and ever! Good-bye!" Click! The phone was dead.

I sat on the floor in the front hall, telephone receiver still cradled in my lap, tears pouring silently down my cheeks.

The rest of eighth grade looked like one long numbed-out haze. The other children, filled with excitement, were looking ahead to the fun of the summer vacation. I could only see eternal loneliness—a return to feelings I thought were back in my sickbed.

That summer proved to be a foggy blur of magazine love stories that I read as I lolled on the old, iron cot on the back porch. The breezes moved softly across my exposed skin, and the sun warmed the outer edge of the screened-in porch. But they only served to strengthen my cocoon of grief. Occasionally, I heard my mother saying, over the internal sadness, "Bitzy, why don't you get up and do something active? You can't waste your days away on trash like this. If you've got to read, read something of value."

Later in the summer, Mother began saying, "Bitzy, why don't you see if you can get yourself a job? Earn a little money for your tuition at college. You know, if you ever want to go, you're going to have to help earn some of the money. Dad and I won't be able to provide it all." My response was to roll over, away from my mother, and go on to another love story.

---

## Looking Through My Therapist Eyes

# Boy and Girl

---

The concluding part of Bitzy's story shows us that she is entering the world of boy and girl relationships with all the confusing and hidden agenda that runs through our society on these matters.

It seems as if we are always picking at the mother, but Mother's handling of the Ray affair was classic and almost cruel. Those of us who have children can understand where Mother was coming from: she felt she had to protect her innocent daughter from a sexual encounter that might happen before the young lady was ready. Certainly, this is a most noble motivation, but what happened to the words that would have explained to Bitzy what was really frightening her mother? Why couldn't her mother have talked about fondling, sexual drive, penetration, and sexual intercourse? Yes, this was the 1950's, her mother was conservative, but Bitzy can tell you that her mother showed her the perfunctory pamphlet on having babies way back when she was a small child. And there was some back and forth discussion on this information between Bitzy and her mother. What happened to the rest of the explanations? (You will have to read the next book, *Hunt the Beloved* to get the answer.)

Bitzy was left to figure out what was driving her mother's orders, an activity that went on often in Bitzy's family, perhaps helping to shape Bitzy for her later career as a therapist. But for the moment, it simply added another layer of pain and confusion for our fourteen-year-old.

Another thing I am able to share with you, now that Bitzy has come out from behind her mirror, is that she kept diaries during this period in her life, and they have resurfaced between the first and second drafts of this story. The amazing and troubling fact is that the story of Ray's dismissal, as it is written in Bitzy's childhood diary, glides over the pain and rage she experienced in this forced break-up. I, as the author, had to hunt for several hours to find the exact day. What do you say; maybe she was afraid someone would read her private book? I know, for a fact, that was not the case. Bitzy had been so carefully conditioned, all unconsciously, to hide her feelings that she even repressed them from herself in her diary. The dream referred to in my Author's Notes triggered the need for this book to be written, and my acceptance of the invitation to reach out and take the inner therapist's hand has caused Bitzy's and my emotional side to begin to unlock.

Now, as an adult, when I am finally able to let the inner child tell her story, the buried feelings come pouring forth. We see the true unrepressed material! This manner of free-flow writing is a very important and very healing tool.

# CHAPTER THIRTY ONE
# Wrapping It Up

B Y NOW, WE know that Bitzy's life was happy and sad, as it is for all of us. But the part not recognized before is that we carry inside ourselves the tools for healing our wounded hearts. We each carry a critical parent and a loving parent internally. We carry a tiny child who can be supportive or destructive, and externally we carry that consciousness that we perceive as being us, the one with the glass of water, half empty or half full.

The energies that we bring with us at the time of our birth, and those experiences of our childhood, shape our perception of the glass of water. This conscious everyday part of our personhood tries to modulate the passionate inner child and the dispassionate critical parent. When these energies clash, the outer response is often depression, as if the critical parent is strangling the child within. Our culture supports the demeanor of the critical parent with our emphasis on "getting ahead." At the same time, the boisterous, disruptive inner child is thrown into the closet to languish in resentment and wounded feelings. By inviting this child to speak about his/her perceptions of events, we unlock the closet door, allowing the inner child to bring its fresh and invigorating energy back into our lives. Bernie Siegel, a pediatric surgeon who worked extensively with cancer children and would talk at workshops about his cancer people, said that the obnoxious patient was his kind of patient because that individual would be getting well. Ego strength, the sense of oneself, is often buried within this inner child. When we give this child voice and empathy for the painful experiences in their lives, this loving attention brings the emotional release that strengthens our sense of ourselves.

It is when these parts of the individual recognize and honor one another that healing begins. If the inner healer will reach out to the wounded inner child, giving a supportive arm-around-the-back (like The Fallen Down Woman in the wake-up-call dream referred to at the start of this book), the inner child begins its journey back to emotional health.

You see this process symbolically when Bitzy comes out from behind her mirror in the dialogue of chapter twenty-seven. She is a complete child, tiny in form, needing only to grow in stature to the size of the individual, forming the conscious self, in this instance, the author, JessieMay.

In my journey, I have been astonished by the feelings of wholeness and completion I've experienced as Bitzy has come to light and told her story, allowing me to put her experiences on paper. But, the larger enlightenment is witnessing the number of adults, many very successful people, who, when I tell them of Bitzy's wounding and willingness to talk, fill up with tears. There is a pain, a sorrow of some kind, in their past, most often in early childhood, that has never been exposed and acknowledged. For some, it is a long-term illness, as with my experience. For others, it is economic circumstances, vagaries of parents, or a brutal invasion perpetrated by another. But it is always a time when the inner child was silenced, cut off from self-expression.

I have written this book for three reasons. The first was my own need to purge, talk about my pain and feelings of profound loneliness, and a feeling of abandonment during my struggle with rheumatic fever. My lingering question has become, was I abandoned, or did I abandon myself? —But these answers are for more sophisticated writing.

The second reason for writing Bitzy's Story is the hope that telling Bitzy's story helps other parents dealing with their seriously ill children. The story helps parents understand that it is important to share their feelings, around their child's illness, to some extent, with their child. My parents came from a generation that felt they needed to "be strong," and they tried to shield me from their anxiety, only making my anxiety greater. As parents, we tend to take good physical care, sheltering the child from information, because we can't tolerate the pain that information causes us. This withholding of information harms our children, for they are left with not understanding what is happening to them, and the whole experience becomes a secret. We forget that for children their physicality and the parameters of their bodies are their knowledge of their existence. They are left with a terror that parts of them will not survive and cannot talk about this fear because the parents are not talking. Children, at some level, realize we parents cannot tolerate the emotions of the situation, so they protect us by burying their questions, fears, and anguish; indeed, abandoning their own Divine Inner Child. Many become cooperative compliant children, even as adults, being eaten from inside by feelings they may not verbalize.

And, the third reason for writing this book is to show that you can conduct therapy, of a sort, even without the supervision of a therapist, **if you do not have a serious mental illness.** You can empower the inner healer, that part of you that continues to search for meaning and emotional growth. This book is an illustration of one technique, using a mirror, to bring forth hidden material. With this method, the caution is to sense when the time is right, be ready to let go, and trust enough to allow the vision of the eyes to distort to the point that images can come forward into the mind. A usual response to the first effort is to say, "I'm imagining this." And yes, this is imagination, but the great psychiatrist, Carl Jung built his life's work on the fact that the unconscious has an uncanny ability to imagine just those things that help the conscious mind to understand life—witness his enduring work with dreams. Or more recently, the work of Roger Woolger, a Jungian psychoanalyst, used focused recall and bodily reenactment to help the individual bring forth past life memories. This process triggers profound healing in the client.

When you look at an artist's paintings, especially a series of their work, you can see their life issues, hidden material with which the artist wrestles. So, relax and let the imaginings come. If you meditate before doing one of these mirror exercises, you will have a better result, for the unconscious has been warmed up and invited to come forward.

There are many good books online and in bookstores that can teach you how to meditate. The simplest starting exercise is to sit in a comfortable straight chair in a relaxed position, feet planted firmly on the floor, eyes closed, and mind focused on one's interior physicality. Take in a deep breath as you count up to the number six, hold the breath for a count of six, let it out audibly through your mouth to a count of six, and hold the breath out for a count of six. Repeat this process at least three times. When you start, you may need to use a shorter count, but as your lungs become stronger, you can lengthen any part of this exercise. It is the exhalation that drops the body into a state of relaxation, and therefore meditation. When the counting is done, breathe normally and "watch" your process of taking in air and letting it out. When your mind wanders, bring it back to your breathing. This exercise, done for five to twenty minutes a day, constitutes an acceptable amount of meditation, both for your health and any imaginative work. If you are doing imaging work, ask before coming out of meditation for those supportive entities or angels who gather around you as protection to bring you only material you are ready to assimilate. Those who work with the unconscious regularly recognize that we carry many energy levels about us, some positive and some negative. In dealing with unconscious material, without the supervision of a trained therapist, it is best to work with those energies having a positive purpose. And, for any of you reading this that have a history of serious or long term mental illness, **these techniques can be dangerous if done without the support and direction of a trained, qualified therapist**.

Another technique of drawing unconscious material into the conscious mind for self-healing is to dialogue with any intriguing character from a dream. I could speak to the Fallen Woman in my dream in my introduction. In that case, I would gather together paper and pen before doing a few minutes of meditation. Upon coming out of the meditation, I would write a question such as, "Fallen Woman, how come you are on the floor and can't seem to get up?" Then, waiting for her answer, I would record what I hear or sense in my mind that she is telling me. She might say, "Why do you want to know; you haven't ever noticed me before?" Given this curt response I'd be disconcerted, and from past experiences with this technique, I would know she was serious and wanted an honest answer.

When doing this exercise, write each party's responses on the paper as you would if you were writing a play. Your inner characters often quibble with your questions, pushing you into deeper and deeper insight. It is important to record it all. Through this evolving give-and-take of written communication, the Fallen Woman's inner being brings understanding to the conscious mind. You can do this exercise completely within your head, but you can refer back to it by writing it on paper, often gaining greater insight with later readings.

Other techniques to retrieve unconscious material involve drawing on paper with any instrument, the emotions that well up from inside you. These pictures may be technical or abstract. The form in which they come forth is not important. You can study these images to make the material more conscious, or you can leave them alone to percolate up through the levels of the mind until they cause changes in the understanding of oneself. Any creative work helps this hidden material to be exposed; be it sculpting, painting, drawing, designing a building, even cooking a meal. We reveal our hidden selves through all of these creative activities; the integration process is hastened when we bring the everyday mind to dwell upon what has come forward so that the messages within can be made cognitive.

I hope that Bitzy will stir something inside you such that you start to take a deeper look at your wounding—your sorrows. You each have a loving inner child wanting to be heard so that she/he can become an assimilated part of your passionate, conscious expression.

Many times, with counseling, it appears that we, the paid counselor, encourage clients to blame their parents for the apparent injustices in the client's life. The sad fact is that this process of blaming often empowers the client to the point where they feel their work is completed, and they leave therapy. But this is only the first half of the healing circle. The client feels they have the answers: it was my mother's fault or my father's fault. But there is seldom fault to focus anywhere. Most parents work diligently from the lessons of their history, and the pressures of the society in which they live, to teach and raise their children in a loving and responsible manner.

The child brings with them into this incarnation a personality program established in a past life existence, by the unconscious, by a set of genes, or by something in between, which we have not yet discovered. The important fact is that the child chooses, by some mechanism, how he/she will approach any event that happens to him or her. Most of these choices are an unconscious knee-jerk reaction. Does this constitute a basis for blame? I think not.

Counseling work moves onward when the client begins to see his or her parents as individual people, a product of their history. This acceptance is the turning point when forgiveness can come forward, creating a healing environment for both the individual and their parents. The timing and quality of this moment is delicate, for it must not come before the inner child has been acknowledged, felt, and even allowed to run rampant for a time, allowing the buried pains and passions to become conscious and expressed. At this juncture, where the individual can say it is not what my parents did to me, but how I have chosen to experience their actions, that forgiveness takes place. When one reaches this place of taking personal responsibility for one's part in one's emotional traumas, healing is close to completion.

In closing, I need to say that Bitzy's wounds, or more truly my wounds, are my responsibility to hold or dispel. Bitzy's parents, or rather my parents, were loving, well-intentioned human beings functioning from the best of their backgrounds. They were and are truly remarkable everyday people with flaws and scares, knots and wrinkles. I love them both intensely. May you, too, achieve self-understanding, forgiveness, and creative release upon your journey!

**Author's Contact Information:**

**Email address:** my2little25bird78@gmail.com
**Blog address:** mylittlebirdbyjmk.wordpress.com